Values Across the Curriculum

+LB1564 .G7 V34 1986

```
LB          Values across the
1564            curriculum
G7
V34
1986
```

	DATE DUE	

Values Across
the Curriculum

Edited by
Peter Tomlinson
and
Margret Quinton

The Falmer Press
(A member of the Taylor & Francis Group)
London and Philadelphia

UK	The Falmer Press, Falmer House, Barcombe, Lewes, East Sussex, BN8 5DL
USA	The Falmer Press, Taylor & Francis Inc., 242 Cherry Street, Philadelphia, PA 19106-1906

© Selection and editorial material copyright P. Tomlinson and M. Quinton 1986

All rights reserved. No part of this publication may be reproduced, stored in a retrieval system, or transmitted in any form or by any means, electronic, mechanical, photocopying, recording or otherwise, without permission in writing from the Publisher.

First published 1986

Library of Congress Cataloging in Publication Data

Main entry under title:

Values across the curriculum.

1. Education—Great Britain—Curricula—Addresses, essays, lectures. 2. Moral education—Great Britain—Addresses, essays, lectures. 3. Social values—Study and teaching—Great Britain—Addresses, essays, lectures. I. Tomlinson, Peter. II. Quinton, Margret.
LB1564.G7V34 1985 370.11'0941 85-10389.
ISBN 0 905273 75 3
ISBN 0 905273 76 1 (soft)

Typeset in 11/13 Caledonia by
Imago Publishing Ltd, Thame, Oxon

Printed in Great Britain by Taylor & Francis (Printers) Ltd, Basingstoke

Contents

Introduction
Peter Tomlinson and Margret Quinton   1

Part 1   Values Across the Curriculum — Specific Areas

Values in Art and Design Education
Brian Allison   11

Values in the Teaching of English and Drama
Peter Hollindale   29

Values in Geographical Education
Patrick Wiegand   51

Values in History and Social Studies
Robert Irvine Smith   77

Values in Home Economics Teaching
Hilary Davies   87

Values in Mathematics Education
Bryan Wilson   94

Use or Ornament? Values in the Teaching and Learning of Modern Languages
Nicholas Beattie   109

Values in Physical Education
Jim Parry   134

Revaluing Science Education
David Layton   158

Contents

Part 2   Values Across the Curriculum — General Issues

Aims, Problems and Curriculum Contexts
Richard Pring   181

Values and the Social Organization of Schooling
Janet Strivens   195

Values Teaching: Some Classroom Principles
Peter Tomlinson   211

Notes on Contributors   225
Index   228

Introduction

Peter Tomlinson and Margret Quinton

The background to this book, and our underlying concern in it, lie with those aspects of education which relate to values. Amongst these, moral and social values are often thought of as central, and they are amongst our prime concerns. But drawing tight boundaries between different kinds of value does not seem to be useful at this point. Without going in for a litany of classic statements and revered sources, we can, nevertheless, say that from at least as far back as Arnold in Britain and Dewey in America, there have been eloquent and persistent calls from modern educationalists for education to be explicitly concerned not only with formal intellectual achievement but also with the formation of the whole person, the preparation of 'rounded citizens' for real life. In the relatively affluent sixties and seventies such concerns found expression in a number of projects and curriculum packages, such as the Schools Council Lifeline, Startline and Humanities Curriculum projects in this country. As regards the day-to-day concerns of teachers and parents, values education, particularly moral and social education, is something to which at least a great deal of lip service is still paid (think of the last school speech day you had to sit through!), though different people seem to mean very different things by these terms (cf Scharf, 1978, Introduction). Their traditional expression has tended to be somewhat narrow and concrete, with specific subject areas being thought of as dealing with values, for instance, RE and possibly English, and particular activities as somehow influencing them, for instance school assemblies. On the other hand, school policy on discipline (or as it could too often be more accurately put, school practice regarding the punishment of indiscipline) is something that has not uncommonly, if paradoxically, been considered separately from its overt stance on moral and social education.

Yet despite all these writings, projects, lipservice and concrete institutions, there is more than a suspicion that the overall effectiveness of social and moral educational provision, such as it is, may be pretty minimal. We are now clear, for instance, that there is no such thing as a 'teacher-proof' curriculum package, and yet only a handful of teacher trainees receive anything systematic by way of education in the theory and practice of values education. Again, one often suspected that social and moral education materials were thought relevant mainly (and then perhaps largely as time-fillers) for the less able, the ROSLA kids, the deviants from that ideal image of the pupil who knows and therefore does the good in its various forms. The non-examination status of such subjects could hardly help, either. Perhaps one of the key points, however, is that teachers, given that they are only human in their reflective capacities, tend to think of teaching in terms of *their subject* and of educational success as achieving subject prowess in their pupils. Values have not been seen as part of their concern. The danger, then, is that, as Hargreaves (1982) has argued, school becomes an institution serving and satisfying only a small, 'committed' minority of its clients. Or as a teacher colleague recently put it to us during a dispute, the nature of the strategies of persuasive action engaged in nowadays by teacher unions and that of the reactions to them by pupils and their parents suggests that a major function of schooling, for an uncomfortably large proportion of children in too many schools, is merely that of child-minding.

Even if one came to such a conclusion, however, a number of types of response are possible. Hargreaves, for instance, makes some rather far-reaching suggestions by way of reform of the curriculum and examination system, which would have consequences for the organization of schooling and the teaching profession. Another reaction might be to encourage the latest expression of the traditional 'whole person' concern, namely the development of new curriculum subjects such as 'Lifeskills' and the integration of pastoral provision — recognizing, nevertheless that we start from a position in which too many teachers have a limited and negative conception of what pastoral care might mean.

Our own stance is more modest (so it stands a good chance of getting us accused of mere tinkering!). It starts from the realistic acknowledgement that children do spend a good deal of time in schools with teachers being taught particular subjects; that such subjects have many value-related aspects; that there are varying degrees of concern by various parties for effective values education; that there may be unintended effects of implicit processes as well as intended effects of explicitly directed activities. And since the tendency is very much for

Introduction

teachers (secondary school teachers, at least) to think in terms of their own subjects, we think it important to recognize this as a necessary starting-point from which to encourage them towards a recognition of the realities and possibilities regarding those values that may be involved in and affected by the teaching of their particular subjects. On the basis of such awareness, teachers may then wish to develop the practical skills that will enable them to pursue actively the realization of those values they think justifiable, or at the very least to develop an effective neutrality to replace any unconscious and implicit biases they may have detected in their previous practices.

Our aim, then, is to provide a practical stimulus to such reflection, together with some positive ideas to inform it, rather than just another abstract piece of analysis and exhortation. However, this area, like education as a whole, offers so many aspects and perspectives that some sort of systematic framework seems necessary in order to relate the parts to each other and to the whole. We are well aware that any such framework will have its limitations and that uncritical application may restrict one's awareness to just those features allowed by that particular viewpoint. We therefore offer the following ideas as a potential but necessarily imperfect resource.

When considering value-related aspects of teaching, a first basis for distinguishing some of the major aspects is yielded by systematically examining the *process* of education as a purposive, intentional activity. Formally speaking, such activities have at least three elements:

(a) *Aims* or intended outcomes;
(b) *Means* or teaching/learning processes;
(c) *Effects* or actual outcomes.

Starting with aims, just as traditional subject teaching has been construed as involving aims thought of largely in terms of cognitive competence (knowledge and understanding, intellectual skills), so one may also consider the values and value-related aspects one might wish to influence in and through teaching particular topics. It is already the case, for instance, that open-mindedness and tolerance have been viewed as value-related aims of social studies and history teaching, appreciation of natural resources has been linked with science, geography and environmental studies, social and personal sensitivity with literature and the fine arts. Later in the book, Richard Pring deals more generally with the matrix of possibilities across various subjects. For the moment, however, note that we do not simply refer here to 'affective outcomes' as in the Bloom taxonomy tradition, because we do not wish to restrict consideration to first-order impulses and feelings, that is, 'affect', since one can value something without getting excited about it. Nor would we wish to align ourselves uncritically with the behaviourist assessment implications of the objectives approach. Rather, by values and 'value-related aspects' we shall mean anything potentially relevant to people's preferences and modes of living (which must include at least certain sorts of knowledge and competence).

Again, just as actual teaching activity constitutes the *means* by which teachers seek to bring about intended learning, that is, cognitive acquisitions in their pupils, with much educational thinking and research directed towards alternative methods and styles, so we may consider classroom processes as activities furthering, perhaps embodying, certain types of value and outlook.

Finally, we may consider the *actual results or outcomes* of our teaching efforts, again with respect to both specific subject competences and values: *do* our pupils end up more open-minded, respectful of persons, sensitive, than they started?

And then, of course, we can try to bring these three facets together. In short, we can ask *what* value-related aspects we can, should or do aim at, *how* our teaching may affect values, and *where* our pupils are ending up with respect to outlooks and preferences. But we can also relate these different phases and elements: how do the values and tendencies our pupils end up with compare to what we had hoped at the outset to engender in them? What role, if any, have our teaching activities played in affecting these outcomes? The latter question is one which, given the complicated and subtle interplay of influences in any educational situation, is not likely to yield simple, general answers, even from the most ambitious research projects. But in addition to such formal research, we have other equally important sources, such as the accumulated experiences, intuitions and reflections of those who have been involved with day-to-day teaching.

For the first part of this book, therefore, we have collected a group of contributors who are experienced in teaching, most of them also in training teachers, in major subject areas of the curriculum. Each in their own way will consider value-related aims, means and outcomes in their particular area. The contributors to the second part of the book will focus on general aspects that are shared to some extent by all the various areas, namely on the nature of potential value influences in classroom teaching processes, on broader effects of school organization and atmosphere, and on the specification of the aims of value-related teaching in relation to the whole curriculum.

But, of course, on its own this formal analysis into educational aims, means and outcomes is unrealistically simple as a guide to understanding the value-related aspects of subject teaching. Everyday intuition and systematic research combine to confirm, for instance, that for much of the time and in many facets of their behaviour, individuals and organizations do not act in systematically explicit and intentional ways. Good practitioners can typically do things more competently than they can articulate how, and teachers are no exception. On the other hand, what one assumes or says one is doing may be a good deal more optimistic, benign or respectable than what one is actually doing (cf. the 'this is going to hurt me more than it hurts you' stance). And there may be various types of relationship between such theory and practice from innocent (if suspect) self-deception to Machiavellian dissimulation: again, neither of these are unknown to human nature as it is revealed in teaching.

It seems, then, that we need to take into account a whole range of perspectives or orders of reality when considering value-related aspects of teaching. Choosing an adequate but economical way of portraying these is not easy, but we propose that to make any sort of positive impact on our chosen domain one must distinguish at least three levels.

1 *How value-related aspects of particular subjects are explicitly thought of and currently construed* by relevant persons. Since teachers and pupils are human beings whose actions will be based sooner or later on the ways in which they grasp reality, and because existing views about value aspects will vary greatly from teacher to teacher, within and across subjects, from pupil to pupil, and so forth, then one is never going to get very far with promoting an intelligent approach to the value-related possibilities of subject teaching unless one gets practitioners to take a reflective look at the ways they and others construe things at present. That is, how they consciously see the value-related aims, means-process, and outcomes of teaching their subjects. We will call this aspect *overt construals* of value-aspects. But people by no means always do what they think or say they are, or should be, doing. We must therefore distinguish another level.

2 *What is actually going* on that relates to values in different areas of subject teaching. Thus, apart from what teachers might explicitly *say* they are aiming at, what do they perhaps also implicitly value by way of desired outcome? Apart from what people say is going on in their teaching, what might critical examination reveal as also tending to occur? In other words, apart from the professed curriculum, what is the *actual or de*

facto curriculum, incuding any *hidden* aspects of its aims and implementation? And finally, what does systematic investigation (if and when available) suggest are the actual effects of current teaching of particular subjects on relevant value outlooks and action: is talking about racial prejudice dissipating it or perhaps strengthening it by rehearsal, for instance? For which pupils? But to consider simply what people think and what is currently happening would be to clear the ground without building any further. We need to consider a third perspective.

3 *What might be possible* by way of values education within particular subject areas: the *potential curriculum.* This is perhaps where a book such as the present one might be most expected to contribute, but it should be stressed that there are no simple recipes or solutions and that practical developments in schools do require that we take account of the existing construals and realities mentioned under the previous two headings. For the meantime, we should point out that like the other two perspectives, the potential curriculum relates to the value-related aims one might construe as possibly treatable within a particular subject, as well as to the possible teaching strategies and techniques one might employ. The potential outcomes would seem to reduce to the potential aims — since they are both only potential — though they might be distinguished in terms of specificity. For example, one might think that biology teaching offers the possibility of considering the values and choices involved in a considerable range of environmental and personal issues (potential aims), but considering limitations on time and their own competence at various techniques (the potential means/process), a biology teacher might have a more modest notion of the potential outcomes of a realistic effort to include at least some value-aspects with biological relevance.

As will have become apparent, one needs to combine the perspectives and process elements we have distinguished. This yields a framework of aspects to which we have already been making part reference, but which is perhaps more usefully presented in matrix form, as in table 1.

We offer the above framework as a way of organizing some of the many strands that become apparent when considering value related aspects of subject teaching. We do so in the hope that it will assist your

Introduction

Table 1:   A matrix of perspectives and elements for considering value-related aspects of the curriculum

Elements	Perspectives		
	Overt Construals 1	De Facto Curriculum 2	Potential Curriculum 3
(A) Aims	What if anything teachers and others say they might or do aim at by way of value-related aspects of a subject area A1	What they actually seem to hold as value-related possibilities of their subject. A2	What value aspects might be promotable via the teaching of this subject. A3
(B) Means Process	The processes and activities whereby they think these value-aims may be effected. B1	The nature of actual value-relevant activities, including implicit ones, in this subject area. B2	Value-related teaching activities that might be tried in this subject area. B3
(C) Effects	The value effects, if any, they think are being realized through teaching their subject C1	The actual effects including hidden ones, being made on pupils' value outlooks, actions and reaction. C2	The subset of A3 that might be attainable under particular conditions in this subject. C3

thinking in this domain and your critical assimilation of the remainder of the book. It should be made clear, however, that whilst our other contributors are aware of this framework, there has been no intention that they should utilize it, whether explicitly or implicitly. In dealing with their subject areas in their own terms, they will hopefully speak more directly to readers who share these specialisms.

Two further comments may be of use. The first relates to the selection of subject areas included in Part I. We have deliberately focused on major traditional curriculum areas, for a number of reasons. One is that limitations of length impose some degree of selection anyway. But more positively, we have chosen to give attention to those subjects traditionally seen as central to the curriculum, but whose value-related aspects are not often considered, especially in collections such as this which attempt to treat a theme across the curriculum. Thus we have not included religious education, precisely because it *has* been traditionally recognized as dealing with values in a central way and much has already been written about this. Likewise, we have not included anything on the more recently developed areas of Lifeskills teaching and tutorial work, because there seems to be clear recognition (cf. David, 1983) of the fact that such enterprises are replete with values. Indeed, books and curriculum offerings relating to moral and social education typically offer relevant material precisely for such integrated activities. What seems notable by its absence is any attempt to treat the value-educative potential of the traditional subjects in terms of which teachers still tend to be trained and to think. So in this book we hope to offer something that may contribute by getting to grips with the various areas (Part I) and by reviewing some general strands common to subjects across the curriculum (Part II).

The second and final comment relates to the central but problematic notion of 'values' and 'value-related aspects', to which we have constantly referred. As we said earlier, our background concern was with moral and social values, that is, those basic preferences, assumptions, principles, forms of sensitivity and competence that relate to the ways people actually live their lives. But this is a domain in which things are highly interconnected and in which clearcut general distinctions between what is basic and what is not are, at the very least, problematic (and even this is a value-laden statement!). Therefore, given that 'values' relates to reaction, preference, decision-making, and actual ways of living, and that social-moral values are seen as a basic concern, we have deliberately left things that vague so that our contributors would be relatively unconstrained in their exploration of the value-relevant potential of their areas. In that sense, Part I of this book is very deliberately subject-centred, though from a particular angle, namely the value dimension. We hope that starting in this way will encourage readers to critically examine their own current construals and actual teaching efforts, and that they may thus go on to consider the possibilities offered in these chapters and in Part II, as a basis for developing ideas and skills with respect to the value dimensions of their teaching.

References

DAVID, K. (1983) *Personal and Social Education*, York, Longman.
HARGREAVES, D.H. (1982) *The Challenge for the Comprehensive School*, London, Routledge and Kegan Paul.
SCHARF, P. (1978) *Readings in Moral Education*, Minneapolis, Holt.

1
Values Across the Curriculum — Specific Areas

Values in Art and Design Education

Brian Allison

Throughout history all cultures and societies have manifested their attitudes, values and beliefs in visual forms. Visual forms can be taken to mean all man-made objects and images and includes everything from pictures to cathedrals, bicycles to aeroplanes, jewellery to statues. Each culture or society produces images and forms which are unique and peculiar to it and even when similar images or forms are common to more than one culture or society they almost invariably have different meanings or values attached to them. To greater or lesser degrees, visual images constitute not only an embodiment of a society's attitudes, value and beliefs but are also a major means by which they are actually formed and realized. A good example of this can be seen in the very influential role played by the visual arts and architecture in the formation and maintenance of religious and spiritual values in all societies since prehistoric times.

It is not only in the formation and realization of societal attitudes, values and beliefs that visual imagery plays a significant role but also in their transmission from one generation to the next. Moral and spiritual teaching has always relied heavily on pictorial imagery and the development of patriotic attitudes has been underscored consistently by banners, flags, medals and other commemorative paraphernalia, statues and a variety of monuments, buildings and dedicated spaces. More covert, but nevertheless equally intentional, attitude-forming images proliferate in newspapers and magazines and through film and television as was clearly identified by Packard (1957) in his influential book *The Hidden Persuaders*.

Almost every aspect of art and design activity, including art and design education, is an epitomization of social or cultural values. In England, for example, the training of artists and designers; the location and organization of colleges and departments of art and design; the complex network of studio and industrial production; the system of art and design marketing; the choice and location of art and design works in homes as well as in public places; the sponsorship and selection of images and other visual man-made forms at local and national govenmental levels all represent a particular value system which exemplifies and recognizes the role and function of visual imagery in people's daily lives.

There is no aspect of the diversity of art and design activities, objects, images and experiences which could truly be described as value-free. Even the amateur 'Sunday painter' who makes a drawing or a painting for no other reason than personal pleasure and pastime can do so because it falls within an accepted and recognizable social value system. Without intending a pun, in this instance of applied values, 'the medium is the message', to use the McLuhan (1964) aphorism.

As with any other subject in the school curriculum, art and design as a school subject owes its existence originally and principally to its role and presence in the social, economic and intellectual affairs of society at large. A primary responsibility of schools as socializing institutions is to introduce the young to the various codes, symbol systems and areas of knowledge such as, at a basic level, developing an ability to read, write and understand number, which will allow them to participate in the society in which they are growing up and to be able to draw upon the experience of those who have gone before. Additionally, and in order to contribute to as well as to benefit from societal development in a dynamic sense, the responsibility of schools can also be taken to include the provision of possibilities and opportunities for the young to question, challenge, reinterpret and consider alternatives to that which already exists. Eisner (1972) described these two particular responsibilities as having 'instructional' and 'expressive' functions.

In practice, of course, the extent to which a school subject corresponds or relates to that 'subject' as it exists in society outside of, and beyond the walls of, the school depends on the ways in which the 'subject' is mediated by teachers and school systems. How 'real', for instance, are or could be the issues raised or the activities provided in, say, a school science lesson in terms of the role and contributions of science and scientists in and to the life of a society and its people would depend upon how the science teacher mediated the 'subject' of science in its broadest sense. As, again to greater or lesser degrees, all aspects of life are value-laden, one measure of the validity of a school subject seen in this way might be taken as being the extent to which it reflects and refers to the range of values which are implicit as well as explicit in the subject field as it exists in life outside school.

Art and Design Education

Whilst this would certainly be a useful way of looking at schools' curriculum content, it could be argued that it represents a rather simplistic view as there are a variety of pressures and influences which can alter the conception of a subject as it appears in school from that which exists in the world outside school. More often than not, however, it would seem that differences can be traced to either the inevitable and understandable difficulties which teachers have in keeping up with developments in society or, more problematically, to the progressive development of the school subject simply as a school subject in an autonomous sense. Either way, they result in curriculum decisions, such as what to include and what not to include, what strategy to adopt and what not to adopt, and these are, in themselves, decisions of value. It is, perhaps, inevitable, that it is often these values which are learned or acquired by young people rather or more readily than the range of values characteristic of the subject in the outside world.

It will be clear that the view of schools as having a primary responsibility to, in a sense, induct the young into social and cultural systems represents a particular conception of the roles and purposes of education. This conception is based on the notion that the teaching of a subject is to provide children with access to a body of knowledge and experience, which has, to a large extent, its origins and existence outside of the school and forms part of social and cultural life. In this conception, the variety of often conflicting values which characterize the subject field as it exists in the world outside school is an essential part of the subject of study. This is implied in the use of the term 'the subject-centred curriculum'.

An alternative but important and prevalent view, which has its origins in the child-study movement earlier in this century, sees the acquisition of particular knowledge through what has been termed 'subjects' as being, in a sense, incidental to the growth and development of the child as a living, human organism. In what has been termed 'the child-centred curriculum', the subjects of study and subject knowledge become means to ends and not ends in themselves. It follows that the value systems implicit in the 'child-centred' approach are primarily related to individual growth and differences.

These two, apparently dichotomous approaches have been described, albeit rather sketchily, because they usefully illustrate the ways art and design in schools is currently being provided. For the last thirty years at least, art and design as a subject in schools has been characterized by the 'child-centred' position and epitomized by Herbert Read's *Education through Art*, which took art as a facilitator for the development of human sensibilities. Similarly, Victor Lowenfeld's book, *Crea-*

tive and Mental Growth (1947), which has been enormously influential on art education in the United States and most English speaking countries, placed the total emphasis on child development, which was defined in terms of intellectual, social, aesthetic, creative, emotional and physical growth. Given the value-laden nature of art works, it is interesting to note that Lowenfeld placed great emphasis on the warning that encounters with, for instance, adult art works might inhibit children's healthy development and growth. For Lowenfeld, all the potentialities for growth were seen as being latent and growth itself was a kind of 'unfolding', which needed to be nurtured by the teacher. This view in some ways resembles that of Herbert Read who saw the teacher as being a kind of 'psychic midwife' who assisted in the releasing of profoundly internal ideas and feelings and, more recently, that of Robert Witkin (1974) as expressed in *The Intelligence of Feeling.*

The instrumentalist approach implicit in child-centred education has been an extremely potent force in primary schools, particularly in the early school years, in which major purposes for engaging children in the use of art materials have been to develop their sensory awareness and provide opportunity for expression or, more specifically, self-expression.

There is a wide range of values and value systems implicit in art activity arising out of the child-centred approach. In the first place, there is the valuing of the self, that is of the child as a person and an individual. In this valuing, efforts are made by teachers to help the children feel that what they do is worthwhile and that they each have a personal and individual contribution to make. Whilst variations in children's abilities in other aspects of the curriculum are often painfully evident, the instrumentalist use of art in schools gives more or less equal recognition to the outcomes of children's efforts and achievements through the application of evaluative criteria which are not art-specific. Even on those not infrequent occasions when a child is not satisfied with what he or she has produced, invariably some supportive comment can be made about some aspect or other of the work in order to help the child recognize some value in his or her own efforts. Putting children's work up on the walls is also considered to be a strong contributor to the development of children's self-esteem and worth.

An extension to the children's valuing of their own efforts is that of the valuing of the efforts of others. Displays and exhibitions of children's art work are considered not only to be ways of developing a valuing of what the children themselves and others have done but also as a useful means of promoting a sense of responsibility towards its care and preservation and so discourage vandalism because of being able to identify personally with the work.

Because of the emphasis in child-centred art and design programmes on individual growth and development, the art and design work which is displayed around the school is almost invariably that produced by the children and this tends to act as a covert form of values teaching. In an indirect but very influential way, the art work put up on display by the teacher gives children a very clear notion of what is approved and acceptable and, reciprocally, what is not. The children also learn in an indirect way that what a teacher puts up on exhibition is as much a reflection of the teacher's taste or preference as it is a choice based on objective educational or aesthetic criteria. As part of learning the value system, children very quickly get to know what needs to be done in order to succeed but they also come to recognize the paradox of the stress on individuality when, at the same time, the learning environment prescribes, to a large degree, what they can, and what is appropriate for them to express.

It is evident, of course, that what art and design teachers do in schools is influenced in a number of ways which are often beyond their control and these affect and, in some cases, determine the values which underpin, either overtly or covertly, the art and design curriculum. The expectations of heads and other teachers about, for example, the display of work around the school, the making of sets and costumes for school theatrical productions, the design and production of posters and school magazines and the entering of children's work in competitions and awards schemes, all contribute to the formation of children's values about art and design in a general sense and about their own art and design activities. One of the most direct influences on the values formed as well as those encountered in art and design in the secondary schools is that provided by the external examinations.

In almost all the external examinations for the GCE or CSE, imaginative interpretation of the topics or themes is encouraged and in many cases there is a requirement to show how ideas were developed through the presentation of working drawings and sketches. However, although there appears to be some attention to contextual matters, formalist criteria tend to predominate when it comes to giving grades or marks. In general, the examinations have not been underpinned by any overt suppositions that the production of artistic images or designs might be, in itself, a value-forming or value-exploring activity. In some GCE 'A' level art history or art appreciation papers, however, there have been occasional opportunities offered to discuss contemporary issues which are value laden but, even then the concerns have tended to be with broad matters such as for example a consideration of the role and effects of the Arts Council.

When the art and design programmes in schools are oriented towards activities such as product or environmental design, there tends to be a firm emphasis on what is described as 'the design process', by which is meant a relationship between elements such as problem solving, materials, technologies and production, or, in other words, the strategies and procedures leading to solutions rather than the values associated with the solutions themselves. Whilst any designing task is almost invariably concerned with problems which have value associations, whether it is concerned with, for instance, meeting some material need such as packaging or a broader issue such as environmental pollution, the criteria for the evaluation of the solution tend to be related principally to the adequacy of the strategy adopted and the procedures followed rather than whether or not the activity or task undertaken has been value-forming or value-exploring. For example, a typical designing task or, as it might be termed, a 'design brief', might be to redesign a child's playpen and this would require a study of the ergonomics of lifting children in and out of the playpen, the suitability and availability of materials, hygiene, material and production costs and the development of technical skills of production. It would be most unlikely that the task would require explicitly a consideration of value issues such as the nature of a society which separates young children from their parents by putting them in a kind of cage on the floor or the priorities and lifestyles of parents in which this would seem to be a desirable thing to do. In other words, the emphasis in designing has been placed on strategies employed in designing and, as a consequence, the focus of the activity has been a concern for meeting the material needs of society rather than giving consideration to the value systems which underly and, to a large degree, create and define those needs.

Given that there has been a predominant emphasis on some ways of producing art and design in schools, there is a problem not only about how value issues can be introduced into the art and design curriculum but also about how the students' abilities to recognize and deal with value issues could be assessed in terms of educational development or progress. It is interesting that the draft proposals for the 16+ National Criteria for Art and Design, which are under consideration as this volume goes to press, reflect this problem. Whilst the broad aims for art and design include the need to give attention to what might be inferred as social and other values issues, the actual assessment objectives relate almost entirely to the strategies of production and the assessment of the resulting products. It is also interesting that the Secretary of State indicated that the assessment objectives should be extended to include a

Art and Design Education

demonstration of 'knowledge about art and design'. No indication was given at that stage as to what knowledge was being referred to but it might be argued that to know about art and design would necessarily include knowing something about its function in terms of value-forming, value-transmission and value-changing. Throughout its existence the Schools Council, which was disbanded in late 1983, was concerned with ways of ensuring the social as well as educational relevance of schools' curricula which were explored through a variety of projects covering all aspects of the curriculum. Over the years the Council's Art Committee moved perceptibly from an almost exclusive concern with the expressive and productive aspects of art and design to an acceptance of the broader social and critical contexts of art and design activities and experiences. One of the early indicators of this shift was in the Committee's working papers for the N (Normal) and F (Further) Examination proposals in 1976 and although the N and F was never subsequently pursued the work which was carried out for it was, nevertheless, influential. As well as commissioning studies into aspects of studio production, it was notable that the Committee commissioned a study into art and design criticism and its relationship to art history. The N and F working papers included what was probably the first comprehensive statement of goals for art and design education to have been made in this country. These were

1. The development of a broad understanding of the meaning of art, craft and design in contemporary culture.
2. The development of perceptual skills leading to a sensitivity to visual qualities, together with an enhancement of experience in art, craft and design.
3. The development of bases for informed aesthetic judgment; personal and community.
4. The ability to value and meaningfully experience the cultural heritage of this and other societies, past and present.
5. The ability to hold, articulate and communicate ideas, opinions and feelings about art, craft and design.
6. The development of particular subject aptitudes and interests, but not exclusively in production and expression.

The activities implicit in these aims could be taken to include making, looking at, thinking about, talking about, feeling about, knowing about and responding to art, craft and design. The achievement of these aims would be dependent on the formation of a range of fundamental concepts regarding the nature of art, craft and design. (Schools Council, 1977)

Brian Allison

This statement of aims for art and design education also carried with it the implication that not only were the aims all and equally important but that they were, almost by definition, interactive and mutually supportive. It was particularly significant that, expressed in this way, the aims placed art and design education firmly in the broader contexts of society and, hence, unavoidably, the value systems within which art and design exists and to which it contributes. The aims also imply a recognition of the extent to which art and design is culturally shaped and, possibly, even determined, both in terms of form and content as well as in the ways it is encountered and experienced. The statement of aims also contributed to opening up the possibilities for developing art and design curricula which embraced the art and design of world cultures and which could be made relevant to the diverse cultural backgrounds of an increasing proportion of the school population. To the extent to which knowledge about the significance and achievements of art and design in different cultures engenders respect for those cultures, the aims could be said to make a positive contribution to anti-racist teaching.

It is, perhaps, not surprising that there has been only a limited acceptance in this country of the global view and responsibility of art and design education represented by these aims. Apart from the 'behaving as an artist or designer' concept of art and design education, referred to earlier, being strongly held by many teachers, for which some partial explanation was given elsewhere (Allison, 1978), many teachers have an enormous investment in what they are already doing and so are steadfastly resistant to all but minimal change. This is further supported by the generally conservative nature of the external examinations which are almost exclusively concerned with expressive and productive activities. Even if this had not been the case, art and design teachers have tended to be extremely cautious when dealing with value-laden issues in the classroom. This has been mainly due to a very genuine concern not to appear to influence or dictate what might be rightly considered to be matters of individual preference or taste. On this last point, it is interesting that when children raise questions about value-laden issues some teachers are able to turn the questions back with 'But what do *you* think?', which, although often a good pedagogical strategy, avoids having to express an opinion or view.

If art and design as it exists in contemporary society is part of the subject as it is taught in schools, then the whole range of value issues which are uniquely identified and expressed in art and design, within and across cultures, historically and at the present time, has the potential for being encountered by pupils. For instance, social, ethical, economic and political issues are inseparable from graphic design in anti-smoking campaign literature, cigarette advertisements or party political propaganda; social priorities and environmental effects are important design issues when considering aeroplane, motorway or car design. As John Berger (1972) cogently argued, the subject matter and form of images are inseparable from the social and political contexts in which they are produced and, reciprocally, the ways in which they are subsequently viewed and the meanings they have for the viewers. On a more overtly influential scale, most religions and political powers have consistently recognized the potency of visual imagery to teach and propogate their beliefs and ideologies. It is not by chance that, in most countries at the present time, there is considerable control over visual imagery, with legislated censorship, to define and maintain moral and ethical codes and standards.

It is, perhaps, not surprising that, as in so many aspects of education and other fields, although England was responsible initially for establishing the place and practice of art in education, the United States of America has been the most active in clarifying its purposes and in pursuing its social as well as aesthetic possibilities. Many art educators have contributed to the groundswell of change which is moving towards the establishment of socially as well as aesthetically accountable curricula. One of the most prominent has been Feldman, who has been making the case for many years for the study of art as a humanistic endeavour. Feldman has argued that art objects serve as a means to understanding the wide parameters of human concerns and issues not only as an enrichment for the individual but also as a means of relating to others. The argument was epitomized in the title of one of his most influential books *Becoming Human Through Art* (1970). Inevitably, there are differences of opinion about the relative values and contributions of practical art and design activities as compared with those leading, essentially, to humanistic understandings. Lanier (1970), for example, went so far as to maintain that 'to teach art is to teach about art as an end in itself, and this is not done only or at best through the production of art', which is a diametrically opposite view to that which is likely to be held currently by the majority of teachers in England. It can be equally strongly argued, however, that what might be characterized as 'production' and 'response' are not mutually exclusive and, indeed, need to be seen as being essentially interactive (Allison, 1978).

Almost all curriculum development in the USA, whether at state level or at federal level, including the recent initiatives being taken by the Getty Foundation (Duke, 1983), stress the importance of giving attention to the societal contexts of art and design as an essential curriculum component. It is interesting that in this regard, if in no other, the United States has much in common with the aesthetic education programmes being developed in some socialist countries, such as Bulgaria.

The potential for giving attention to the social as well as individual values in art and design is, perhaps, most clearly demonstrated in the work of Laura Chapman (1978), who has been very influential on much of the curriculum development work in the USA. Chapman, following up on her earlier work with Barkan, Efland and Kern in Ohio, identified three parallel functions of art education as being to encourage

1 Personal fulfilment through art.
2 Awareness of the artistic heritage.
3 Awareness of art in society.

Each of these functions was seen as having an expressive or productive dimension and a response dimension so that, for instance, 'personal fulfilment' was derived as much from experience and involvement with art works from past and present times as from being expressive or creative in the use of art media. Similarly, learning how artists create works was as equally important as looking at and evaluating what they had created. 'Awareness of art in society' was seen as being concerned with learning about how one's own culture and other cultures expressed beliefs and values through art as well as providing opportunities to interpret and evaluate art works as social expressions. Chapman developed a curriculum structure and described teaching strategies which addressed these three functions at each age level from pre-school (three year olds) upwards to the end of secondary school education. The age range is particularly interesting because it has been one of the persistent myths of art and design education, in theory and in practice, that matters such as art appreciation and history are inappropriate at primary school level and even before the latter years of secondary school.

Although, as indicated throughout this chapter, art and design works are inestimably rich as embodiments of social, moral, economic and ethical values, they are open to a wide range of levels of interpretation and meanings. Simply because art and design works and objects are visible and/or usable does not necessarily mean that they are, in themselves, understandable beyond a minimal or superficial level. Indeed, most art and design works have several layers of meaning which can only be peeled away by adopting relevant strategies or contemplating them from different viewpoints. Much has been done in the field of semiology, the study of signs and symbols, which is extremely helpful in getting beneath the immediately apprehendable imagery to more profound but, nevertheless, exciting and rewarding aspects and meanings of man-made visual forms.

Despite the variety of constraints and influence on art and design activities in schools, an increasing number of teachers are beginning to explore the possibilities of dealing with social and other aspects of art and design and are attempting to get away from the singular conception of art and design as only a 'making and doing' activity in an Anglo-European sense. A small number of systematic research studies and curriculum projects have been carried out in this country into the nature, possibilities and practicalities of what may be termed 'aesthetic education' and they have yielded significant outcomes which hold considerable potential for the future. Generally, the research projects have been mainly concerned with exploring and trying to understand something about the abilities of children and young people to engage in informed and meaningful criticism and to develop a sense of the broader social as well as aesthetic values in art and design, with consideration given to the practical teaching and learning as well as the curriculum implications (Allison, 1974; Kelsall, 1982; Major, 1970; Moloney, 1984; Pearce, 1974; Sherry, 1983; Simpson, 1972). These studies, along with curriculum projects such as the 'Using Pictures with Children' project in the North Riding of Yorkshire (Bowden, 1983), the Schools Council 'Art and the Built Environment Project' (Ward and Adams, 1982) and the 'Critical Studies in Art Education' project funded by the Schools Council, the Crafts Council and the Arts Council (Taylor, 1982a and b), have demonstrated clearly that a critical approach to art and design works is not only within even young children's capabilities but that children can find the activity enjoyable and illuminating. It is particularly significant that there is strong evidence from these studies that children have the potential to confront the value issues related to art and design as readily as they have been expected to address the formal aspects and production processes.

A further significant outcome of these and other studies is that, as a consequence of children's analytical and critical appraisal of art and design works drawn from various historical and cultural contexts, children's own expressive and productive activity has been shown to develop in a number of important ways. This, of course, reflects the truism that 'art comes from art' and demonstrates that art and design works are a major source for learning how to make art and design. At the same time, it challenges the long held myth that exposing children to adult art and design works has negative or inhibiting effects. For example, Wilson and Wilson (1982) showed that drawings of heroes and superheroes, based on comic strip cartoons, by children in different countries projected wide ranges of social observations and value issues which would not otherwise be likely to have been explored.

Despite many calls for greater degrees of social, industrial and economic relevance in the school curriculum, relatively little attention has been given so far to identifying the range and kinds of values and value systems which can be encountered, perhaps uniquely, through art and design in schools. It seems ironical that visual images are used extensively as illustration by other subject areas in schools in addressing values and value-laden issues, such as human rights, social inequalities, ecological and environmental problems, yet the development of an understanding of the interaction between image and value has hardly figured at all in art and design programmes at any level except, perhaps, in some degree level art and design history courses.

The increasingly multicultural constitution of the population of many schools, which, in some, is almost entirely non-European, raises extremely potent values issues affecting all aspects of the school curriculum as well as organization. Given the legislative support of the EEC directives, the Race Relations Act and, more recently, the Equal Opportunities Act, these value issues have wide-reaching implications for all subject areas and may be the single, most important agency in moving the balance of the art and design curriculum from being based predominantly on process/product-based activity to one which emphasises value-based activity. However, it needs to be acknowledged that prevailing practices are deep-rooted and the dominance of British culture and conceptions of art and design, which are held more as being facts of life than as manifestations of a particular culture, are undeniably resistant to change. The evidence would seem to indicate that, without any conscious projection of cultural or racial superiority on the part of teachers, minority group children in some schools are covertly or even overtly directed into western-European modes of representation and imagery from the early years of school as if it was simply a matter of 'normal' development. All the influences on children's work referred to earlier, such as selected wall displays and teacher acknowledgement, contribute to what is seen as 'normal' development. This constitutes a direct if unintentional form of values teaching, which was epitomized by the comment of an art teacher about immigrant children when he said that 'we try to encourage them to work in their own art forms but it is only when they use western conventions that they are creative' (Schools Council, 1973). The recent study commissioned by the Schools Council, as part of a broad enquiry into the appropriateness of external examinations for the multi-cultural society, showed that, to a substantial degree, art and design examinations are racially prejudiced and culturally biased (Leary, 1984).

Art and Design Education

It is important to note that many of the GCE and CSE examinations are not only culturally biased in terms of the skills and knowledge expected to be demonstrated or in the subject matter or topics upon which the skills and knowledge are to be exercised, but also in the western European conceptions of art and design upon which the examinations are based. Drawing from observation and the following through of 'the design process', for example, are both peculiarly Anglo-European conceptions of art and design and their singular pre-eminence in examinations forms or reinforces the values attached to them as well as, by their omission, to the art and design forms of other than Anglo-European cultures.

A number of projects currently in progress, such as those at Leicester and Birmingham Polytechnics and by Oxfam, are not only questioning the essentially Anglo-European concept of learning in art and design which predominates in schools but also the exclusivity of Anglo-European perception and forms of representation. Not least important in these projects is the recognition given to the role of the visual arts as a contributor to the realization of value-issues relating to, for example, cultural identity and self-esteem. The evidence available suggests that whilst, on the whole, little has been done so far in this country to move to a multicultural conception of art and design and art and design education, there is an encouraging level of interest by teachers to develop curricula which can meet the needs of children in both monocultural and multicultural schools.

As a refinement of the broadly expressed aims for art and design education referred to earlier, a number of objectives have been put forward for the 'cultural' domain but which interact with objectives in the expressive/productive, perceptual, analytical/critical and historical domains (Allison, 1972). It will be evident that these objectives would be very difficult to achieve in an exclusively process/product based curriculum.

The objectives of the cultural domain are to help develop understandings of:
(a) the ways different cultures embody and communicate their beliefs in the visual symbols they produce.
(b) the sources of imagery and symbolism, and that these sources vary from the ritualistic, mythical and magical to representations of visual responses to the environment.
(c) the variety of ways art and design forms or symbols to be found in a culture influence the lives of people in that culture.
(d) the ways in which the art and design forms and materials

used in different cultures influence, and are influenced by, the particular kinds of imagery and symbolism.
(e) the ways in which both the art critic and anthropologist can help in providing ways of understanding the art forms of different cultures.
(f) the differing criteria which need to be employed in responding to and comparing and contrasting the art and design forms of different cultures.
(g) the ways artists and designers in one culture derive symbols and images from other cultures and attach new meanings to them.

Expressed in this way, it is clear that these objectives do not refer exclusively or specifically to the art and design education of children in England or even to particular ethnic groups within this country. The perception of art and design activity as a humanistic endeavour can be seen as a fundamental concern of art and design education across the world. This was maintained, for example, in a policy document, submitted by the International Society for Education through Art (INSEA) to the UNESCO World Congress on Culture held in Mexico City in 1983, which gave emphasis to the role of art education in promoting cultural realization and development whilst, at the same time, contributing to intercultural understanding and respect. The INSEA policy document included the objectives for the cultural domain of art and design education given above.

To consider art and design education, its purposes and practices, as an international endeavour rather than simply as a national, English or even local education authority matter can provide valuable perspectives on some of the larger moral, social, political and economic value issues with which it might properly be concerned. It is very evident that there are marked differences in the role art and design education is seen to play within general education by national governments. It is significant that a large and increasing number of countries have made ministerial appointments in government with specific responsibilities for 'culture'. When central government makes 'culture' an important part of its administration, carrying with it commensurate political as well as administrative resources, the contributions of artists, designers, musicians, actors, dancers, architects, town planners, conservators and curators, spectators and participants and so on, including art and design teachers at all levels, are given a coherent sense of relationships.

The attention given to art and design education at national leadership level is an indicator of the value given to it by governments. At the opening ceremony of a relatively small INSEA conference in Portugal in 1984, for instance, it was significant that the speakers included the Ministers of Culture and Education. Similarly, the senior governmental representative at an INSEA ceremony in Bulgaria, also in 1984, was the Minister of Culture. In both these countries, as in many others which place culture in the centre of national affairs, the role and responsibility of art and design education and its interaction with contemporary life is a fundamental educational concern.

There are, of course, other and varying values which relate to and, in a direct sense, are an essential part of the content of art and design education when it is seen as having a broad cultural responsibility. Art and design education in the Republic of Cyprus at the present time, for example, is inextricably related to concerns for the cultural heritage and Greek-Cypriot identity, which is felt by the Greek-Cypriots to be threatened by the invasion and subsequent occupation of the northern territory by Turkish forces. Similarly, human rights, economic survival and the necessity of individual expression are major concerns of art and design education in Brazil, despite the enormous social, ecological and environmental problems which beset the country. Brazil, incidentally, has probably the most evenly balanced multicultural population in the world. In Israel there is a positive national investment in art and design education, as well as in museum and gallery education services, so that aesthetic and cultural concerns interrelate with technological, industrial and economic developments. Many other examples could be given of the kinds of national, cultural and social values which are being addressed by art and design education throughout the world.

The themes of World and Regional Congresses of INSEA give some indication of the kinds of value issues which would seem to be of international as against specifically national importance. Recent World Congresses have taken as their themes 'The Arts in Cultural Diversity' (Australia, 1978), 'Art Education: Process and Product' (Holland, 1981) and 'Creative Education and the Challenge of Socio-Cultural Transformation' (Brazil, 1984) whilst more localized concerns are addressed in Regional Congresses such as 'Art Education and Environmental Consciousness' (Cyprus, 1982), 'Humanistic Concerns in Art Education', (Bulgaria, 1983) and 'Many Cultures, Many Arts' (England, 1985). The 1982 Cyprus Congress forwarded a resolution to UNESCO calling for all countries in the world to take positive action on the protection of the environmental cultural heritage and to develop educational programmes to increase environmental awareness and understanding.

The potential of art and design education to address humanistic concerns is being recognized increasingly in different countries across the world. To a large degree this is because of an increased awareness of differences in cultures and lifestyles but its importance is due, in no small measure, to world tensions and inequalities and the need to find ways of resolving them. As an example of a response to this awareness, a unique initiative was taken in Bulgaria in 1978 with the establishment of the 'Banner of Peace' movement. The movement has the triple themes of Unity, Creativity and Beauty and embodies the belief that harmony and peaceful co-existence can be helped to be achieved through personal and shared creativity. 'Banner of Peace' centres have been set up throughout Bulgaria as creativity centres for young people but the international dimension is the holding of an Assembly every two years which brings children and young people from over 100 UNESCO countries in all parts of the world for two weeks to work together in arts activities. The movement hopes that collaboration and cooperation at an early age in arts activities, in ways which seek to transcend language, national, religious and ideological barriers, will lead to greater respect, tolerance, support and understanding for other human beings, whoever and wherever they are, as the young people grow older and as they contribute to shaping the present and the future of the world in which they live.

Summary

As art and design, throughout time and in all cultures, has both reflected and contributed to the formation, maintenance and transmission of values, art and design education in schools and colleges is in a particularly vital position to contribute to the expansion of children's awareness of values at a personal level and in society. It has been shown that there has been a continuing concern in art and design education to develop a sense of valuing individual worth and achievement but that the identification of art and design education more directly as a mediator of art and design in contemporary society would bring a clearer focus on broader value issues as they affect and influence everyday life. Personal expression and response is undoubtedly important but it is also necessary for young people to be aware of and to be able to contribute to societal expression about humanistic concerns.

Art and design education in many countries is moving increasingly to broader conceptions of its role and responsibilities than that which, traditionally, has been based almost entirely on individual expression and production in art and design. Even within these broader conceptions, however, expressive and productive activity is still an important and essential element. Nevertheless, it is recognized that, in other respects, art and design processes and practices can be regarded only as means to ends and it is important that those ends relate to the kind of understandings which will enable young people to have access to and to be able to contribute to the important humanistic concerns of the contemporary world. Environmental, social and racial issues and equality of opportunity are but a few of the concerns which art and design education could readily address.

Acknowledgement

I am indebted to Mr D.G. Hutson and Mr T.F. Simpson, Leicester Polytechnic Centre for Postgraduate Studies in Education and Dr N. Stanley, Birmingham Polytechnic Department of Art, for their valuable comments and suggestions on the draft of this chapter.

References

ALLISON, B. (1972), *Art Education and the Teaching About the Arts of Africa, Asia and Latin America* ..., London, VCOAD.
ALLISON, B. (1974), *Intellectual Factors in Art Education.* Unpublished PhD thesis, University of Reading.
ALLISON, B. (1978), 'Sequential learning in art' (orig. 1972). *Journal of the National Association for Art Education.*
ALLISON, B. (1980), 'The "Either-Or" and its effects on education,' *Journal of Aesthetic Education*, Vol. 12, No. 2, pp. 85–91.
BERGER, J. (1972), *Ways of Seeing*, Harmondsworth, Penguin.
BOWDEN, J. (1983), *Using Pictures with Children*, Art Advisers' Association.
CHAPMAN, L. (1978), *Approaches to the Study of Art in Education*, New York, Harcourt Brace, Jovanovich.
DUKE, L.L. (1983), *Programs of the Getty Centre for Education in the Arts,* paper presented at the NAEA Convention, Detroit, USA.
EISNER, E.W. (1972), *Educating Artistic Vision*, New York, Macmillan.
FELDMAN, E.B. (1970), *Becoming Human Through Art*, Englewood Cliffs, NJ: Prentice Hall.
KELSALL, R.T. (1982), *An Empirical Study in the Development of a Teaching Strategy Designed to Alter the Appreication of Art by Some Primary School Children*, unpublished MPhil thesis, Leicester Polytechnic.
LANIER, V. (1970), *Essays in Art Education: The Development of One Point of View*, New York, MSS Educ. Pub. Co.
LEARY, A. (1984), *Assessment in a Multicultural Society: Art and Design at 16+*. London, Schools Council.
LOWENFELD, V. (1947), *Creative and Mental Growth*, New York, Macmillan.

McLuhan, M. (1964), *Understanding Media*, London, Routledge and Kegan Paul.

Major, D. (1970), *An Investigation into Teachers' Attitudes Concerning the Importance of Developing Aesthetic Sensitivity and the Ability of some Secondary School Children to Make Informed and Sensitive Aesthetic Judgments*, unpublished DipArtEduc dissertation, Leeds Polytechnic.

Moloney, K.M. (1984), *Concept Definition. Analysis and Assessment*, unpublished PhD thesis, Leicester Polytechnic.

Packard, V. (1957), *The Hidden Persuaders*, London, Longmans.

Pearce, T. (1974), *An Investigation into the Effects of a Course of Study on the Abilities of some 12 year old Children to Respond to Designed Objects*, unpublished DipArtEduc dissertation, Leeds Polytechnic.

Read, H. (1945), *Education Through Art*, (2nd edn), London, Faber.

Schools Council (1973), *Multiracial Education: Need and Innovation*, Working Paper No. 50, London, Evans.

Schools Council (1977), *Schools Council Research Programme. Studies based on the N and F Proposals: Art*, London, Schools Council.

Sherry, S. (1983), *An Experimental Teaching Strategy Planned to Develop the Levels of Discernment and Discrimination of Some Secondary School Children Towards the Functional Aspects of Man-made Objects*, unpublished MA thesis, Leicester Polytechnic.

Simpson, T.F. (1972), *An Experimental Strategy Developed to Alter the Qualitative Responses of Some Secondary School Children to Various Aspects of Design*, unpublished DipArtEduc dissertation, Leeds Polytechnic.

Taylor, R. (1982a), *Broadening the Context. Critical Studies in Art Education Occasional Paper No. 1*, London, Schools Council.

Taylor, R. (1982b), *The Illuminating Experience. Critical Studies in Art Education Occasional Paper No. 2*, London, Schools Council.

Ward, C. and Adams, E. (1982), *Art and the Built Environment: A Teacher's Approach*, London, Longmans.

Wilson, B. and Wilson, M. (1982), *Teaching Children to Draw*, Englewood Cliffs NJ, Prentice Hall.

Witkin, R.W. (1974), *The Intelligence of Feeling*, London, Holt Rinehart and Winston.

Values in the Teaching of English and Drama

Peter Hollindale

The very title of this chapter may seem to declare at the outset an unexamined value-judgment, namely that English and drama are linked and inseparable areas of the curriculum which share a common set of values and can be readily approached in simultaneous discussion. In many schools and for many teachers this is in practice true, even self-evident. Drama is commonly a sub-division of the English department's activities, possibly supported by its own qualified specialist but often dependent on the enthusiasm and haphazardly garnered skills of English teachers generally. In these circumstances it may be represented in the school programme by the annual production of a scripted play, some casual and arbitrary acting out of plays in English lessons, and perhaps one period a week in the hall (when not in use for examinations) for first and second year pupils. In other schools, however, any such link with English would seem tendentious and provocative. When a separate drama department exists, it usually draws clear lines of demarcation to separate itself from English, occupies specialist premises in the form of a drama studio, conducts systematic work in mime and movement which untrained English teachers could not attempt, and works for different curricular goals such as public examinations in theatre studies. The relationship between English and drama in terms of status and subject content is varied, unresolved and often controversial. So much must be admitted at the beginning in an article which will partly argue that what is urgently needed in this curriculum area is a clearer pattern and coherent rationale to relate activities which already exist. English and drama alike at the present time need to search not for innovations but for a convincingly inclusive structure.

An enquiry into values very quickly begins to reveal how much the two areas have in common. Both are concerned with language (that is,

Peter Hollindale

with forms of lucid, mutually understood communication between one person and another); and with a language (English); and with a set of 'languages' (the conventions of utterance in word and physical expression from which individuals must learn to make appropriate choices in the diverse life-situations we all face). Both English and drama are concerned with language (thus broadly conceived) in the 'participant' and 'spectator' role, in the terms of D.W. Harding's contentious but widely-used distinction. English and drama explore, and indeed *are*, both art forms and sets of utilitarian skills. Both are intimately concerned with the affective as well as the cognitive elements of human behaviour and relationships. As educational activities, both are concerned with both process and product, with the act of making and the thing made, with fluctuating priorities between the two which differ from teacher to teacher and school to school. Both are preoccupied with explicit and implicit values; as language subjects they are necessarily and unavoidably so preoccupied since language is itself the repository of values.

There are some obvious differences. Drama is invariably a social event, embodying the paradox that its most intense encounters with privacy and individualism, such as Beckett's one-person plays and plays without words, can be realized only in theatrical performance; they have currency only as product, not as process; they require the spectator as co-participant. There is no direct equivalent in drama of the 'self-to-self' individual transactional quality that English in certain of its forms can have (diaries; notebooks; poems written without intent or desire for publication). Only such eccentricity as secret mime before a mirror would equate with the commonplace introspective privacies of expressive English. It follows that the value attached to the term 'experience' by English teachers has dimensions with no counterpart in drama. More obviously but less importantly, if the sense in which I have used 'language' is accepted, drama does not require the verbal.

Nevertheless, if we look at major formulations of priority, aim and value in both English and drama we find strong similarities between the two. Dixon (1967) reporting on the Dartmouth seminar on English teaching sketched three accepted models of English:

> Among the models or images of English that have been widely accepted in schools on both sides of the Atlantic, three were singled out. The first centred on *skills*: it fitted an era when *initial* literacy was the prime demand. The second stressed the *cultural heritage*, the need for a civilizing and socially unifying content. The third (and current) model focuses on *personal*

growth: on the need to re-examine the learning processes and the meaning to the individual of what he is doing in English lessons. Looking back over the history of our subject, we see the limitations in the earlier models and thus the need to reinterpret our conception of 'skills' and 'heritage'.[1]

This model has been much criticized, notably by Whitehead[2] and Allen[3] for its promotion of child language at the cost of the teacher's authority to intervene, its promotion of a 'value-free' concept of language, and its displacement of literature, and hence for its erosion of established values embodied in literature itself and represented by the informed intelligence of the guiding teacher. However, it has also been influential and widely accepted, as a later formulation such as that of Paffard (1978) makes clear:

> English is mainly concerned with doing rather than knowing, in a word, with skills (which makes it like physical education) and more particularly with skills of expression, communication, discovery and evaluation (which makes it even more like Art). Like them, too, it is concerned with personal growth and with our cultural heritage. It deals with levels of personal experience and the matrix of language from which all other specialist subject concerns develop.[4]

We are directly confronted here by the major debate about values which has characterized English teaching since the mid-1960s. It is strongly reflected in the Bullock Report (1975), for example in a passage which omits the 'cultural heritage' but includes what had by then become a fourth competitor in the contest of priorities:

> Some teachers see English as an instrument of personal growth, going so far as to declare that 'English is about growing up' ... Others feel that the emphasis should be placed on direct instruction in the skills of reading or writing ... There are those who would prefer English to be an instrument of social change.[5]

The importance of this debate about values, with its implications for subject content, classroom method and educational objectives, will be considered below. For the present I wish chiefly to stress its parallel in drama. The Report of the Schools Council Drama Teaching Project (10–16), *Learning Through Drama* (1977) asks and answers the question of teaching objectives as follows:

> What then is the role of teachers in the arts and in drama? It is two-fold:

1 To encourage the child to deepen and challenge his perceptions of himself and his world so that he gradually begins to make sense of the complexities and subtleties of his experience; acknowledges, accommodates and reassesses his world-view in the light of new experience.
2 To do this through enabling the child to use and express himself through the symbolic process of the arts.[6]

There is clearly much in common here with Dixon's objective of 'personal growth', and with Paffard's 'skills of expression, communication, discovery and evaluation'. Similarly Way (1967) observes:

the achievement of skill in all human activities is dependent, in the final analysis, on practice; skill at living is equally dependent on practice, and the intention of this book [*Development Through Drama*] is to suggest ways of providing practice at this particular skill. In this sense, a basic definition of drama might be simply 'to practise living' ... The aim is constant: to develop people, not drama.[7]

He proposes an expanding concentric method which moves outward from personal discovery towards awareness of other people and of the environment at large. Way's view of drama is manifestly akin to Dixon's 'personal growth' model for English, and his concept of skills is compatible with what are increasingly accorded curricular recognition as 'life-skills'. The sequence of skill development proposed by Pemberton-Billing and Clegg (1965)[8] has rather more in common with Dixon's 'skills' model for English, in that they begin with movement and work progressively through carefully structured activities towards speech, improvization, and so to more advanced dramatic activities which require the exercise of contributory skills simultaneously and interactively. The object is a form of dramatic literacy, in which the elements of dramatic skill are systematically exercised and developed both as a training in dramatic expertise in its own right and also for their social usefulness in the business of effective living. Finally, very few commentators on drama exclude the value of the scripted play, of going to the theatre, and hence sharing as a member of the audience in our national dramatic heritage, and — for those children with the necessary skill, confidence and motivation — of acting in productions. The 'cultural heritage' model thus has its counterpart also. It seems, then, that whilst some activities in drama are interchangeable with those of English there are others which are separate and distinctive, yet this separateness concerns content, and specific skills, rather than state-

Values in the Teaching of English and Drama

ments of aim and value. The three models of English teaching proposed by Dixon have their equivalent in drama, as does the fourth, the desire to fashion an educational 'instrument of social change.' Although it is relatively uncommon to find any one of the four omitted, the priorities of individual teachers are often single-mindedly intensive and forcefully defended. Each has its logic of continuity into classroom method, and each has its predominant explicit and implicit values. When these are discussed in the following pages with specific attention to English, a parallel situation in drama can be guardedly assumed. Certainly the aims stated by drama teachers, as summarized in *Learning Through Drama*, would be warmly endorsed as subject values equally by those English teachers who concur with Dixon's 'personal growth' model and those who place greater emphasis on literature and the 'cultural heritage':

> ... what are the aims of such work? The teachers involved in the project listed such aims as 'developing the child's powers of self-expression', 'developing self-awareness, self-confidence, encouraging sensitivity and powers of imagination'. They showed a clear concern for the individual child's life of feelings and emotions and sensed that these are areas of the child's development that may be overlooked in a great deal of curriculum work. They also emphasized the importance of structuring work which encouraged the 'use of imagination'.[9]

Although there would be widespread agreement amongst English teachers about the qualities of mind and personality which work in English and drama is designed to encourage, and about the preferred social and moral values implicit in such aims, the various models referred to nevertheless represent markedly different priorities and values when scrutinized more closely. The four broad centres of interest defined above are not of course either comprehensive or mutually exclusive, and many teachers would perceive the formulations as simplistic. Nevertheless, they are widely current and widely recognized, and certainly provide a broadly accurate depiction of the way English teachers (and, I have suggested, drama teachers also) have perceived the choices and opportunities open to them. Most teachers have attempted to take some account of each in planning their work, and much of the apparent confusion and uncertainty in English teaching since the mid-1970s may flow from the effort to embrace all the 'official' purposes of English teaching without the aid of a coherent theory which notices and integrates their discrepant underlying values. Ormell (1980) sets out a possible divergence of values between school and

33

Peter Hollindale

school in Classics teaching which closely reflects and illuminates the kind of dilemma facing teachers of English.

> The intellectual values of a classical syllabus may be mental-training, discipline, knowledge of words, syntax and verbal accuracy. An institution which adopts such a syllabus aims to please those who care about these things. On the other hand, a rival scheme may claim that its values are awareness of our Graeco-Roman heritage, imaginative reconstruction of the past, classical poetry and legend, and an appreciation of the great ideas of the ancient world. No one is in any doubt that this scheme operates with different currencies from the other. It aims to please those who care more about the cultural content of a classical education and less about its form.[10]

Ormell goes on to point out that teachers strongly committed to one scheme or the other may feel guilty about the omissions forced upon them as a result, and this is particularly true in a curriculum area with such diverse aims as English.

The burden of controversy has centred heavily on the value of literature. In other words it is the 'cultural heritage' model which has felt itself most neglected and has stated its claims most forcibly. The case in favour of literature as an educational medium is ancient, but for its specific place in modern educational thinking it need be traced back no further than Matthew Arnold, and derived greatly renewed force in the 1930s from the work of Dr F.R. Leavis and his colleagues and followers in the Cambridge English School. Teachers in this tradition have always made very great claims for literature; for example Wilson (1980) refers to it as 'mankind's greatest, most flexible, and most generally useful art form', and 'supremely important among subjects'. It is represented above all as 'supremely educative, being grounded in values.'[11] The stress in claims for literature in English teaching has always lain from this standpoint on its moral value. In established classical literature, it is argued, we find language at its best, its most mature, its most scrupulous, its most discriminating, engaging with the realities of human experience and subjecting them to the scrutiny of a delicate and searching moral intelligence. The morally educative power of literature can take place only in the felt response of the reader to the work *as a whole*: the encounter of the reader with great literature makes demands upon his intelligence, his feelings, his moral insight, his capacity to respond to the values and shades of value embodied in language. Moral questions cannot be 'extracted' from literature, because form and content, language and meaning, are unique and inseparable.

By their experience of literature children encounter a *quality* of imaginative and linguistic experience which has no parallel or substitute. Its representations of human experience have a uniquely civilizing power: they enact the moral dimensions of human experience; they enrich our awareness of the otherness of other people, and extend our sympathies; they free us from the limitations of our egotistical perspectives of what it means to be human; they exercise a civilizing influence on our own beliefs, values and behaviour. It is commonly argued that as an instrument of moral education literature has been rendered still more important by the decline of religious education and religious belief, and by the corruptive influences of a materialistic post-industrial society and debased commercial culture.

These are large claims, and in some important respects the case for the moral value of literature teaching can easily be overstated. The causal connection between literary sensitivity and morally responsible behaviour is obviously naive; only a fool would claim that reading good and moral literature maketh the good and moral man. Again, in so far as great literature is an 'achieved' event of the adult moral intelligence, it requires in turn a mature and tutored intelligence in the reader; it is an overlooked paradox in the pedagogy of literature teaching that the desired fullness of response in the reader requires the *completion* of a process which English lessons in school are merely developing. There is a frequent confusion between the kind of learning which occurs in the mature and the immature intelligence: the most we can expect from children is a good response to simple literature or a partial, unformed 'insensitive' response to major work. This misconception has had the practical effect of discouraging potentially valuable encounters with less distinguished but more accessible fictions, and instigating premature, deterrent confrontations with difficult classics. In turn this has implications for children's writing about literature. The study of literature in schools is habitually associated, especially for older pupils, with the ability to make lucid appreciative or critical statements about it, and indeed the entire public examination structure depends on this association. One could suppose the entire profession of English teaching to be ignorant of Wordsworth's 'How the art of lying may be taught'. In much argument for literature teaching there is also an implicit but questionable equation of literary with moral excellence. In such problems as these, to some of which I shall return later, there is some discrepancy between the ideology of literature teaching and its actual practice and results.

However, the criticisms of those committed to other 'models' of English teaching have been mainly directed at other aspects of litera-

Peter Hollindale

ture. Dixon, in arguing for 'personal growth', criticized the stress 'on culture as a *given*', and went on:

> Literature itself tended to be treated as a given, a ready-made structure that we imitate and a content that is handed over to us. And this attitude infected composition and all work in language. There was a fatal inattention to the processes involved in such everyday activities as talking and thinking things over, writing a diary or a letter home, even enjoying a TV play. Discussion was virtually ignored ...[12]

The emphasis preferred by those teachers who aim for 'personal growth' is on the experience brought to the English lesson by the child himself. What is valued above all is the impetus of the child to use language in order to give shape and meaning to his own knowledge, his own interests, his own feelings. Instead of teacher-initiated attention to established literature, the stress is on pupil-initiated sharing of direct experience through talk and through informal writing tasks. Writing done by the children becomes the 'literature of the classroom', and there is a continuum which links the 'literature' which the child produces with the 'literature' of the classical repertoire, rather than the customary distinction, involving different categories of value, between the achieved literature of recognized adult work and the immature apprentice efforts of the child.

The word 'literature' is being effectively used in a different sense here. It has become a more neutral, descriptive term to denote something more widely and prematurely achievable by ordinary people. A value is placed on primary experience, the original conversion of individual choice and interest into language, rather than the value of secondary experience, a gradual initiation into appreciation of 'other men's flowers', the best and most durable products of the inherited culture. The values of developing self-awareness and self-expression, through the vivid ephemera in experience (such as short-lived hobbies) and the vivid ephemera of language (such as notes and talk) replace the values of mature adult achievement, established public esteem and permanence. While the approach through literature is overtly concerned with values and evaluation both in the content of literature and in the language which expresses it, the approach through personal experience requires a more egalitarian, more value-free and less judgmental attitude at once to language and to the experience it explores.

Here too there are exaggerated claims. Children's writing will sometimes, but not often, support the kind of analysis, the praise for originality, or the comparisons with adult work to which it has been subjected in recent years. In particular we need to review the increasing practice of placing children's poems together with those of adults in anthologies: the ambiguous status they enjoy there, partly challenging equal attention as literature and partly offering conspiratorial encouragement to the child reader, reflects both a proper respect for children's writing and a reluctance to face the implications of evaluating it. Moreover, the neutral definition of literature *does* often mean that children are deprived of access to the past and the cultural context they inherit, and that they are not invited to explore the moral universe of major literature. The approach can also mean that language which is value-laden is treated as if it were value-free.

Each of these approaches has strengths and limitations. But it is hard to see why they should be regarded as alternatives, especially when we see how much they share in their hopes for the maturing child. They need not polarize, except for practical convenience, into 'literature' and 'language' approaches, as they so often have in recent discussions. Literature is, after all, a particular quality of language. Its defenders have been provoked and understandably irritated by formulations which demote or neglect it as merely one of several 'Englishes', the prestigious dialect of a minority culture with no higher claims to value than any other kind of English.

These formulations are particularly current in research projects with the primary and entirely reputable aim of defining and providing a means of teaching a complete spectrum of language skills. It is true of course that children need to develop extensive and varied language skills in both speech and writing in order to function competently as adults in a society where English becomes steadily more complex, sophisticated and manipulative. Two such projects, the *Nuffield Programme in Linguistics and English Teaching* and the Schools Council Project, *Writing and Learning Across the Curriculum*, have certainly propagated a notion of equivalence as between 'literature' and other forms of English, and the Linguistics Programme in particular has suggested that its role is peripheral. It is quite possible in my view to accept that literature is a product of language, categorically indistinguishable from other kinds of language, and is not an entity which has somehow transcended what it is made from, and yet to accept that it represents the quality of that language at its most complex and achieving. A test of that quality is its intrinsic concern with values, conducted in such a way that those values are inextricable from the wholeness of the language which explores them.

In this sense the whole 'language v. literature' debate of recent years is unnecessary. Participants in the controversy have almost all taken the view that literature both *is* and *is not* 'language', but have attached radically different evaluations to their sense of its distinctiveness. The expedient division of school English into 'Language' and 'Literature' is one of the crudest, most divisive instances of this artificial dichotomy. Literature is a qualitative sub-division of language, with boundaries and definition that can never be precise. What can be confidently asserted is that literature is that part of English which is most profoundly occupied with values, and English work in school which neglects literature is as impoverished and one-sided as that which concentrates on it to the exclusion of children's personal language and utilitarian linguistic needs.

In some quarters — those referred to earlier who see English and drama primarily as potential instruments for social change — the attack on literature and the switch of emphasis to pupils' own language has a different emphasis and a more explicitly political intention. The change discussed earlier, from a 'cultural heritage' to a 'personal growth' model, certainly has a political dimension in itself, and it would be naive to ignore it. Underlying it is the ideal of a living democracy of language, something in which all can share, which binds and unifies the community, and works against such definitions of literacy as produce arbitrarily selected élites. For other teachers, a comparable devaluation of literature in educational currency, together with the new coinage of valued pupil language, has a more overt political context. Mathieson (1975) defines the standpoint of those teachers she characterizes as the New Left:

> Great literature, it is now being argued, is not only inappropriate and inaccessible to the majority of our pupils whose time should first be spent on extension of their linguistic competence; its inclusion in all pupils' curricula, with the inevitable exclusion of working-class culture, implicitly supports the present social structure with all its inequalities ... From their standpoint, the Cambridge School's insistence upon the value of great literature and disparagement of commercial culture represents endorsement of middle-class values.[13]

There is some force in this argument, though it has more to do with literary criticism and the implications of conventional literature teaching than with the nature of literature itself. Those who believe as I do in the educational value of literature, and believe moreover that sensitively taught it can have much of the maturing and civilizing influence described earlier, can yet acknowledge that in practice literature is a

Values in the Teaching of English and Drama

radical phenomenon which is treated conservatively. To some extent this is inevitable. That valuing of the past and the cultural inheritance which is involved in the choice and teaching of established literature does usually imply (though it *need* not) a resistance to major social change. The values embodied in much great literature, by virtue of its survival and acceptance, have often been absorbed into the general framework of assumed and uninspected social values. Merely by virtue of its historicity, literature is sentenced to a passive conservatism which only the continuing process of 'revaluation' (there is irony in our debt to Dr Leavis for this key term) can overcome. The New Left — a term I borrow as a rather unsatisfactory shorthand — is correct particularly in accusing the Cambridge English School of *reinforcing* the conservative function of literature in its educational role. In many respects the contemporary teacher's debt to Leavis and the Cambridge School is immense, not least for its 'disparagement of commercial culture'. The involvement of English as a school subject in the critique of advertising and other commercial, manipulative language uses (which crucially include *political* language, in view of its growing fusion with commercial deception techniques) is directly traceable to the Cambridge School, and in particular to Leavis and Thompson's seminal work *Culture and Environment*.

However, the dubious counterpart of this constructive process has been the presentation of major literature as the voice and embodiment of permanent and desirable moral values. There is in effect a category error in the Leavisite approach to its approved major literature, in that much critical discussion in this school has treated values as if they were *facts*, with the same authority of unbreachable truth that scientific truth can claim. Moral values are not 'true' in the same precise and durable sense that scientific facts are 'true', but Leavisite discussion habitually speaks as if they were. Hence in this formulation by Q.D. Leavis (1981) we find the significantly corrective phrase denoting factuality and permanence in what is otherwise a fine statement of the major writer's endemic interaction with his time. The gifted writer is 'peculiarly sensitive to national tensions and conflicts and one who, by the accidents of his personal history, is specially qualified to feel and register the characteristic and deeper movements of the life of his time, *has a true sense of values*, and has the wisdom and insights which make him a warning voice for his generation.'[14] By extension the great writer is the spokesman of 'true' values as a condition of his greatness. Ben Jonson remarked on 'the impossibility of any man's being the good poet, without first being a good man', but what he intended as a piece of combative rhetoric has come to be idealized in some critical circles as a truth. There is no adequate allowance for the proposition that the 'true' values of one period may not be the 'true' values of another, or that a great writer may voice the legitimate values of one generation which are repugnant to a later one and still remain a great writer, still less that a major writer may in his *own* time have an 'untrue' or undesirable sense of values. The temporary eclipse or obsolescence of important values as the result of historical aberration is overridden by the ahistorical and defining term 'human' as a mark of approval. Leavisite criticism has established a vocabulary of value-permanence by abducting the term 'human' and attaching it to values of supposedly fixed validity, those which — in a repeated and characteristic phrase — are 'central to our humanity'. Viewed from this perspective, literature is certainly a conservative phenomenon.

If the established ideology and practice of literature teaching is rooted in the Cambridge School, that of the New Left is rooted in structuralism. Structuralism questions many of the assumptions on which traditional literature teaching is based: whether literature is more 'valuable' than other kinds of writing, whether it truly registers or organizes human experience, whether it has value as a 'humane' (or 'human') study. Its diametric opposition to Leavisite practice is clear from an excellent discussion by Hollingworth (1983):

> The theory of value on which structuralist arguments rest is relativistic. Basically, since the observation of human societies suggests to us that values are not permanent entities — that what is valued by one civilization or one historical epoch is not necessarily valued by another — it seems reasonable to infer that value lies in the eye of the beholder and, by extension, to argue that one set of values cannot be demonstrably better than another.
>
> The theory of language on which the arguments rest is that of extreme subjectivism. We shape our own reality, or, rather, society shapes it for us — there is no objective reality to which we fit our language as experience comes upon us. On the contrary, language, which society gives us, gives us the means to make patterns of meaning in the chaos of experience — to make sense of our world. By extension, language *is* meaning, and without language there is no meaning at all.[15]

Hollingworth goes on to summarize the development of this argument which offers a threat to traditional literature teaching: 'the extension to the ideological argument that man is a victim of a society which ruthlessly inculcates its arbitrary values through language. Society controls its members ideologically — shapes the value perceptions of its citizens — through language: it necessarily must do so since there are no external standards of value or reality which the individual can legitimately appeal to'.

The kinship is evident between this critical ideology and 'language-centred' theories of English teaching. Its political radicalism goes further than that of most English teachers who would align themselves with the 'New Left', but in its stress on the historical fluctuation of values, on the entrenched political systems which determine them, and on the personal construct of reality which we shape from language, it has fundamental points in common.

The plight of the English teacher, who is not concerned directly with antagonistic critical ideologies but is nevertheless influenced by their seepage into the everyday debate and practice of teaching, is that in seeking to be eclectic, to find space for a set of recommended and convincingly purposeful activities, he may be in practice juxtaposing disparate and even incompatible value-related activities. For example, a teacher who is more or less simultaneously teaching *Great Expectations*, encouraging autobiographical writing, and discussing political reportage of a BL strike in the tabloid press, would seem to have an agenda of interesting, diverse and educative activities, but may in practice be dealing in concealed discrepancies of value which perplexingly deny to him and to his pupils any sense of unity and purpose in the subject. At the same time, all but partisan ideologues will feel that a potential unity is there, waiting to be discovered and explained. English and drama need a coherent theory of eclecticism to account for discrepant values and justify the diversity of what they do.

The war of critical ideologies is, however, a distraction from the radical nature of literature itself. Creative writers are on the whole more radical than critics, and works which appear (or can be made) conservative in retrospect are often in their contemporary setting deeply challenging to prevailing political and moral orthodoxies and, even more disturbingly, to man's conception of his own nature and biological status. Even works which appear in the end to vindicate conservative values seldom exempt them from a fundamental testing which takes nothing on trust. One characteristic of what I have called the 'qualitative sub-division of language' which is literature is that it is a testing-ground, characterized by imaginative experiment which allows for any possible result. And even when creative writers themselves regard certain values as fundamental to human well-being, they tend to recognize their shifting and unstable status in the affairs of mankind at large. D.H. Lawrence observed the temporality of values: '. . . all morality is of temporary value, useful in its time ... Art must give deeper satisfaction. It must give fair play all around' (*Phoenix*); and again, 'Everything is true in its own time, place, circumstance, and untrue outside of its own time, place, circumstance. If you try to nail everything down, in the novel, either it kills the novel, or the novel gets up and walks away with the nail' (*Phoenix*). Whatever may be asserted elsewhere, it is in the very nature of literature, in exploring the human dilemmas from which fictions take their life, to show that not a single moral value is so basic, so necessary as the bedrock for other values, that it admits no exceptions and is always right. Not even the widely canvassed 'respect for other people' is that; a creator of fictions can readily imagine circumstances when the welfare and even the lives of other people should not be respected. The same radicalism applies to conditions of the spirit: despair may be a mortal sin, but literature can vindicate it; there is no attestation of faith in either life or after-life which is proof against the relentless pessimistic vision of *Jude the Obscure*. Nor is the moral compunction of the individual always to be taken as evidence of a higher humanity than egotism. In John Fowles' novella *The Ebony Tower*, a gifted and successful artist, intelligent and scrupulous in his private life, compares his own fine, second-rate accomplishment with the greatness of a selfish and amoral painter he has visited.

> He felt a delayed but bitter envy of the old man. In the end it all came down to what one was born with: one either had the temperament for excess and a ruthless egocentricity, for keeping thought and feeling in different compartments, or one didn't; and David didn't. The abominable and vindictive injustice was that art is fundamentally amoral.

And the lack of amorality, of creative egotism, is felt as a failing and a loss.

Patently it is not true that literature is inherently 'conservative', that it reinforces middle-class or establishment values. On the contrary, its potential radicalism is limitless. *Gulliver's Travels*, *Northanger Abbey*, *Wuthering Heights*, *Middlemarch*, *The Mayor of Casterbridge* and *A Passage to India* are all in their way profoundly radical in their values, though each can easily be misrepresented as escapist or as bourgeois fiction. It is not literature, but schools of criticism and traditions of teaching, or even simple historical mutation, which make of literature a counter-force to personal creativity and social change.

Teaching English and drama is therefore a multiple and complex process, in which concealed discordances of value may set one classroom activity at odds with another, or even with itself. However

Values in the Teaching of English and Drama

abstract or academic the issues seem, they surface in the everyday negotiations of the classroom, its misunderstandings and its failures of direction. Their typical obfuscations are beautifully caught in a passage from Iain Crichton Smith's novel about a middle-aged English teacher, *An End To Autumn*.

> One day he had a discussion about *King Lear* with his class, and it seemed to him that the play had taken on a new meaning for him, as if it were trying to teach him something. He found that for some odd reason his sixth year consisted almost exclusively of girls, which he didn't really mind, for though their minds lacked the penetration of those of boys — a certain ruthlessness — they compensated by a sensitivity that boys didn't have. They found *King Lear* not very interesting, which surprised him, but at least they had things to say about the king whom they considered little more than idiotic: nor did they condemn Goneril and Regan as much as he thought they might have done. No, there was no law inscribed on eternal tablets, which stated that one must look after the old, no matter what the latter were like. It all depended really on the individual old person. Certainly the bleak majesty of *King Lear* was very unlike the passive appeal of his own mother, and certainly the transformations and murders and wars belonged to a much earlier more barbaric world, but wasn't the principle timeless? No, they repeated, there existed no timeless decree by which we could all set our compass, no eternal moral north. And as he looked at them — young, pretty, earnest — he sometimes wondered what would happen to them, which ones would be stranded by the storms of life, and eventually live on the scraps of charity distributed by a family busy with their own concerns.

The temporality of values is there, the moral relativism and the moral ruthlessness. In this case the conservative principles of compassion, duty and family responsibility are not reinforced by conservative literature; rather their fragile hold on the self-determining conscience is exposed by the radicalism of the play. These girls, after all, are not voicing opinions wholly extraneous to the drama, however little it interests them. They have responded to it, but in a limited, self-pleasing, 'insensitive' way. In *King Lear* Shakespeare depicts the rationality of callous egotism, and this they have taken from it because it speaks to them 'where they are'. The play shows rationality at odds with moral intelligence. The girls have seen only the rationality, without responding to the moral repugnance which surrounds it or the cataclysm which its exercise releases. There is no way for them to understand the play at an adequate level of response; its complexity as literature is beyond their compass. (But how can it not be? Is there not inherent absurdity in confronting teenagers with *King Lear*?) Consequently, their perceptions of relevance and their available language are 'far, far wide' from the play as literature — as drama — yet their adolescent intellectual ruthlessness is actually closer to the play (to Goneril and Regan) than to the bourgeois decencies of classroom discussion or the reality of their own potential experience. When classroom English seems at cross purposes, as it often does — at cross purposes between text and response, between language received and language spoken, between principle and feeling, between intrinsic meaning and extrinsic relevance, between teacher and pupil, the aimless perplexities which result are usually traceable to deeper confusions of value rooted in both the content and the ideology of English.

The teaching of English and drama, then, is clearly rooted in explicit and implicit concern with values. Their nature and definition appear to differ widely depending on the teacher's centre of emphasis, but the divergences are not perhaps so incapable of reconciliation and mutual consistency as may appear. Yet the practice and effects of much English teaching have to be acknowledged as disappointing. The ambitious objectives of English in the curriculum are not discernible in many actual results, even amongst pupils who go on to study English in further and higher education. Amongst possible reasons for this, I would wish to propose three: pupils' perception of the nature and utility of the subject; discrepancies and contradictions between professed aims and classroom practice; and the failure of teachers to hold a rational theory of eclecticism to unify the diverse work they undertake.

Amongst pupils, English and drama are not exempt from the preoccupations which pupils bring to all their school work. If they are to respect a school activity, they must be able to 'see where they have been' as a result of it. They must be able to do things they could not do before, and feel that as a result they exert greater control over their own lives and destinies. Ironically drama, the less obviously utilitarian of the two subject areas, is often more successful in achieving such a purpose. English, however, works at a disadvantage in pupils' esteem at precisely that point where teachers assume that positive advantage is most evident. Teachers see language as a fundamental skill. In its utilitarian ('transactional') forms it is necessary for the successful performance of numerous disparate life-tasks; in its pleasurable ('poetic') forms it offers increased access to recreation, cultural enlightenment and individual expression. Its development is thus clearly associated with economic, social, moral, intellectual and aesthetic values. And teachers are right to formulate the importance of language in this way. Many pupils, however, do not see language as a form of knowledge (in the same sense as mathematics, or a *foreign* language); nor do they see it as a skill (in the same sense as gymnastics or woodwork). The advantage of drama is that it is more readily perceived as a skill. English, however, is something you have already, something you employ unselfconsciously without any awareness of the knowledge and skill you have already accrued as a child in order to manage everyday life. For most pupils, their present command of English is already sufficient for their everyday purposes, gathering increments of specialized language for private hobbies and technical skills as they are needed. Usually they also have sufficient recreational language for reading popular literature and watching television drama. The purposes of *extending* language competence which are so obvious to the teacher are far from obvious to many pupils. A case needs to be made, and often goes by default, for taking English seriously.

That case must include questions of control. This in turn involves *showing* (not stating) that most language is value-laden and potentially manipulative, and that manipulation can take both desirable and undesirable forms. A fundamental aim of English teaching is to develop pupils' capacity to manipulate language, and to recognize language which seeks to manipulate them, in such a way that their control of their lives is enhanced and their ability to distinguish legitimate from improper manipulation is strengthened. The place of literature in this process should not be taken for granted: teachers disappointed by the failure of pupils to take pleasure in literature must have an answer to the spoken or unspoken question, 'What's the use of it?' Much progressive inertia in English teaching stems from under-estimation of children's pragmatism in their attitude to learning.

It should also be apparent to children how seemingly discrete activities are coordinated in their purpose. For example, it is not instantly obvious what connects the reading of literature (a study of affirmed values) with a critique of popular media (a questioning of implicit values) and in turn with personal writing (a discovery and articulation of values). The teacher must be able to establish such connections and hence to unify his subject.

English is also undermined by discrepancies between aim and practice, which at worst can have the effect of exposing dishonesty in the teacher and encouraging dishonesty in the pupil. For instance, it is widely accepted that pupils' writing must be meaningful, produced from a real situation which in turn determines its kind, length and appropriate form, and emerge from a need for expression. Keen (1978) has shown how the standard English essay is influenced by questions of expediency, such as the length of the school period and the demands of coordinated grading, and frequently directs the pupils' writing to artificial tasks which have no purpose beyond that of satisfying the teacher. He analyses contradictory elements in a school essay on 'A Fairground at Night' and comments:

> She [the pupil] dutifully relates some thoughts and feelings of the kind that English teachers seem to like. Unfortunately, in her desire to invent some feelings that will make her teacher happy she trips herself up and writes down two sets, which happen to contradict each other. There is no reality to these feelings; they exist only in the rules that determine what mark you get for your essays. Yet the student is responding as best she can to a task that forces her to respond with bewilderment and dishonesty.[16]

The same kind of problem arises with comment on reading and critical response to literature. The 'fullness of response' which is most valued in literature teaching is regularly vitiated in practice by imposing on the pupil an obligation to produce a response where none was felt or a premature demand that it should be expressed in a formal critical idiom. Jackson (1982) discusses a comprehension question which directs children's attention to a real and interesting but difficult literary effect, and comments as follows on the way the task is phrased: 'But the facility for manipulating that kind of critical apparatus isn't necessarily tied into a feeling experience of any sort. And often, in schools, we go for the premature critical approach without the lived-through dimension to make it real.'[17] The results at examination level of such premature demand (and such contradiction of declared value) are cogently described by Paffard (1978):

> Anyone who has marked a public examination in English literature has endured many teachers' model answers to anticipated questions at second hand only distinguishable from one another by being more or less successfully remembered or literately presented: the teacher virtually takes the examination by proxy. Requiring students to read certain critics and commentators is open to the same objection and abuse; hang-dog reproductions of standard literary evaluations, clichés of criticism, pirated eulogies from the text-books and imitation-indignant castigation of faults are all too likely to result. It is doubtful if in any other subject the student is so persistently

tempted and even encouraged to compromise his integrity as a reader and rewarded for acquiring an examination technique which negates the most essential feature of that subject's discipline.[18]

Yet why should the pupil not compromise his integrity when the teacher habitually does the same? The Schools Council research report *Children and their Books* (1977)[19] found a widespread reluctance amongst English teachers to engage with complete books, and hence with the wholeness of response which literature is supposed to develop. Instead, they habitually made use of extracts. Admittedly the teaching of complete books is difficult, organizationally as well as pedagogically, but that is scarcely a reason for abandoning an activity so fundamental to the declared purposes of English. It appears to be, like the misuse of the school essay, a compromise made in response to the routine pressures of school organization. That should not obscure the importance of the sacrifice involved. It emerges again in the widespread choice and use of class readers which bend to the topical extrapolation of 'themes' and 'issues' at cost of the wholeness of their fictional worlds: the use of such novels as *Walkabout* and *To Kill a Mockingbird* as 'kits' for thematic work on racism is a common everyday example of this approach.

These are instances of the erosion of values in the process of transmission from principle to practice. At the level of principle itself, however, English needs to devise a rational eclecticism underpinned by theory. Although ideologues of various persuasions may argue strenuously for a single model of English teaching and a heavy emphasis upon it, the teacher in the classroom will continue to link and blend a diversity of activities which he rightly sees as contributing to the whole federation of English work. Literature, personal writing, talk and listening, media studies, work on 'non-literary' language skills, may each be partly self-governing states in such a federation, as will movement, mime, role-play, improvization, and possibly script performance if drama comes within its union. But where is the capital or centre, which the teacher may not explicitly describe to his pupils but which he needs to identify nonetheless if his presentation of the subject is not to be fragmentary and disjointed?

The case for literature as a part of English perhaps needs to be restated and redefined. Major literature represents the fixed points of human interaction between values and historical experience. The greater the literature, the more searching and the more durable is its presentation of that interaction. But because values *do* change in their context and priorities from period to period, because literature is itself

Peter Hollindale

the index of such change and at best registers a particular alertness to it, it follows that no literature, however great, is finally detachable from the period which produced it. Even the greatest literature is the prisoner of its time, and with the movement of history may become temporarily inaccessible or permanently lost. In the longest perspective, shifts not only of values but of language mean that even the great classics (even Shakespeare!) will finally be irrecoverable to all but a handful of scholars. We should value literature, then, as much for its *impermanence* as its supposed permanence. It is valuable above all because it offers still points of reference in the flux of human experience; it is the place where we find values embedded in the full context of historical locality.

The greater the work, and the greater its separation from us in time, the more inaccessible it becomes for inexperienced readers. The process of learning to read it is slow, and difficult, and not for everyone. (Drama again enjoys an advantage, retaining an ease of historical accessibility denied to poetry or the novel, because it offers more varied points of contact and entry). A 'full response' to literature is strenuously won; I have tried to demonstrate the absurdity of an educational procedure which demands that such a response should be articulated before it can with any probability be achieved. Along with discreet and carefully timed attention to the 'classics', therefore, we need in English a more generous attention to the less profound but more urgent minor literature of our own period, together with a more inclusive *definition* of literature which has space for the non-fictitious. If we perceive all literature as finally ephemeral, we can be more accommodating to the immediate ephemera with which (importantly) we happen to share a decade, or a year.

On such a view, literature is potentially *more*, not *less* interesting to teachers who accept the mutability of values than to those who look for fixity and permanence.

There is no incompatibility between a sense of fluctuation and evanescence in language and values, and the acceptance of educational worth in accessible works where episodes of interaction between language and values are comprehensively registered by a major writer. There is no essential discrepancy between the use of language to promote social change and attention to those works which have formerly observed it, whether as partisan or opponent. There is no essential discrepancy between respect for the child's personal construct of reality, as he fits language to his experience, and care for past great efforts to do the same.

English and drama are both concerned to enrich experience, and they do this crucially when they transform secondary experience into primary experience by giving it linguistic and expressive shape. Secondary experience may be that of other people, potentially available in literature or the theatre; it may be news, documentary experience whether of Northern Ireland or Poland or El Salvador, which has been dulled to indifference by the distancing familiarity of television; it may be inchoate observation or experience of our own, which needs to be shaped by language into understanding. The business of English and drama is to use the languages of speech and body to make experience truly our own, and integrity is its essence. That is not the *only* business of English and drama, nor yet the way our pupils will most quickly understand or respect it, but it is, nevertheless, at the centre. The teacher who has formulated his own values into some such unifying pattern is more likely to avoid the aimlessness and fragmentation which undercut so much teaching of English, and more likely to avoid teaching procedures which contradict or deny the essential goals of his subject.

Notes

1 DIXON, J. (1967) *Growth Through English*, Reading, National Association for the Teaching of English, pp. 1–2.
2 WHITEHEAD, F.S. (1976) 'Stunting the growth', *Use of English*, 28, 1, pp. 11–17.
3 ALLEN, D. (1980) *English Teaching Since 1965: How Much Growth?* London, Heinemann Educational, pp. 28–44.
4 PAFFARD, M. (1978) *Thinking About English*, London, Ward Lock Educational, pp. 11–12.
5 The Bullock Report, (1975) *A Language For Life*, London, HMSO, p. 4.
6 MCGREGOR, L., TATE, M., and ROBINSON, K., (1977) *Learning Through Drama*, London, Heinemann Educational, p. 23.
7 WAY, B. (1967) *Development Through Drama*, London, Longman, p. 6.
8 PEMBERTON-BILLING, R.N. and CLEGG, J.D. (1965) *Teaching Drama*, London, University of London Press.
9 MCGREGOR, L., TATE, M. and ROBINSON, K., (1977) *op. cit.*, p. 4.
10 ORMELL, C., (1980) 'Values in education', in STRAUGHAN, R. and WRIGLEY, J. (Eds.) *Values and Evaluation in Education*, London, Harper and Row, p. 77.
11 WILSON, R. (1980) 'Literature,' in STRAUGHAN, R. and WRIGLEY, J. (Eds.) *Values and Evaluation in Education* London, Harper and Row, pp. 124, 129 and 133.
12 DIXON, J. (1967) *op. cit.*, p. 4.
13 MATHIESON, M. (1975) *The Preachers of Culture: A Study of English and its Teachers*, London, Allen and Unwin, p. 140.

14 LEAVIS, Q.D. (1981) 'The Englishness of the English Novel', *New Universities Quarterly*, 35, 2, p. 150 (my emphasis)
15 HOLLINGWORTH, B. (1983) 'Crisis in English teaching', *Use of English* 34, 2, p. 4.
16 KEEN, J. (1978) *Teaching English: A Linguistic Approach*, London, Methuen, p. 16.
17 JACKSON, D. (1982) *Continuity in Secondary English*, London, Methuen, p. 129.
18 PAFFARD, M., (1978) *op. cit.*, p. 77.
19 WHITEHEAD, F. *et. al.* (1977) *Children and their Books*, London, Macmillan Education, p. 278.

Values in Geographical Education

Patrick Wiegand

Oh, the hammer ponds of Sussex and the dew ponds of the West,
Are part of Britain's heritage, the part we love the best,
Every eel and fish and millpond has a beauty all can share,
But not unless its got a big, brass, broken bedstead there.

The English, the English, the English are best,
I wouldn't give tuppence for all of the rest.

(Flanders and Swann, 1964)

A few years after Flanders and Swann were entertaining audiences of *At The Drop of Another Hat* with their 'Song of Patriotic Prejudice' and 'Bedstead Men' school geography departments in Britain began slowly to respond to revolutionary changes that had swept geography departments in the universities. With the publication by Chorley and Haggett of *Frontiers in Geographical Teaching* in 1965 and the revision of geography examination syllabuses in the 1970s, school geographers turned their attention away from regional geography towards the scientific, hypothesis testing, model-building geography of the so-called 'quantitative revolution'. At the same time, some university geographers were, in turn, moving away from an objective consideration of the relations between people and environment. The 1970s saw much 'alternative' writing from university geography departments. Foremost amongst these were 'humanistic' and 'radical' approaches to geography (Johnston, 1983). Humanistic geography rejects the scientific approach of positivism and builds instead on the philosophies of phenomenology and existentialism. Understanding is achieved not through theory building but by studying the lived world of people's subjective experience. Humanistic geographers attempt to understand places through human feelings and values. Rowles, for example, (1980) has explored the geographical experiences of growing old, not by a conventional approach such as measuring migration patterns of the retired population but by an in-depth case study of a few elderly people, probing their feelings and memories for places past and present.

The 1970s also saw an increasing number of claims that geography should become more relevant to social problems. Welfare approaches to geography asked the question 'Who gets what, where and how?' (Smith, 1978), by mapping the distribution of social goods. Maps of medical facilities for example in relation to the distribution of population reveal spatial inequalities. Radical geographers go further. To paraphrase Marx: 'The point of geography is not just to interpret the world but to change it'. Radical geographers have turned their attention towards social justice in the operation of housing markets, development policies in the Third World and environmental issues.

Despite the search for personal meaning and social relevance in the universities, those of us teaching geography in schools in the 1970s could, naturally enough, only cope with one revolution at a time. In any case the new geography offered enhanced scientific status amongst our colleagues and gave us greater bargaining power in our claims for further resources for new textbooks, statistical tables, calculators and more sophisticated fieldwork equipment. Ironically, although Pahl (1967), in one of the most influential books of the quantitative revolution, had said that geography was not, and never could be, value free, the challenge and attraction of an *apparently* value free new geography blocked a proper consideration of the role of values in our classroom. Indeed, it could be argued that the really important value issues in geography were taken up more effectively in the 1970s by, for example, environmental education, development education, peace and world studies, leaving geography a squeezed-out lemon of map skills, regional description and over-simplified models. There were, of course, important exceptions but it is only since the 1980s that the role of values education in British geography has been broadly recognized and explicit teaching strategies and teaching units for dealing with values become more widespread.

There are some grounds for optimism in the present situation of teaching about values in relation to environmental and global issues. Without wishing to be overly partisan, geography is a long-established subject in the school curriculum and has a more secure foothold than the newer subjects mentioned above. More widespread adoption by geographers of values teaching could have more effect therefore throughout the system. A move in this direction is indicated by the editorial of the

Values in Geographical Education

most recent issue of *Teaching Geography* (Bailey, 1983) which raises the values debate and invites contributions from readers on how they handle value laden issues in the classroom. Another development at the time of writing is the formation of a new association: 'The Association for Curriculum Development in Geography' with a journal entitled *Contemporary Issues in Geography and Education*. This Association was launched with a conference on geography and education in a multicultural society in March 1983 at the University of London Institute of Education which explored the political context and ideological content of geography teaching in school. It remains, of course, to be seen how much impact these initiatives will have.

The two songs by Flanders and Swann at the beginning of this chapter are about values central to geography: values about places and people. This chapter is essentially a review. It describes why values about the relationship between people and places are central to the subject matter of geography. Some reference is made to recent changes in university geography as without this the present tensions in teaching the subject cannot be fully understood. Overt values in geography syllabuses, schemes of work and teaching materials are then explained together with some recent criticisms of bias in geography education. Finally a review is made of teaching strategies that have been proposed to deal with the question of values in the geography classroom.

Value Laden Landscapes

Geography is concerned with the interrelationship between people and places. Values enter into geography in two main ways. Firstly, places are (at least in part) determined by people's decisions. These decisions are taken on the basis of the values held by the decision makers. Places, therefore, may be the spatial expression of human values. Secondly, places have value for people, that is they are valued by them. This in turn will affect what the places themselves become. Landscapes may be conserved, developed or neglected on the basis of their perceived value. This brief section illustrates how landscapes cannot be fully understood without reference to human values.

The values held by individuals and groups are significant in explaining landscapes. Cowie (1978) has noted that many features of landscapes may be the spatial expression of underlying religious, social and economic values. She illustrates as examples of religious values the distribution of places of worship and the attitudes of religious groups towards certain kinds of food finding spatial expression in the distribu-

Patrick Wiegand

tion and type of agricultural land use. Social values are expressed in, for example, the designation of areas as National Parks reflecting the value placed on leisure by the national community. Note that this value might conflict with local value priorities which may place employment higher than leisure. Economic values find expression in, for example, migration of population where people move to seek work.

In addition to places being the spatial expression of values, people find value in places. Brief mention was made in the introduction to humanistic geography. One of the major areas of research in humanistic geography concerns the relationship between people and places at the level of subjective experience. The phrase 'sense of place' has been widely used at the academic level and recently taken up as the title of a series of school texts (Beddis, 1981). Relph (1976) in some of the most convincing and accessible writing of humanistic geography has distinguished between place and placelessness: 'To be human is to live in a world filled with significant places'. Place is a difficult concept to define briefly but it involves qualities of authenticity, character, distinctiveness, personal significance and meaning. Places are directly experienced, they stand out in our memory because, for example, we were happy or lonely or experienced something new there. Relph contrasts this experience with that of placelessness: abstract places that have no personal meaning or significance either because they have not been directly experienced or because they are monotonously uniform or planned without feeling or mass produced. Some central city architecture with uniform multi-storey carparks, street lamps and underpasses exhibit placelessness. Tuan (1974) has coined the phrase *topophilia* to describe the 'affective bond between people and place or setting'. Drawing on a great richness of cultural experience he illustrates the ways in which people respond to the environment, taking us through landscape paintings, the romantic poets, patriotism and homesickness. Places are undoubtedly valued by people but are their absolute values to be attributed to environments? Much of the controversy of modern planning hinges on relative environmental values and value conflicts between, for example, professional planners and grass roots opinion. The collection of essays entitled *Valued Environments* (Gold and Burgess, 1982) explores some of these themes.

A familiar example will help to illustrate the complexity of the relationship between people, values and the environment. One of the most important decisions people make is where to live. Accepting that some people have less choice than others, the residential location decision is governed by two sets of factors: individual preferences and the availability of housing stock. The distribution of housing in a town is

Values in Geographical Education

a reflection of a number of values. Classical urban theory relies on an economic model to explain the location of land use types in the city. Competition for the most accessible places leads to the location of shops, offices (who can afford to pay) in the central area, forcing housing into an outer ring. Other mechanisms may be superimposed on this pattern. For example, wedges of housing of high, medium or low quality may develop, often linked to the relative attractiveness of local terrain. Local authority housing estates may be built on cheaper land on the edge of the town. Other factors affect the availability of housing too. Consider, for example, the values underlying the removal of areas from the Green Belt for housing, or the demolition of back-to-back terraces compared to their renewal as 'through' terraces. The choice as presented by estate agents reveals attitudes towards what counts as quality or desirable housing. The details as circulated by agents reveal subtle differences between locations (there is often a right side and a wrong side of the railway line), styles (stone faced or stone built) and accessibility to prestigious amenities (for example, independent schools or golf courses). Residents want to be near but not too near the amenities they need. A cynical view is that we all want access to local bus routes but we would prefer the bus stop to be outside someone else's house. Similarly the local primary school and convenience shops need to be within walking distance but we don't want to overlook them. The local authority dump should be ideally placed in someone else's neighbourhood. The influence, for good or bad, on the local community of such facilities as discotheques, football stadia, launderettes, or restaurants are an important aspect of welfare approaches to geography. The negative or positive effect of these 'externalities' depends to a large degree on where they are located in respect to residents. Mapping the favourable and unfavourable facilities may reveal who benefits from the parks and who suffers from the sewage works. Both Bale (1981) and Slater and Moeller (1981) have devised pupil exercises on the impact of different types of land use in residential areas.

Values change: areas go 'up' or 'down'. Mews properties become gentrified. 'Mews' itself is a value laden word — note also the values implied by terms like cottage, villa, slum or inner city. The desirability of city life itself has long been challenged. Whereas the Greek tradition represents the city as the epitome of civilization, the Judaeo-Christian tradition is dominantly anti-urban. With the industrial revolution this intensified. 'God made the country, man made the town'. Victorian landscape painters and novelists habitually represented the bucolic peace of the countryside in contrast to the horrors of urban life. As a compromise the suburb acquired some of the values of the country

Patrick Wiegand

(Tuan, 1974) with front lawns and back gardens as substitutes for open space. Place names in the suburbs reflect the values of the time. Note the use of aristocratic names and major battles in Victorian suburbs. However, values change. A recent attempt to name streets in a Welsh housing estate after engagements in the Falklands campaign faced bitter local opposition. Modern suburbs frequently no longer use the words 'street' and 'road' but prefer instead the more evocative 'Larchwood' or 'The Birches' or 'Parklands'.

Residential areas reflect a web of underlying values both of the individual and of groups which operate to control the 'quality' of areas: for example estate agents, building societies and local authorities. Many residential areas exhibit social or cultural segregation as a response either to prejudice or the desire by some groups to live together. Once occupied homes become territories (Gold, 1982) which convey messages to the outside world about the people living within. Gardens, replacement doors and windows and spaces for cars all act as a silent language for the values of the resident. Even the built form of each 'Dunroamin' reflects the values of the residents (Oliver *et. al.*, 1981). Rappaport (1982) reports on the significance of the front lawn as an indicator of the 'status, taste and lifestyle of the family who owns it' and describes how a woman who decided to grow vegetables instead in her suburban front garden faced local outrage. The implications of all this are that addresses, post codes, details of homes and gardens all have meanings that can be decoded by those familiar with the subtle variations involved.

The adoption of a particular paradigm within which to work in geography is clearly a value decision and reference has been made to contrasting positivist, humanistic and structuralist approaches (Johnston, 1983). All geographers, however, use maps. What gets mapped, how and why? The choice of phenomena to be represented in map form and the means of its representation are not value free. As a contrast to the conventional distributions represented in atlases, Kidron and Segal's *State of the World Atlas* (1981) includes maps of military spending, sex discrimination in relation to work, the number of calories available per head of the population, the extent of illiteracy and access to safe drinking water. The startling contrasts revealed between north and south, rich and poor and powerful and weak make this atlas compelling browsing. The distributions shown not only reflect values but provoke political involvement by geographers. Choice of map projection is crucial for an unbiased view of distributions. Mercator's projection, though ideal for navigation, has been responsible for a distorted impression in the minds of many of the size of the northern continents. Peters' projection puts the southern continents into a more accurate perspective. Ordnance Survey maps, though excellent in many respects, reflect the needs of a particular group in society with leisure interests such as historic houses, museums and ancient monuments. The identification of beauty spots and viewpoints on Ordnance Survey Landranger and other maps is largely a subjective one. As an antidote to official maps and atlases it is worth looking at, for example, local maps in 'alternative' university and college prospectuses or maps based on imagined group perception such as that in the *Sloane Ranger Handbook* (1982). Even titles to maps can reflect attitudes to content. Contrast, for example, the titles 'Distribution of Nuclear Power Stations' with 'How Far do you Live from a Nuclear Power Station?'

Overt and Hidden Values in Geographical Education

An examination of syllabus documents and teaching material for geography reveals two sorts of values. Firstly, there are those overt value statements which indicate the values that are to be taught or the values that are to be analyzed in the geography course. Secondly, there are hidden values which are implicit in curriculum statements or teaching materials. The terms behavioural, procedural and substantive values introduced by Fenton (1967) are helpful in the examination of values in the geography curriculum.

Behavioural values refer to the way classroom learning experiences are conducted and the way in which pupils and teachers interact. Procedural values relate to the ways of thinking considered important in geography. Blachford (1972), for example, states that geographers lay heavy emphasis on the value of fieldwork, the use of maps, the desire for comprehensive explanation, topic studies, systems thinking and the desire for spatial order. Whether geography in fact has a distinctive, central procedure is open to question (Smith, 1978). Substantive values may relate to procedural values. For example they may govern the selection of a topic for study or they may relate to the intrinsic worth of ideas or people or phenomena. Setting aside for the moment the view that all values may be substantive ones (Cowie, 1978) we may consider the value statements made explicit by syllabus and teaching materials.

Examination syllabuses and the documents of the recent 16+ examination debate are instructive about the substantive and procedural values of teaching geography. A rapid survey of the geography 'O' level and CSE syllabuses for 1982 reveals little mention of the substantive value implications of geography. Most syllabuses are statements of geographical content, themes or regions to be studied. Where examination objectives are stated these are, as may be expected, almost entirely expressed in terms of the cognitive domain. Candidates should, for example, be able to demonstrate knowledge of geographical features and processes together with the ability to understand and interpret geographical information in written, pictorial, map and statistical form. Where values are mentioned it is at a broad level of generality, for example, the compilers of the Northern Ireland CSE syllabus aimed to test a 'Course of study which will help to develop informed and responsible attitudes at both local and world levels.' An exception to this general rule is provided by the syllabuses for the *Geography for the Young School Leaver* project which will be discussed later. The examination syllabuses do provide evidence of procedural values related to geography. Much value, for example, is placed on fieldwork and the logical presentation of geographical information in maps and diagrams, as well as in writing. Most boards give emphasis to the candidates' ability to work with a variety of unseen resource material. Those who have invigilated geography examinations will recall that the papers are often accompanied by Ordnance Survey maps, photographs, diagrams and tables of statistics. Projects and local studies, especially of the local area, are seen to be an important part of learning geography.

While candidates were preparing for the 1982 examination based on these syllabuses the debate over a proposed common examination at 16+ was well under way. Whereas the syllabuses above saw geography in terms of knowledge, understanding and skills, the reports of the working groups charged with providing the criteria for ground rules for the new examination had added values to the list. The geography working party of the GCE and CSE boards' Joint Council for 16+ National Criteria thought it necessary to elaborate on why values were introduced into the definition of geography which prefaced their report. 'The term "values" is included to indicate that important topics in geography syllabuses have obvious social and political dimensions and cannot properly be understood without taking account of the attitudes and values of those involved' (Geography Working Party Report, 1982 p. 1) They were right to anticipate that not all geography teachers would accept the role of values as a natural part of the geography curriculum. Responses to the questionnaire sent out to teachers and national organizations for comment on the Working Party's draft report indicated that many school geographers thought social and political issues inappropriate to geography teaching. The HMI Geography Committee on the other hand accepted the inclusion of values as part of the criteria for a common examination at 16+. In addition to the 'official' Joint National Council Geography Working Party Report there were at the time other unofficial statements of criteria drawn up by other interested bodies as a further contribution to the debate. These included the GCE Boards working together, the Schools Council Geography Committee and the Geographical Association. Whilst these reports also stressed the importance of values in the geography curriculum, they were all reticent about how exactly values in geography might be assessed.

The reports were similarly vague about the precise substantive values that geography might propagate. Typical criteria relating to values that were suggested for the new groups of examination boards to adopt were that 'aims should consider the need for people to be aware of and to reflect constructively upon, conflicting values, as well as to decide upon their own values preferences and any appropriate action which might follow from such decisions.' (Geographical Association Working Party Report, 1982, p. 3) Assessment objectives usually require a more impartial, less committed stance towards values:

> The student will demonstrate an awareness of the significance of attitudes and values in some current social economic and environmental issues which have a geographical dimension; for example, an understanding of the role of decision making, and of the values and perceptions of decisions makers, in the evolution of patterns in human geography (Joint National Council Working Party, 1982, p. 3).

This is natural enough, for whilst one might wish pupils to have liberal or caring attitudes towards other cultures or the environment, it would surely not be feasible to withhold a certificate from student members of the National Front or pupils guilty of vandalism.

Geography teachers presumably have behavioural values that are indistinguishable from other subject teachers, although it might perhaps be claimed by some that the fieldwork element important in geography teaching requires a firmer level of control for the class's safety out of doors. Behavioural values may vary with the procedural values implicit in teaching and learning relationships. In the teachers handbook to the Geography 14–18 Project, Tolley and Reynolds (1977) identify three alternative styles of classroom geography. In the transmission-reception model pupils receive ideas transmitted by the teacher. In the behaviour-shaping model the teacher provides structured learning sequences for pupils assuming that they have common learning styles. The Geography 14–18 Project team favour the interactionist model in which pupils engage in processes of enquiry similar to those which geographers themselves engage in when solving problems. Obviously, the behaviour pattern expected of pupils will vary according to the model of

Patrick Wiegand

Figure 1: A route for geographical enquiry

FACTUAL ENQUIRY	ROUTE AND KEY QUESTIONS	VALUES ENQUIRY
Achieve awareness of a question, issue or problem arising from the interaction of people with their environments.	Observation and Perception What? Where?	Achieve awareness that individuals and groups hold differing values with regard to the question, issue or problem.
Outline and define the question, issue or problem. State hypothesis where appropriate. Decide on data and evidence to be collected. Collect and describe data and evidence.	Definition and Description What? Where?	List the values held or likely to be held by different individuals or groups with interes and/or involvement. Classify values into categories. Assess the actions likely to be linked with each category.
Organize and analyze data. Move towards providing answers and explanations. Attempt to accept or reject hypothesis. Decide whether more or different data and evidence are required.	Analysis and Explanation How? Why?	Assess how the values can be verified by evidence, i.e. to what extent are the values supported by facts? Produce ranked list of own preference or those of interested groups represented.
Evaluate results of enquiry. Attempt to make predictions, to move towards generalizations and theory construction. Consider future alternatives.	Evaluation Prediction and Theory Construction What will? How ought?	Relate predictions and future alternatives to the preferred values.
Base decision on results of enquiry, and relate to results of values enquiry.	Decision-making What will? How ought?	Base decision on results of enquiry, and relate to results of factual enquiry.

Decision

Source: Schools Council *Geography 16–19 Project*, London Institute of Education, 1982. Reproduced, by permission, from Clive Hart's *Values Enquiry in Practice*.

Values in Geographical Education

the teaching and learning that is taking place. All the Schools Council projects value enquiry styles of learning. The Geography 16–19 Project established a 'route for enquiry' (Fig 1.) This is similar to the classic model of the scientific method (for example, observation, description, analysis, evaluation and prediction) but encompasses 'not only the handling and analysis of "hard" geographical data, but also the analysis and classification of attitudes and values relevant to the problem or question under consideration' (Rawling, 1980). Although the term has been used specifically for the Geography 14–18 Project all the projects imply a 'new professionalism' in respect of the teacher's role. The projects see the teacher as fully involved in and responsible for the planning, teaching and evaluation of the curriculum rather than just the teaching alone. By building school-based assessment into the examination's scheme and testing and the candidates' ability to think geographically rather than work with a fixed corpus of content, the projects ensure that the door is kept open for the entry of 'new geographies' into the curriculum (Wiegand and Orrell, 1982).

Procedural values are also visible in the way the core content of the project curriculum is specified. *Geography for the Young School Leaver*, for example, lists the objectives of the course under the headings: Ideas, Skills and Values and Attitudes. Each unit of work is preceded by a summary of the key points related to the teaching topics. Typical attitude and value objectives listed in the *Geography for the Young School Leaver* unit 'Man, Land and Leisure' include:

> An awareness of the probable benefits and problems arising from a general increase in the amount of leisure time.
>
> A consideration of the inequality of holiday opportunities within society.
>
> A consideration of the individual's response towards the use of the countryside in the pursuit of leisure activities. (GYSL Teachers' Guide, 1974)

Helpful as the statements are, however, they are not in themselves statements of values. The identification of the values held by other people is essentially an activity within the cognitive not the affective domain. Fenton (1967) believes that the teacher's role in regard to substantive values is to keep within the cognitive domain, that teachers should teach *about* substantive values but not teach the values themselves. However, to ignore substantive values altogether is in fact to teach a value. Lawton and Dufour (1973), however, believe that there are certain substantive values which the schools have a duty to transmit.

Patrick Wiegand

For example, murder and rape are wrong. Are there substantive values in geography that teachers ought to teach? This question will be returned to in the conclusion.

A more detailed study of geography syllabus documents reveals implicit or hidden values. One of the most interesting of these is in connection with the type of assessment used. Tolley (1983), in a stimulating paper on project work in 'A' level geography, has revealed that teachers and examination boards most favour projects which adopt a hypothesis testing approach, that is those which are firmly positivist in nature. He draws evidence from examination board guidelines on project work to illustrate that the message being put over by the boards is that geographical research can be objective and value free.

Tolley lists some alternative titles for 'A' level projects, for example:

> Promoting a good image: an examination of the published materials used by a town to attract new industry.
>
> The industrial landscape of North West England as depicted by Lowry.
>
> Spatial aspects of the economic recession, for example, regional variations in unemployment and factory closure.
>
> Britain's railway network: a comparison of the policies of the major political parties and the railway unions. (Tolley, 1983)

Sections of geography examination syllabuses traditionally bear titles such as 'British Isles', 'North America' or 'Physical Geography'. Increasingly though these have been replaced by potentially more interesting and value laden themes such as 'Contrasts between the developing world', 'Problems of population growth', 'Problems of the environment' etc. It is difficult to prove but one suspects from reading examination scripts that potentially value-laden topics are, in fact, taught in the same way as more neutral regional ones. Many of the hidden values of the geography curriculum have been brought to light recently under the label 'Bias' (Kent, 1982a). Bias can be said to exist when a geography course promotes one set of values over another. Several types of value bias have been detected in geographical education, notably race bias and sex bias.

Race bias has been found to be the subject of a number of papers by Hicks (for example, 1980). Hicks has done a good deal to alert geography teachers of the presence of ethnocentrism and racism in geography textbooks. Ethnocentrism is the assessment of other cultures against the norms of one's own culture whereas racism considers one's own culture to be superior to that of another. Clyde's *School Geography* (1898) devotes a section on each country to the inhabitants of that country. For example: 'The Chinese ... are a quiet, orderly, and intelligent race not given to violent crimes but in the highest degree to lying and petty frauds ...' (p. 366). Whereas 'No people surpass the English in moderation and love of fair play' (p. 90). Such crude stereotypes are obvious and even amusing but Hicks demonstrates that bias in today's text are more subtle and insidious. Of particular concern are references to development which, for example, imply that the third world needs to 'catch up' with us or that the population problem is due to 'their' irresponsibility. Wright and Pardey (1982) have also reinforced this criticism of bias in texts by an examination of visual images or distorted use of maps and statistics particularly with reference to South Africa. Inevitably such criticism will lead to acrimonious exchanges between author and critics (for example that in *The Times Educational Supplement* between 6 November 1981 and 11 December 1981) despite the good intentions of textbook authors.

In September 1982 ethnocentricism and racism in geography became a focus of attention in the educational press with the rejection by the Schools Council of Gill's (1982) *Geography Report on Assessment in a Multicultural Society*. The Report had been commissioned along with a number of other subject reports to investigate how syllabuses and examinations at 16+ could meet the needs of all pupils in a multicultural society. The reasons for the rejection of the report by the Schools Council were not made entirely clear ('failure to take into account criticism from the Steering Group') but criticism of a successful Schools Council project at a sensitive time for the Council could not have helped. In the event, the Report became widespread through its distribution by the Commission for Racial Equality and received more attention than perhaps it would otherwise have done. In the report Gill criticizes the *Geography for the Young School Leaver Project* for its ethnocentricism and the implicit racism of its early classroom resources. Unfortunately the press coverage did not refer to her praise of the project's more recent materials. She also criticized the criteria documents of the 16+ debate for their neglect of a more radical treatment of the causes of global inequality. The 'People Place and Work' unit of the *Geography for the Young School Leaver Project* has also been criticized for its failure 'to explain adequately, even at a simple level, the real basis for work today, namely as a reflection of the needs of capitalism' (Cook, 1983). Cook goes on to suggest an alternative whereby, for example, a study of work could illustrate how capitalism creates underdevelopment through the exploitation of the Third World. 'Although certain benefits spin off from capital investment in the Third World economies, this investment concentrates development into islands of export orientated industries in seas of largely subsistence agricultural economies'. (p. 79). Although GYSL had been criticized much earlier for its consensus view of society (Gibson, 1976), it would be unjust if any criticism were too extreme. Firstly, it is in any case easy to criticize teaching materials with hindsight, especially in the light of the changing priorities for geography education that became established in the 1970s. Secondly, the Project has made perhaps the single most significant recent contribution to the teaching of values in geography. Although it was probably true to say about the project's early materials that potentially controversial issues were sometimes reduced to the level of differences of opinion that were permissible and even expected in society (*ibid*) this is not true of the recent materials developed by the Project team. The continued ability of the project to change and be responsive to new needs is reflected in the GYSL Development Education Project funded by the Overseas Development Administration. The Project acknowledges the unacceptability of earlier thinking on development issues and has as its aims the emphasis of North-South interrelationships (Brandt, 1980) the incorporation of welfare issues in geography and the raising of questions which challenge eurocentric and value-laden assumptions and involve students in ethical dilemmas (GYSL, 1981). Like the earlier materials, the organizing principles of the course are listed under key ideas, skills and values and attitudes. A number of the section headings from the books will give the flavour of the contents: *Money and happiness, Distribution of power, Do rich countries help poor countries?, Who benefits from tourism?, It depends on whom you ask, Who makes the profits?* and *Through Western eyes.*

Another aspect of bias to receive recent attention in geographical education is that of sex bias. The last ten years have seen a growing interest in gender by geographers and to a lesser extent those concerned with geographical education (Bale, 1982; Larsen, 1983). Much human geography has been recognized as being the geography of men, despite women's role in agricultural innovations (Hayford, 1974). The invisibility of women has been furthered by the use of the household as the basic unit of much geographical research in which women have been assigned to social classes on the basis of their husbands' occupation. Women are also spatially disadvantaged and spatially restricted. Mobility is often retarded by the presence of young children and women have less access in general to the 'family's' car. Girls may be disadvantaged in the geography curriculum. Their 'home range' is less than boys. They thus tend to know less of the local environment and they may feel inhibited by the requirements of fieldwork. Several studies show that boys are better at map and atlas tests than girls (for example, Boardman and Towner, 1979). Many geography teaching materials have been shown to be sexist. Monk (1978) illustrates how, in a sample of geographical games, the main decision-making roles were allocated to men. If women had roles at all they were subordinate ones. It is also now clear that the frequent use of *man* to mean *people* in geographical phrases such as 'economic man', 'man and the environment' and so on can give offence. Topics for study in, for example, economic geograpy also frequently centre on male-dominated industry such as iron and steel or motor vehicle manufacturing. Less attention is given to the predominantly female occupations, for example, in the service sector. Sex bias is further underlined by pictures in geography textbooks which either omit women or imply that women's roles are more passive than men. The illustrations in *Foods, Farming and Famine* (Jones and Wales, 1982) by contrast acknowledges the substantial contribution of women to agriculture in the third world.

In addition to sex and race bias other areas of value bias have been explored. Wiegand (1982) has commented that visual bias may become widespread. Bias may be accentuated when because of cuts in public spending teachers are forced to rely more heavily on publications — booklets, pictures, posters etc. — from tourist offices, government agencies and multinational corporations. These materials cannot be relied upon to give a neutral impression of the places represented pictorially. Kent (1982) has drawn attention to the imbalance in the scales at which geographers study the world, noting a surfeit of local, intermediate scale, western, developed world knowledge and a deficit of global scale, communist, and third world knowledge.

Values in the Geography Classroom

A number of models for teaching geography through values strategies were suggested in the Australian and North American teacher handbooks and journals of the 1970s (Martorella, 1977; Kracht and Martorella, 1970; Kracht and Boehm, 1975; Cole, 1976; Banks, 1974). Although the importance of values was recognized in British school geography at this time (for example, Marsden, 1976) models for values teaching specifically in a British context were not generally accessible to teachers until the 1980s (Fien and Slater, 1981; Slater, 1982; Hart, 1982). All the models referred to serve as a theoretical framework to a number of classroom activities. Most of these involve the clarification of alternative value positions in respect of a problem. After balancing the merits and demerits of the values of the protagonists the student is in a position to make a suggestion or recommendation. Some strategies stop at the cognitive level, others demand some involvement or personal response from the student. The *values clarification* strategy is based on the work of Raths *et. al.* (1966). The basis of this approach is that values are based on three processes; *choosing* thoughtfully and freely from a number of alternative value positions, *prizing*, that is resting content with the choice made and being prepared to publicly affirm that choice and *acting* on the basis of the value choice made. In the classroom this model usually takes the form of a handout that presents a value-laden episode, perhaps a newspaper extract that refers to a local problem of boundaries (Martorella, 1977) or a dispute about where to locate something undesirable (Slater, 1982). A sequence of questions then leads the student through the value clarification process, for example, 'What would you do to resolve the problem?' (choosing) 'Justify your selection to the class' (prizing) 'Devise a plan to prevent the problem occurring again' (acting).

The *value analysis* strategy is based on a procedure suggested by Chadwick and Meux (1971). A problem topic is selected for study, for example, should the local airport be extended? and the necessary source material is provided by the teacher. The individual pupils then list positive and negative statements about the problem. For example:

> The journey time to the capital will be cut.
> Construction of the extension will reduce local unemployment.

As against:

> Local agricultural land will be lost.
> Larger, noisier aeroplanes will use the extended runway.

Positive and negative statements for the class are then grouped and ranked. Solutions are found to the major negative statements, for example:

> Double glazing for local residents.
> Compensation for farmers.
> Prohibit night flying.

Positive and negative statements about each of the solutions are then listed. For example, double glazing brings further benefits to residents' property, such as heat retention, but there is a difficulty in defining precisely who might be eligible and the solution in any case is expensive. Residents are also unhappy about noise effects when they are out of doors. The solutions and negative and positive statements are then used as the basis for a report which includes recommendations for action.

The *values enquiry* strategy is that adopted by the Schools Council Geography 16–19 Project. The approach is illustrated in an excellent booklet by Hart (1982). The main organizing structure is based on the sequence of operations in the scientific method (see Fig. 1) but the strength of the model is that it links enquiry into both facts and values. Although separated for the purpose of the diagram the Project team emphasize that both areas of enquiry are, of course, closely associated in practice. In the practical example illustrated by Hart a landslip has closed a main road. One solution is to divert the road through a small village. The example neatly links the physical geography that is the cause of the landslip, the human geography that is the effect on the area's route network and the values of those involved in the proposed solution, i.e. tourists, local residents with varying interests in the route and the country councillors. The values of those involved are clarified and analyzed in ways similar to those described above. Students are then asked to indicate to what extent they sympathize with the individuals involved in the issue. The personal attitudes and opinions of the students themselves are then connected to the issue. The exercise concludes with the students assessing and justifying their own decisions regarding the route of the proposed road. During this exchange the teacher helps students 'to try to pinpoint what values and beliefs have had an influence on their decisions'.

Fien and Slater (1981) criticize many of the teaching techniques proposed for the examination of values in geography simply because whilst they do explore attitudes they do not allow access to the deeper underlying values. Fien and Slater suggest a *values probing* procedure in which these deeper personal beliefs about, for example, human dignity, justice, equality, and self interest versus the greater good may be explored. According to Rokeach (1968) we hold relatively few such values. Their procedure is to introduce an issue about which there may be two opposing views. One way of doing this is to present the issue in petition form. Students divide on the basis of whether they agree or disagree with the petition and groups then select the most convincing arguments for and against. Then comes the difference. The groups of students then probe for the values that underly their arguments. Here also might come the difficulty. For distinguishing between superficial attitudes and deeper values may be a demanding task for students. Values are then recorded by the teacher and discussed in a plenary

Patrick Wiegand

session. Consideration may then be given to putting values into practice by investigating how those values could be operationalized into involvement and action in the local community.

These models of pursuing values have been applied to a number of geographical situations. Often these have been environmental issues, for example, the location of new transport facilities or some other public utility. The weakness of the values education approach, however, has been laid bare by Huckle (1983a) who illustrates his critique with specific reference to nuclear power issues in geography. The difficulty is that values education assumes that society functions in the same way as a geography lesson. In fact, the logic and moral reasoning described in the strategies above don't match decision making processes in the real world. 'Values education seeks morally optimal choices based on a formal logic, but politicians seek politically feasible choices based on substantive logic' (p. 60.) Huckle points out that political decisions are more complex than can be allowed for in classroom exercises and that the moral choices in the real world are rarely as clear as values strategies imply. Values education adopts too liberal a stance and Huckle suggests, instead, a radical programme of political education through geography. A consideration of nuclear power in the geography classroom might consist of identifying the major protagonists in the dispute, clarifying not only their underlying values but also the ways in which they seek to achieve their ends. It is the latter aspect of the issue which leads to a more realistic understanding of society and the processes of social change. The proper place for values education may be a location within the political decision making process (Huckle, 1982). Barton (1983) has provided an example of how values may be examined in a real political context. The Kirkhamgate/Dishforth motorway scheme is intended to establish a major link from West Yorkshire to North East England (Barton, 1982). In this example a real planning issue forms the content of a simulation game designed to demonstrate the complex technical and political aspects of the planning process. The objectives of the simulation are not just to develop students' empathy with those involved in the scheme but also to develop their political awareness of the planning process as it relates to a trunk road planning scheme. There are three phases in the role play:

1 Public consultation following the initial publication of road proposals. A consultation document outlining optional routes for the motorway is read in the light of the role the student is to play, for example, local resident, councillor, businessman etc. Pupils must then prepare a written reply to the Secretary of

Values in Geographical Education

State (or teacher!) arguing for one of the routes or proposing some other strategy.
2   The decision of the preferred route by the Secretary of State. The 'Secretary of State' (geography teacher) announces the preferred route.
3   Public enquiry. This is conducted according to the Department of Transport guidelines. Evidence is presented by the 'Department of Transport' and then by objectors.

The simulation concludes with a consideration of the following issues:

1   In what way did the participants' decisions differ from those taken by their real counterparts?
2   Is there a genuine need for the road? Note that need is argued by the Department of Transport to be a question of national policy and therefore not appropriate for discussion at a local enquiry. Is a non-road solution viable?
3   Are the provisions for public participation of the enquiry 'democratic'?
4   What values were held by each of the participants in the simulation?

In addition to the various values strategies described above, there are a number of activities of a more personal, experiential character which have been applied to geography. These activities usually have a strong affective component. They are not designed to examine or clarify values in a structured way but to provide first hand experience of the tensions of the world and the significance of places. By giving the students opportunities to be receptive to and respond to their feelings, geography teachers thus build the basis for valuing. Activities in respect to the environment include town trails and acclimatization. Trails are guided walks which attempt to draw out the distinctiveness of the town and give the trailee a coherent image of the place being trailed. Goodey, (1982) an early promotor of the town trail movement, has noted, however, that the domination of local historians and architects in the writing of trail leaflets has given a stereotyped 'heritage' flavour to most trails. Instead a more experiential approach is suggested, less structured and focusing more on the individual's response to places. The fixed route might be replaced by a strategy such as that suggested by the *Art and the Built Environment Project*: steering by cards (Adams and Ward, 1982). A number of cards with symbols indicating instructions such as turn left, straight ahead, listen, touch, imagine, or ask, are used to give a random walk through the urban area. Trailees shuffle the cards and respond in turn to the directions on the next card.

Acclimatization is a similar sort of procedure designed to loosen up the senses but this time to the natural rather than to the urban environment (Van Matre, 1972). Students are immersed in the natural environment and given the opportunity to explore their emotional reaction to it. Ecological concepts are stressed but the emphasis is on understanding through feeling. Teachers encourage pupils to participate, play roles (like frogs, roots, fish and dead logs) and release emotion spontaneously. Clearly this approach is not suited to all teachers.

Activities which attempt to establish empathy with other peoples rather than places have been collected by Hicks (1981) and the *World Studies Project* (1977). Bafa Bafa is a game produced by Christian Aid. It simulates two cultures. Students divide into two groups, each one practising a culture. One culture uses playing cards in an elaborate form of social interaction. Cards are used to open conversations with other members of the group. The other culture exchanges tokens according to a strict ritual. The aim of this cultural group is to accumulate wealth. Students from each group visit the other culture zone in turn and discuss their experiences. Typical outcomes are that students experience the strangeness of a different culture, that first impressions are misleading, that they can give offence without realizing it and that other cultures cannot necessarily be interpreted in terms of their own values (Hicks, 1981).

Exercises designed to give classroom experience of cooperation, empathy, participation and sharing are not without opposition from the establishment. 'Getting it together' (World Studies Project, 1976) is an exercise whereby students in groups of five are each given irregularly shaped pieces of card. The aim of the exercise is to assemble five squares from the pieces. Members of the group may *pass* pieces to each other but are not allowed to reach out and *take* pieces. What usually happens is that one square is quickly formed by one member of the group. This member is then usually reluctant to dismantle his square so that everyone in the group can form a square of their own. The World Studies Project believe that this exercise 'dramatizes something about sharing, about aid (the difference between real, insightful generosity on the one hand and merely describing something on the other) and about democratic participation' (p. 74). The Minister for Schools, Dr. Rhodes Boyson, was reported by *The Times Educational Supplement* (24 December 1982) as saying: 'This seems to be an extension of the nursery school up to the age of 16 or 17. I wonder what effect it will have on the rest of the curriculum. It is a return to so-called child-centred education which brought illiteracy and innumeracy'. The value clash here is plain.

A final class of value-based activities in geography is that of focussing directly on the value-biased material present in the classroom. Values are explored by directly challenging the materials used for teaching. Students could, for example, look at contrasting descriptions of places; perhaps using the contrasting first hand experience of travellers in conjunction with a conventional textbook account. Who wrote the passage? Why was it written? What did the writer stand to gain? How did the writer feel when he wrote it? How soon after the visit was the account written? Pupils could explore the development and persistence of geographical myths in connection with this sort of activity, for example that of the Great American Desert. For about 100 years large tracts of the North American high plains were considered to be desert. The myth began with early nineteenth century explorers who through individual misfortune, misinterpretation of the absence of trees and ambiguous reporting, established the idea of a desert in the American mind. Later travellers and amateur geographers reinforced the idea and 'unexplored desert' appeared on atlases over Nebraska and Kansas. This area now constitutes the great wheat lands of the North American continent. An important lesson here for the critical reading of accounts about places!

Another possibility is to investigate the bias in the visual images of places. Pupils examine the location of photographs from their regional texts and mark them on a map. What areas are over or underrepresented? What are the areas like that are now shown? Attention can also be focussed on individual photographs. Who holds the copyright? Many texts contain a large number of photographs collected from government agencies or commercial interests as these are either free or have low reproduction fees. However, these photographs may well show a particular country or industry in a more favourable light than other photographs would. As a consciousness raiser to these questions pupils could consider postcards of their home area. Which one is the most representative? Reasons are discussed. What aspects of the local area are not available as postcards? Are there questions of value involved in the selection of photographs used as postcards? What values lie behind a choice of a postcard that we send to friends? These values will be linked to notions of landscape attractiveness and the use of stereotyped images to represent places. For example, Leeds is generally represented by the Town Hall, Edinburgh by the Castle and Durham by the Cathedral.

Patrick Wiegand

Conclusion

Greater consideration of values would undoubtedly lead to a more relevant geography curriculum. The geographical literature of the 1970s and early 1980s provides a respectable base on which to found such a curriculum. The inclusion of values will be crucial to the survival of geography as a subject. On the debit side the competition in the last decade from more energetic and committed approaches to people and environment (such as development education, art and the built environment and peace studies) together with the restrained recognition of the subject from the DES and HMI in the late 1970s have left geographers less than confident. On the credit side, however, is the fact that geography is a popular and established part of the school curriculum. Curriculum change, therefore, with greater attention paid to values, could perhaps come more effectively from within geography than without.

The question of whether to teach values or about values has not yet been resolved however. Attention has been paid to techniques of teaching for analysis or clarification of values. Mention has also been made of the need to raise pupils' awareness of the bias that may exist in teaching materials. Although many geographers would resist the teaching of substantive values it seems to me that at least three are inescapable. Firstly, that the study of people's interrelationship with the environment is necessary and worthwhile. Secondly, that experience of places enriches human existence and therefore we must teach towards interest in and concern for the quality of place. Thirdly, that the different human traditions and patterns of behaviour throughout the world merit understanding and tolerance. These underlying high order values relate to the most basic values of all: those of survival and the quality of life. Resistance to values teaching has perhaps been on the grounds that such teaching is difficult and involves controversy. The affective domain also poses problems for the evaluation and assessment of pupil learning; although Carswell (1970) has applied the assessment of attitudes to geography. The difficulties found by values teaching must, however, be set against the unreal nature of much positivist geography. It is as difficult to encourage pupils to use the eye of faith to see hexagons in settlement patterns in East Anglia or to explain why the simple theoretical models of land use don't 'work'.

Geography involves study of the values that shape decisions which influence the quality of life in places. It is also about the meaning that places have for us. If we view geography in this light we will undoubtedly discover that there are not only value issues but political issues which we cannot ignore in the geography curriculum.

References

ADAMS, E. and WARD, C. (1982) *Art and the Built Environment*, Harlow, Longman, for the Schools Council.
BAILEY, P. (1983) 'Editorial: Values', *Teaching Geography* 9, 1.
BALE, J. (1981) 'Teaching welfare issues in urban geography — a work unit on externalities', in WALFORD, R. *Signposts for Geography Teaching*, London, Longman pp. 51–63.
BALE, J. (1982) 'Sexism in geographic education', in KENT, W.A. (Ed.) *Bias in Geographical Education*, University of London Institute of Education, pp. 3–10.
BANKS, J.A. (1974) *Teaching Strategies for the Social Studies: Inquiry Valuing and Decision Making*, Reading, Massachusetts, Addison-Wesley.
BARR, A. and YORK, P. (1982) *The Official Sloane Ranger Handbook*, London, Ebury Press.
BARTON, R. (1982) *The Kirkhamgate-Dishforth Trunk Road Scheme: An Analysis of the Politics of Trunk Road Planning*, School of Geography, University of Leeds, Working Paper No. 322.
BARTON, R. (1983) *The Kirkhamgate-Dishforth Motorway Scheme: A Simulation*, unpublished method unit submitted as part of the Leeds University School of Education Graduate Certificate in Education.
BEDDIS, R. (1981) *A Sense of Place*, (Book 1–3), Oxford, Oxford University Press.
BLACHFORD, K.R. (1972) 'Values and geographical education', *Geographical Education*, 1, pp. 319–30.
BLACHFORD, K.R. (1979) 'Morals and values in geographical education: towards a metaphysics of the environment', *Geographical Education*, 3, 3, pp. 423–57.
BOARDMAN, D. and TOWNER, E. (1979) 'Reading Ordnance Survey maps: some problems of graphicacy', unpublished, School of Education, University of Birmingham.
BRANDT, W. (1980) *North-South*, (Report of the Independent Commission on International Development Issues, under the Chairmanship of Willy Brandt), London, Pan Books.
CARSWELL, P.J.B. (1970) 'Evaluation of affective learning in geographic education', in KURFMAN, D.G. (Ed.) *Evaluation in Geographic Education*, Belmont California, Fearon, pp. 111–30.
CHADWICK, J. and MEUX, M. (1971) 'Procedures for values analysis' in METCALF, L.E. (Ed.) *Values Education* (41st Yearbook of the National

Council for the Social Studies), Washington D.C., National Council for the Social Studies.
CHORLEY, R. and HAGGETT, P. (1965) *Frontiers in Geographical Teaching*, London, Methuen.
CLYDE, J. (1898) *School Geography*, Edinburgh, Oliver and Boyd.
COLE, R. (1976) *A New Role for Geographic Education: Values and Environmental Concerns*, San Diego, National Council for Geographic Education.
COOK, I. (1983) 'Radical geography' in HUCKLE, J. (Ed.) *Geographical Education: Reflection and Action*, Oxford, Oxford University Press, pp. 74–81.
COWIE, P.M. (Sister P. Dominic L.S.U.) (1978) 'Geography: A value laden subject in education', in *Geographical Education*, 3, pp. 133–46.
FARBSTEIN, J. and KANTROWITZ, M. (1978) *People in Places*, Englewood Cliffs, Prentice Hall.
FENTON, E. (1967) *The New Social Studies*, New York, Holt, Rinehart and Winston.
FIEN, J. and SLATER, F. (1981) 'Values-probing: An integrated approach to values education', in WILSON, P. et. al., (Eds.) *Research in Geographical Education*, Brisbane, Australian Geographical Education Research Association, pp. 46–56.
GCE and CSE Boards Joint Council for 16+ National Criteria (1982) *National Criteria for Geography: Geography Working Party Report*.
Geographical Association Working Party on Examinations (1982) *Report on Criteria for a 16+ Examination in Geography*. Sheffield, The Geographical Association.
Geography for the Young School Leaver (1974) *Teachers Guide: Man, Land and Leisure*, London, Nelson.
GYSL Development Education Project (1981) *Geography and Change: Teachers' Guide*, London, Nelson for the Schools Council.
GIBSON, M. (1976) quoted in MACDONALD, B. and WALKER, R. *Changing the Curriculum*. Open Books.
GILL, D. (1982) *Assessment in a Multicultural Society: Schools Council Report: GEOGRAPHY*. Unpublished report submitted to the Schools Council, distributed by the Commission for Racial Equality.
GOLD, J. (1980) *An Introduction to Behavioural Geography*, Oxford, Oxford University Press.
GOLD, J. (1982) 'Behavioural Geography', in WIEGAND, P. and ORRELL, K. *New Leads in Geographical Education*, Sheffield, The Geographical Association.
GOLD, J. and BURGESS, J. (Eds.) (1982) *Valued Environments*, London, Allen and Unwin.
GOODEY, B. (1982) 'Values in place: interpretations and implications from Bedford', in GOLD, J. and BURGESS, J. (Ed.) *Valued Environments*, London, Allen and Unwin, pp. 10–34.
GOODSON, I.F. (1983) *School Subjects and Curriculum Change*, Beckenham, Croom Helm.

HART, C. (1982) *Values Enquiry in Practice*, University of London Institute of Education, Schools Council Geography 16–19 Curriculum Development Occasional Paper No. 3.
HAYFORD, A.M. (1974) 'The geography of women: an historical introduction' in *Antipode*, 6, 2.
HICKS, D. (1980) *Images of the World: an Introduction to Bias in Teaching Materials*. University of London Institute of Education, Centre for Multicultural Education. Occasional Paper No. 2.
HICKS, D. (1981) *Minorities*, London, Heinemann.
HICKS, D. and TOWNLEY, C. (1982) *Teaching World Studies*, London, Longman.
HUCKLE, J. (1982) 'Teaching environmental issues; a workshop on nuclear power', in WIEGAND, P. and ORRELL, K. *New Leads in Geographical Education*, Sheffield, The Geographical Association, pp. 53–56.
HUCKLE, J. (1983a) 'Values Education through Geography: a radical critique', in *Journal of Geography* March/April 1983, pp. 59–63.
HUCKLE, J. (Ed.) (1983b) *Geographical Education: Reflection and Action*, Oxford, Oxford University Press.
JOHNSTON, R.J. (1983) *Philosophy and Human Geography*, London, Arnold.
JONES, B. and WALES, R. (1982) *Food, Farming and Famine*, London, Nelson for the Schools Council.
KENT, W.A. (Ed.) (1982a) *Bias in Geographical Education*, London, University of London Institute of Education.
KENT, W.A. (1982b) 'Scale and Regional Bias', in KENT, W.A. (Ed.) *Bias in Geographical Education*, University of London Institute of Education, pp. 11–24.
KIDRON, M. and SEGAL, R. (1981) *The State of the World Atlas*, London, Heinemann.
KRACHT, J.B. and BOEHM. R.G. (1975) 'Feelings about the community: Using value clarification in and out of the classroom', in *Journal of Geography*, 74, 4, pp. 198–206.
KRACHT, J.B. and MARTORELLA, P.H. (1970) 'Simulation and inquiry models applied to the study of environmental problems', in *Journal of Geography*, 69, 4, pp. 273–8.
LARSEN, B. (1983) 'Geography', in WHYLD, J. (Ed.) *Sexism in the Secondary Curriculum*, London, Harper and Row, pp. 165–178.
LAWTON, D. and DUFOUR, B. (1973) *The New Social Studies*, London, Heinemann.
MARSDEN, W.E. (1976) *Evaluating the Geography Curriculum*, Edinburgh, Oliver and Boyd.
MARTORELLA, P.H. (1977) 'Teaching geography through value strategies', in MANSON, G.A. and RIDD, M.K. (Eds.) *New Perspectives on Geographic Education*, Dubuque, Iowa, Kendall Hunt, pp. 139–162.
MONK, J.J. (1978) 'Women in geographic games', in *Journal of Geography* 77, 5.

OLIVER, P., DAVIS, I., BENTLEY, I. (1981) *Dunroamin: The Suburban Semi and Its Enemies*, London, Barrie and Jenkins.
PAHL, R.E. (1967) 'Trends in Sociology', in Chorley and Haggett, pp. 81–98.
RAPPOPORT, A. (1982) *The Meaning of the Built Environment: A nonverbal communication approach.* Beverley Hills, Sage.
RATHS, L., HARMIN, M. and SIMON, S. (1966) *Values and Teaching*, New York: Merrill.
RAWLING, E. (1980) 'Enquiry learning for the 16–19 year old' in RAWLING, E. (Ed.) *Geography in the 1980s*, Sheffield, Geographical Association.
RELPH, E. (1982) *Place and Placelessness*, London, Pion.
ROBINSON, R. (1982) 'What is Truth?', in *Times Educational Supplement*, 3 December, 1982, p. 31.
ROKEACH, M. (1968) *Beliefs, Attitudes and Values*, San Francisco, Jossey-Bass.
ROWLES, G.D. (1980) 'Towards a geography of growing old' in BUTTIMER, A. and SEAMON, D., *The Human Experience of Space and Place*. London, Croom Helm.
SINGLETON, L.R. (Ed.) (1983) *Tips for Social Studies Teachers: Activities from ERIC*. Boulder, Colorado, Social Science Education Consortium.
SLATER, F. (1982) *Learning through Geography*, London, Heinemann.
SLATER, F. and FIEN, J. (1981) 'Exploring values and attitudes through group discussion and evaluation', *Classroom Geographer*, April, pp. 22–5.
SMITH, D.L. (1978) 'Values and the teaching of geography', *Geographical Education*, 3, pp. 147–61.
TOLLEY, H. (1984) 'New Directions for project work in 'A' level geography' in WIEGAND, P.A. and ORRELL, K. (1984) *Evaluation in Assessment in Geography*, Sheffield, The Geographical Association.
TOLLEY, H. and REYNOLDS, J.B. (1977) *Geography 14–18: A Handbook for School Based Development*, London, Macmillan.
TUAN, YI-FU (1974) *Topophilia*, Englewood Cliffs NJ, Prentice Hall.
VAN MATRE, S. (1972) *Acclimatization*, Martinville, Indiana, American Camping Association.
WALFORD, R. (1981) *Signposts for Geography Teaching*, London, Longman.
WIEGAND, P.A. (1982) 'A biased view', in KENT, W.A. (Ed.) *Bias in Geographcial Education*, University of London Institute of Education, pp. 25–36.
WIEGAND, P.A. and ORRELL, K. (1982) *New Leads in Geographical Education*, Sheffield, The Geographical Association.
World Studies Poject (1982) *Learning for Change in World Society: Reflections, Activities and Resources*, London, World Studies Project.
WRIGHT, D. and PARDEY, D. (1982) 'Bias in statistics and statistical maps: the example of S. Africa', in KENT, W.A. *Bias in Geographical Education*, University of London Institute of Education, pp. 37–45.

Values in History and Social Studies

Robert Irvine Smith

A class of fourteen year olds in an expensive independent school is studying the matchgirls' strike and the Dockers' Tanner. A girl reads out her homework, a spirited and well-informed speech to a meeting of workers, urging them to join the union. The teacher compliments her on the historical understanding this shows. The girl looks pleased but has something to add: 'Of course it's different now, Miss. The unions were all right then but now they've become too powerful and hold the country to ransom.'

Teachers of history, geography, economics, and any other form of social science course are familiar with situations like this, and most of us have ways of explaining to ourselves what is happening and deciding what to do about it. When as a young teacher of history I first read Edwin Fenton's (1966) *Teaching the New Social Studies* I was pleased to find an analysis of values in the classroom which 'rang true': i.e. something explicit, coherent, and confident which corresponded with my own half-formed intuitions. It is always gratifying to find that one has had a theory all along without realizing it. In working with teachers I have found his analysis to be widely accepted, and could probably be taken as the conventional wisdom of modern classrooms.

Fenton distinguishes between *behavioural*, *procedural*, and *substantive* values. He argues that we must teach the first two but not the third. In the example I gave, the girl *behaved* beautifully, entering into the spirit of the classroom exercise in a cooperative and lively manner; she made a commendable effort at adopting historical *procedure*, feeling her way into the mind of a historical character, drawing on primary sources, recreating the world of Victorian London: and she demonstrated that on the *substantive* issues of trade union power she (and by implication her teacher) valued independent thinking.

I am not arguing against this way of looking at values in the classroom, but rather suggesting that the analysis can mislead as well as illuminate, and that in this, as in other aspects of classroom life, we need to reflect carefully on the categories we use for interpreting what we see and hear.

Behavioural Values

There are certain minimum conditions for study and discussion which, it is argued, students must recognize as important. Fenton modestly suggests that 'Students must keep quiet when others have the floor ... they must not defenestrate the teacher.'

The problem here is that what starts out as a minimum framework of rules for an orderly room can grow into something that is heavily contaminated with particular social conventions. Many studies of classrooms have suggested that teachers construe certain types of behaviour as 'cheekiness', 'lack of motivation', or 'evidence of linguistic deprivation', when very different interpretations might be possible. Nell Keddie (in Young, 1970) claims that the successful pupils are those who conform to the teacher's notions of appropriate behaviour and do not question the content of the lesson. They do not misbehave even if they find no meaning or satisfaction in their work. They trust the school, and play its academic games — history, English, and the rest — assuming that the meaning will be revealed in the end. Other children are not so patient — or so gullible. They want their gratification now. In Fenton's terms, those who behave badly may be the very pupils who are hungry for useable procedures and meaningful substance in their work, qualities which the well-behaved have learned not to expect.

Whether or not one goes the whole way with this argument, it is undeniable that the language and manners of scholarly debate do not come easily to many children. Another classroom illustration, this time from a comprehensive school in a rural part of Yorkshire:

> The teacher is going over the main events of Stephen's reign: 'The King found he couldn't take the castles, so he burnt the farms and crops in the countryside all round them.' A yell of protest goes up from the back row: 'Hey, that's stew-pid!' The teacher asks the boy to explain, which he does: 'Well, it's not fair, is it? I mean, well, them farmers, they were innocent like ...' The teacher comments that history is full of unfair things, but that he must get on if they are to finish Stephen by the bell.

Values in History and Social Studies

The boy has drawn attention to something in this dry old tale which is morally alive — the enduring issue of ends and means in politics and war. The trigger, perhaps, was the image of his farm going up in flames. The teacher accepted as a contribution something which other teachers might have punished for its unseemly manner (with something on the lines of 'John, how many more times? Put your hand up and ask your question properly'). So far so good. But the conventions of the classroom are too strong to allow the teacher to make anything of this moment of insight.

A few seconds later, a well-spoken boy sitting near the front asked, in a thoughtful and helpful voice, a question that the teacher spent the rest of the lesson talking about: 'Sir, couldn't the king have got the common people on his side against the barons?' Commenting afterwards, the teacher pointed out it was a mixed ability class, with some really good little historians in it.

The teacher considered that the second boy's question was more relevant to the subject being taught, so he took it up for procedural reasons: his decision had nothing to do with his reading of the behaviour of the boys. But if the first boy had signalled by his words, his tone of voice and his body language that he was really interested in twelfth century attitudes to life, property and authority . . . ?

In those forms of social or general studies where the demands of an academic discipline are not of paramount importance, questions of tone and manner are, if anything, even more difficult. There is no obvious touchstone of relevance, external to the discussion: we can't say, 'very interesting, but let's get back to our economics'. It is difficult to unscramble what is meant from how it is expressed, especially where the talk centres on feelings and attitudes that are important to the student. In the discussion of such matters it is rarely obvious what the idea of 'appropriate classroom behaviour' should be taken to mean. The dangers of misreading students, and of being misread by them, is at its most acute in courses that centre on real-world problems and claim to be developing students' social and life skills. This point might be made clearer by an illustration from a technical college liberal studies class, where day-release motor vehicle technicians are discussing social security issues.

> 'What about these scroungers, then', says one lad. 'There's this bloke on Dartmoor with fifteen kids and he gets far more on the dole than he would working.' The teacher points out the difficulties of keeping fifteen children, and their two mothers (appreciative laughter, shouts of 'Wayhay' and admiring gestures

with upright forearms), and of finding a job on Dartmoor. Attempts at forming a joke about the prison die out as a student comes forward with a positive idea: 'People who can't get a job shouldn't be allowed to breed. You can't stop them having sex, like, but they shouldn't have kids.' 'That's right,' says another, 'Sterilize 'em, like they do in India.' The teacher, unruffled, suggests that might be a bit drastic and unpopular. 'Here's the answer,' says a student, 'You can make it reversible. Tie the bloke's tubes and untie them when he gets a proper job.' This technical solution to a social problem is greeted with shouts of approval from his mates.

What was going on in that room? We might say it was no more than messing about, having a few laughs, surviving liberal studies. But it is also possible that this is one way of exploring embarrassing value problems in areas of urgent concern to these young men: sex and family commitments; unemployment and self-respect.

The teacher is trying to help the students to think more rationally, to find a language in which to talk about serious matters, to develop coping skills, and to behave with more consideration for other people's interests and feelings. It is not always obvious what sort of classroom behaviour is appropriate for these purposes. A teacher needs, first of all, delicate antennae to know when something serious is being said among the wisecracks and repartee; second, the ability to focus a discussion without deadening it; and third, the courage to risk, on occasions, criticism from other members of staff for running what sounds like a rowdy classroom.

Procedural Values

Here again Fenton has no doubts, and he speaks for many, perhaps even most, teachers of history and social sciences in his emphasis on the value of disciplined enquiry. 'We ought to teach procedural values,' he declares. 'Critical thinking is better than uncritical thinking ... students should be forced to subject (their prejudices) to the test of evidence and to defend them in the face of the full array of scholarly arguments ... they must accept the method by which social scientists and historians arrive at conclusions.' A brave stand against the forces of irrationality, perhaps: but it needs a closer examination of actual circumstances.

When we look at a pupil's curriculum we see only a small selection of the possible disciplines by means of which a world-view can be shaped and complex value questions handled. In practice, most 15 year olds have access only to the disciplines of history and geography — and often only one of those subjects, given the option system. The assumption must be that it doesn't matter which disciplines are studied — it is the process that counts. This argument requires a touching faith in the spontaneous transfer of learning. All-round critical thinking is hardly likely to develop as a by-product of learning CSE geography or history. To have any chance at all transfer needs to be worked for. And that probably means a compulsory section in public examinations to make sure that the task is taken seriously.

A second reason to pause before embracing procedural values is the nature of the disciplines as human activities. Are we all talking about the same thing when we refer to the methods and procedures of our disciplines? Specialists are in fact deeply divided not only about conclusions but about ways of working. This is not a trivial technical matter: the divisions in the social sciences reflect important differences in the way people see the world, and in the value they set on different methods of interpreting reality. The full array of scholars looks orderly only from a distance: close up it presents a scene of lively civil war.

If the academics were united, rather than being keen to point out each other's shortcomings, we would still need (all the more, perhaps) to look critically at their disciplines for any hidden messages before transmitting them to captive school-children.

The political bias of traditional history is well known, as studies of text books in adjacent countries have revealed (try listing the battles of the Hundred Years War from French and English schoolbooks: each country was clearly fighting a different war, which may explain how they both won it). Racism and sexism have been similarly exposed in a subject which claims to develop empathy and fair mindedness, and there has been some progress towards eliminating the grosser forms of bias. But history teachers might like to estimate what proportion of their syllabus is still concerned with the deeds and views of rich white Western males. Where the poor, the black, the non-Western and the female enter the history texts, how are they presented? As persons with minds and interests of their own, or as problems for white Western male leaders?

Even that most scientific of the social sciences, economics, is far from value free. Nigel Wright, in the *Handbook for Economics Teachers* (Whitehead, 1979), argues that

> Positive economics has been supposed to be a value free science ... Many of us taught it for years in the conviction that we were

being quite neutral before we realized that it contained a whole set of implicit values which probably rubbed off on students in quite insidious ways ... If I invited a professor of economics from Peking University and asked him to speak up as soon as I strayed from neutrality, how long would he keep quiet? You may counter that such a person would be operating from an entirely different paradigm. But this is precisely the point: growing numbers of people within our own community are operating from different paradigms. It is because we live in a society without consensus that values have become such a burning issue.

One last question about procedural values in the social subjects, from the many more one could ask: how far do the conditions under which school learning takes place allow for the critical and disinterested study of human issues? If we really rated this highly as an aim, there would be less telling, less note taking, fewer stereotyped exercises and bogus research projects. Syllabuses would not be so loaded with other people's judgments masquerading as 'facts' to be learned and reproduced in examinations. Teaching materials would look very different.

There are some cheering counter-currents. The Schools Council 13–16 History Project has admirable units on evidence; Geography for the Young School Leaver has generated enquiry into important contemporary issues; some social and general studies courses stimulate critical and reflective thought. But mass compulsory schooling, with its priorities of containment, selection, and socialization, can happily do without the questioning spirit. The procedures of schooling are one thing; the procedures of critical enquiry are another. The two may not be irreconcilable, but their marriage is at best an uneasy one.

Substantive Values

At first sight there is no problem about either defining what we mean by substantive values or deciding whether to teach them. A closer look, however, suggests there is room for debate on both questions.

Fenton is emphatic in his advice not to teach substantive values, and he gives examples: 'We must not teach that democracy is better than totalitarianism, that religion is a good thing, that the family is the basis of society, or that money is more important than anything else.' In Britain, the Humanities Curriculum Project, the General Studies Project and other projects in the humanities have taken a similar stance, arguing

Values in History and Social Studies

that we should raise controversial matters as open questions for study, discussion and informed personal judgment. The teacher should be impartial in the classroom, and where he knows he is strongly committed to a viewpoint, do everything possible to compensate for his bias by giving alternatives a fair run. He should insist on fair play and impartiality, on the moral autonomy of each student, on respect for persons and the importance of seeing life through other people's eyes. In this way he provides the classroom conditions within which individuals may shape their own views on particular substantive issues.

But the commitment to fair play and all the classroom practices that stem from it can look to students remarkably like a cluster of substantive values. They may be held at a generalized level, but they seem to lead inexorably to predictable viewpoints on specific issues. For example, it is not hard to guess what such a teacher would think about media censorship, or apartheid, or gender discrimination: all issues which he would of course handle impartially in his fair-minded classroom. He is committed to rationality and the pursuit of truth, but he also values alternatives which he knows are less reasonable than others. He does so in the name of divergence, which he values for reasons that make as little sense to students as they would have done to J.S. Mill, for whom toleration of divergent views was a temporary tactic in the search for truth (see Charles Bailey's essay in Bridges and Scrimshaw, 1975). The philosophical nuances fill shelves in the education section of the library: my point is that even if they are properly understood by the teacher, they may not be obvious to students, or to their parents.

The work of such a teacher can be seen as the transmission of culture. He is defending a precious inheritance, a set of qualities that Orwell noted as redeeming features of British life, which are threatened by the forces of bigotry, authoritarianism and greed. But it can also be seen as an attempt to transmit the values of a sub-culture. The technical college apprentices I referred to earlier see it this way: liberal studies is staffed by members of an odd-ball minority, a splinter group from the middle class, who read *The Guardian*, would have knuckled under to the Argies, can't make their minds up about nuclear missiles, and vote for the Alliance. The independent school pupils I quoted belong to the world of the commercial and bureaucratic middle classes, of *The Telegraph* and *The Times*. It is a different world in some respects from that of the apprentices but similar in its decisiveness, its practicality, its robust ethnocentrism and its contempt for airy-fairy fence-sitting intellectuals. They see their teachers as Greeks in their fathers' Roman Empire, interesting gadflies whose ideas should be courteously attended to but never confused with reality.

83

Robert Irvine Smith

The liberal-minded teacher is, in Michael Frayn's phrase, a herbivore in a carnivorous world. He may be liked, even admired, but he is rarely taken as a model for behaviour. The predators of boardroom, shopfloor and street are more potent moral educators.

Teachers who find that they are being labelled and thereby neutralized by their pupils have a number of options. They can accept the label of herbivore and go on playing the part, hoping that some of the fair-mindedness they display in their classroom will be assimilated by something akin to osmosis, a process in cell liquids by which the weak dilutes the strong, in spite of an intervening membrane. Another strategy is that of the sheep in wolf's clothing, by which the teacher becomes street-wise (or boardroom-wise, or shopfloor-wise, as appropriate), keeping *The Guardian* out of sight and adopting the dress and manners of the carnivore.

For the teacher who dislikes both these alternatives the following may be useful as focussing ideas for self-evaluation.

1. Is our selection of *content* appropriate to the aims of value education? History offers us an almost infinite choice. We do not always choose those bits which raise significant value questions: indeed, many syllabuses seem designed to exclude them, in the ill-founded belief that they make it more difficult to learn historical objectivity. In social studies, the issues selected may be real and controversial to us but leave our students cold.

2. Our selection, too, of *resources* may help to distance students from the issues. If general studies is identified with a particular value position it could be that too many sources are taken from *The Guardian* (as was the case in many of the General Studies Project units). If we are talking about real issues in a community the obvious source is real people, engaged in direct talk with students. It may mean complex arrangements and considerable risk, but this is the price of authenticity.

3. Some teachers have found defining *objectives* a useful exercise, though there is no agreement about the form this should take. Whatever one's views on the issue of behavioural objectives it seems a good idea to discuss with students what they will be able to do at the end of the course that they were unable to do at the beginning.

4. This means taking a fresh look at the notion of *skills* in relation to value questions. What do people need to enable them to understand complex human situations, weigh up alternative policies, reflect on implications, and make intelligent and

sensitive decisions? How can we tell if a student is making progress in these directions? Keith Webb (1980) points to ways of combining understanding with skill in political education, as does Len Masterman (1980) in media studies. Schools could learn from the experience of industry and further education in the development of lifeskills training (Further Education Unit, 1980), and related moves towards profile reporting (Balogh, 1982). There are dangers here: industry may be more interested in skills of problem-solving within controlled company boundaries than with the spirit of free enquiry. But schools would be unwise to ignore a movement which demonstrates the practical usefulness of certain aspects of social education.

5 Most important of all is attending closely to the *learners' perceptions* of what values education is all about. It is too easy for teacher and taught to drift apart on a matter in which the closest collaboration is essential, as a study of a social and moral education course by a Yorkshire teacher, Fred Middleton, (1979), showed in stark terms. One of his 14 year old pupils described the innovatory course thus: 'Social and moral is like any other subject. Teachers talk about it, write it on the board, and we copy it down in our books'.

Learners are active agents, and they will find ways of making their own sense of whatever teachers provide. This can be unproductive and disabling, if the work is mentally filed as 'just another school subject', or 'pinko propaganda', or 'riding his hobby horse again'. But it can also be a powerful force for valuable learning, if the teacher finds out what systems of ideas already exist in the learner's head, and how new material is likely to be construed and assimilated. There may be surprises here, and teachers need to be sensitive and quick on their feet. In a final classroom illustration an 11 year old York girl reminds us that the best laid plans of the curriculum designer may need swift adjustment.

The lesson was on primitive societies, part of a first year humanities course in a comprehensive school. The underlying values were those of universal humanism: respect for different cultures was to emerge from studying ways of coping with hard environments. The teacher is explaining sex roles. A little girl puts up her hand: 'Sir, if the women get the food and look after the children, what do the men do?' The teacher is pleased to have this cue to the next part of the lesson, the concept of division of labour. 'Well,' he says, 'They are responsible for religious ceremonies — you know, the dance rituals we saw on the film, and they also take part in wars with neighbouring tribes.' The girl tosses her head with the accumulated scorn of a thousand generations of women: 'Dancin' and fightin': typical!'

References

BALOGH, J. (1982), *Profile Reports for School Leavers*, Longman, for Schools Council.
BRIDGES, D., and SCRIMSHAW, P. (1975), *Values and Authority in Schools*, Hodder and Stoughton.
FENTON, E. (1966), *Teaching the New Social Studies in Secondary Schools*, Holt, Rinehart and Winston.
Further Education Unit (1980), *Developing Social and Life Skills*.
MASTERMAN, L. (1980), *Teaching about Television*, Macmillan.
MIDDLETON, F.R. (1979), *A Case Study of the Teaching of Variety of Social Studies*, MA thesis, University of York.
WEBB, K. (1980), *Political Education and the Development of Political Skills*, MA thesis, University of York.
WHITEHEAD, D.J. (Ed.) (1979), *Handbook for Economics Teachers*, Heinemann.
YOUNG, M.F.D. (Ed.) (1972), *Knowledge and Control*, Collier-Macmillan.

Values in Home Economics Teaching

Hilary Davies

Home economics is an area much neglected by educationalists. It has, however, been criticized by feminist writers in their analysis of influences affecting the position of women in society (Coote and Campbell, 1982; Marks, 1976; Sharpe, 1976). The education system, the hidden curriculum and specific subject areas such as science, CDT and home economics have all been criticized for transmitting attitudes and values which reinforce sex-role stereotyping so limiting personal and vocational opportunities on the basis of gender. These are political issues and teachers have often failed to recognize the influences in society which give rise to the values and assumptions which are then transmitted through the formal and informal curricula in schools. They should be recognized as the power base from which all educational decisions, curriculum patterns and subject studies are derived.

In this chapter consideration will be given to home economics in the curriculum today. A detailed historical development of the subject will not be undertaken but important educational issues will be raised in an attempt to identify influences which are reflected in the content of present-day syllabuses. An analysis of home economics teaching will then be undertaken from an educational perspective and, finally, strategies for the future will be proposed from the belief that education in home economics can enhance rather than restrict the personal development of individuals whatever their sex.

Values in Home Economics Education — past and present

Many historical perspectives on the changing role of women have been adopted (Mitchell and Oakley, 1976; Oakley 1974; Sharpe, 1976), but whatever additional responsibilities and activities women undertake, the affairs of the home have been seen primarily as the responsibility of women in our society. This acceptance of women's role in homemaking led to the inclusion of needlework, and later domestic economy, into the curriculum for girls over 100 years ago.

Accounts of women's lives in the nineteenth century show clearly that working class girls were expected to assume major responsibilities for homemaking and the care of young children from an early age, particularly in times of sickness, childbirth and unemployment (Burnett, 1974 and 1982; Llewellyn Davies, 1931/1977). It has been argued that the education of girls received low priority in this period (Burnett, 1982) but factual accounts suggest that however limited the educational provision overall an element of sewing or needlecraft was included in the curriculum for younger girls which was extended in later years to give the rudiments of plain cooking, home management and laundry work for older pupils if facilities were available (Van der Eyken, 1973). This acceptance of a 'vocational' element in girls' education is in marked contrast to the powerful and passionate liberal vocational education debate of the late nineteenth and early twentieth century (Layton, 1973; Simon, 1960 and 1965; Tawney, 1964). The acceptance of a curriculum for girls as recently as 1965 suggests that this debate had little effect on the nature of the education deemed suitable for future wives and mothers.

The women's education movement was, and still is, divided on the issue of education for homemaking. Those seeking an education for girls identical to that of boys rejected it. Others argued that home economics could form part of the curriculum being of value in itself but also being a vehicle for widening and increasing womens' opportunities, particularly in science, by building on knowledge and experiences of the home environment which are familiar to girls but are seldom used as a base for learning in traditional science teaching.

The first home economists were concerned to improve the quality of life for working class families (Ehrenreich and English, 1979). The values transmitted were those considered to be accpetable to society at that time: living within one's means, frugality and simplicity in everyday life, concern for others, selflessness, self respect and personal responsibility. Domestic economy in schools consequently comprised of the theory and practice of *plain* cookery, hygiene, home management and needlework. In a century of rapid political, social and technological change the content of the subject today is, nevertheless, similar to that taught 100 ago. Some change has taken place — the educational developments of the post-war period laid stress on the pleasures of homemaking, the creation of a loving, caring and aesthetically pleasing

Values in Home Economics Teaching

environment for one's family, and the influence of the social sciences is recognized in that more attention is paid to the needs of people as opposed to care and maintenance of the home, but these are changes in emphasis. The fundamental values transmitted through home economics education today are basically the same as those transmitted to pupils over a century ago:

> homemaking as primarily the responsibility of women.
> care and concern for others — at home and in the community.
> the pleasures of homemaking and the joy of family life.
> a frugal and simple life-style.
> the encouragement of independence and personal responsibility.
> high personal standards in every area of life.

Many would argue that these values are 'good' and 'right'. Others would argue that they are exerting a powerful form of social control on young people — girls in particular, and that some of these values taken to extremes are not acceptable within the framework of education as personal development and the encouragement of personal autonomy. These traditional values do not encourage a respect for individuals as ends in themselves, nor do they encourage respect for differences, for the subject prescribes an 'acceptable' way of life and proscribes alternatives.

Increasing numbers of home economics teachers are expressing concern at the content of courses and at the quality of the educational experiences which are offered to pupils within the traditional subject framework. There is concern:

- at the sexist assumptions underlying the whole subject area that home affairs are the concern of women. Education for everyday life at home is seen as essential for boys as well as girls. (DES. 1975, 1979 and 1980; EOC, 1982).
- that care and concern for others should be an important area of boys' education.
- at the perpetuation of 'family' as representing father, a dependent non-working mother and two children — an image which represents only 5 per cent of households today.
- that women get 'joy and pleasure' from homemaking — whereas for many these tasks are chores.
- that women do not work.
- that the complexity and reality of interpersonal relationships is

seldom discussed and that mental health, in contrast to physical health, is frequently ignored.
— that the family is always regarded as a force for good.
— that alternatives to the 'family' are seldom mentioned.
— that individual difference is not respected.
— that different ways of life are either not accepted or cannot be accommodated within existing syllabuses.
— that decision-making on the part of pupils is not encouraged — preferred outcomes only being approved.
— that the process is still more impartial than the people.
— that the subject, which is an obvious vehicle for social and political education, is stripped of all controversy and alternative perspectives.

These criticisms raise important educational, philosophical, social and political issues. How can 'education for everyday life' meet the educational outcomes which we hope to effect in young people today and for the future?

Values in Home Economics Education — an alternative view

The home economics teacher with reservations about existing syllabuses and courses is faced with a series of dilemmas. Her expertise lies in the traditional areas of the subject and the introduction of unfamiliar material and different learning strategies could be so threatening that the individual denies the need for change. In this way traditional knowledge and skills are perpetuated in schools. Other teachers work within existing structures in an attempt to reflect change, but inevitably a point is reached when the traditional values are imposed be it at the level of course approval, moderation or examination. It is all credit to the teachers who feel anger at the denial of important *educational* principles: that a candidate's reasoned decision is not accepted, and that alternative ways of life are not approved.

It has been argued that change is only possible if a philosophy is adopted and educational aims are identified (Davies, 1981). Only by working from a level of principle can progress be made: content can be determined from the philosophical stance, and educational aims can be matched with content to meet the educational needs of individuals and groups, for example:

Principle
'Home economics is concerned with the way diverse household groups

Values in Home Economics Teaching

organize and manage available resources to meet human needs within the overall community context (the socio-economic environment)'

From this content areas can be identified

a study of diverse household groups — in this country and in other countries' value systems.

resources, human, financial, time: the availability of resources.

identification of human needs: food, clothing, housing, warmth, others, emotional needs, love, care security, self esteem, human relationships needs and wants.

organization and management of resources to meet needs.

the household in the community: interrelationship.

The educational aims for home economics education are then determined

1. Education in home economics should develop an awareness of the needs of individuals.
   [needs, wants, identification of basic needs in our society, changing needs throughout life: meeting needs within the household and within the community.]

2. Education in home economics should encourage an appreciation of the complexity and reality of life within households.
   [people together: living and working with others: caring-sharing: giving and taking: mental health.]

3. Education in home economics should encourage an awareness of the many varied value systems of people within household groups.
   [values — an appreciation of different value systems — personal, cultural, religious, regional, national.
   an appreciation of similarities and respect for difference.]

4. Education in home economics should encourage individuals to recognize and appreciate the relationship between values and the organization and management of available household resources.
   [different ways of life — ways of life other than your own, an appreciation of similarities and respect for difference in the way others live].

5. Education in home economics should enable men and women to make reasoned and informed decisions for themselves and for their dependants in everyday life — decisions related to the organization and management of available resources such as time, money and human potential to satisfy needs and priorities within the household group.
   [Knowledge of food, nutrition, housing, materials, fuels, health,

safety, money, time matched with needs, values and relationships. Decision making — alternative courses of action.]
6 Education in home economics should enable individuals to reorganize the interrelationship between the household and the community.
[the influence of national/local policy on households, the influence of households on local and national policy]
factors affecting the 'availability' of resources.
7 Education in home economics can provide meaningful educational experiences and opportunities for personal fulfilment FOR SOME in aesthetic, creative and scientific skills in areas associated with home and family life.
[traditional homemaking skills for those who choose to.]

So what values are transmitted through a scheme such as this which is only one teacher's attempt to make home economics an *educational* activity?

Home Economics as an educational experience for all irrespective of sex.
The importance of human relationships.
Care and concern for others.
Respect for difference — for individuals as well as groups.
Encouraging personal responsibility in everyday life.
To understand the working of a democratic society.

These values can be defended educationally if education is defined in terms of personal development, increasing confidence and personal autonomy and developing insights and skills in dealing with others.

References

BURNETT, J. (1974), *Useful Toil*, Allen Lane, London.
BURNETT, J. (1982), *Destiny Obscure*, Allen Lane, London.
COOTE, A. and CAMPBELL, B. (1982), *Sweet Freedom, the Struggle for Women's Liberation*, Pan Books, London.
DAVIES, H. (1981), 'Let's start with people', *Housecraft*, 54, 5, pp. 117–20.
DES (1975), Educational Survey No. 21, *Curricular Differences for Boys and Girls*, London, HMSO.
DES (1979), *Aspects of Secondary Education in England*, London, HMSO.
DES (1980), *Girls and Science*, HMI series: Matters for Discussion, London HMSO.

Equal Opportunities Commission (1982), *Equal Opportunities in Home Economics*, EOC Manchester.
EHRENREICH, B. and ENGLISH, D. (1979), *For Her Own Good — 150 Years of the Experts' Advice to Women*, Pluto Press, London.
LAYTON, D. (1973), *Science for the People*, George Allen and Unwin Ltd, London.
LIEWELYN DAVIES, M. (Ed.) (1931/1977), *'Life as we have known it'*, Vintage, London.
MARKS, P. (1976), 'Femininity in the classroom', in MITCHELL, J. and OAKLEY, A. (Eds.) *The Right and Wrongs of Women*, Penguin Books, London.
OAKLEY, A. (1974), *Housewife*, Penguin Books, London.
SHARPE, S. (1976), *Just like a Girl — How Girls Learn to be Women*, Penguin Books, London.
SIMON, B. (1960), *Studies in the History of Education 1780–1870* — retitled (1974) *The Two Nations and the Educational Structure 1780–1870*, Lawrence and Wishart, London.
SIMON, B. (1965), *Education and the Labour Movement 1870–1920*, Lawrence and Wishart, London.
TAWNEY, R.H. (1964), *The Radical Tradition* ed. Hinden, Allen and Unwin, London.
VAN DER EYKEN, W. (1973), *Education, the Child and Society*, Penguin Books, London.

Values in Mathematics Education

Bryan Wilson

Why Mathematics?

At first sight it may come as a surprise to find a chapter on mathematics in a book concerned with values in education. Surely mathematics, of all subjects, is value-free?

Mathematics stands apart as a subject in the school curriculum, universally regarded as important, the only subject taught in practically every school in the world, and apparently sublimely impervious to the constraints of the cultural environment and social value-system within which it is being taught. Numbers are numbers are numbers ... $2 + 2 = 4$ is true in precisely the same way in Idi Amin's Uganda as it is in the tranquility of a Pacific island. The angle in a semi-circle is a right angle, as much for a child in the rectilinear world of the inner-city as for a child in the meandering, circular world of much of rural Africa. Cos x integrates to sin x, whether you are living under communism or capitalism, although the proportion of school-leavers who know it may vary enormously: over 90 per cent in USSR, less than 10 per cent in USA.

Mathematical truths are objective, external, unchanging, independent of the particular people who happen to be teaching or learning them. Whether mathematics is discovered or invented is a philosophical question perhaps outside the scope of this present book, but, on the face of it, it certainly seems that if all written mathematics were to be destroyed and the whole complex edifice had to be developed again *ab initio*, then the same truths would in due course reappear. Notations would of course differ, so much so that in written form it would not be immediately recognizable to anyone familiar with the 'old' mathematics. But this is no more than saying that you cannot read literature written in a language that you do not know, even if it is a book with which you are

Values in Mathematics Education

already familiar. In the case of mathematics, the facts and the structures would be the same, even if expressed in a different system of notation.

Mathematics, then, has an absolute quality. In this it differs from every other subject in the school curriculum; indeed, it could be argued that it differs in this respect from every other field of human study. There is an essential arbitrariness about literature, history, geography ... things *could* have been different, people could have acted differently, chosen differently, written differently. Values are everywhere, underlying those actions and choices. Even the scientist's constructs are dependent on the external world; theories have to be checked, and predictions tested against observation. In this sense, science is a dependent activity in a way in which mathematics is not. Popper, Kuhn and others have enabled us to realize that science depends upon an interpretive framework that is itself supplied through value systems and beliefs. Within education, curriculum content has to be decided against a background of public debate on nuclear weapons, CND, conservation, vivisection and so on. People do not argue in similar ways about the social implications of matrices, or whether developments in abstract algebra threaten human survival.

Mathematics, then, is unique in the school curriculum. It is true that mathematics educators may argue about the merits of including certain topics and excluding others, and overtones of the 'traditional-modern' dichotomy still distantly echo, but these are purely technical issues, as neutral and as value-free as mathematics itself. Mathematics is important, and schools and parents world-wide give it high priority. Every child ought to master as much of it as possible. 'Values', in the sense of those principles of selection and of action which vary from society to society, and from one individual to another, are nothing to do with it.

Such at least is the popular view. It is the function of this chapter to question it. Other voices have already raised a similar question. For example, CASTME, the Commonwealth Association of Science, Technology and Mathematics Educators, was established in the early 1970s explicitly to consider the relation between the teaching of those subjects and the varied social and cultural values across the Commonwealth within which such teaching takes place. To quote from the introduction to the report of the CASTME Caribbean Regional Seminar (1983):

> No longer may the teaching of science and mathematics be seen as value-free, independent of the society which sustains it and which it is designed to serve. (p. 1)

Wilson (1981) gives over 200 references to studies on the interaction of

Bryan Wilson

mathematics education with its cultural context. Many of those concern the value-systems implicit in those contexts.

Part of a Total Curriculum

The first point to make is a very obvious one. Mathematics is part of the education of all pupils and cannot be considered in isolation. Nor can the rest of an education be considered apart from its mathematical component. All schools have their own sets of values, usually implicit but, nonetheless, real and powerful. These values become explicit through the attitudes and actions of the people involved, mainly of the teaching staff in their various roles. Mathematics teachers are primarily teachers. They contribute to or detract from the overall purposes of the school, through which a value-system is mediated, by the way in which they teach mathematics as much as by the spirit with which they take games or by whether they volunteer to do dinner-duty. The mathematics teacher who is content to mark work simply by putting ticks and crosses, who makes a pupil feel stupid when he gets something wrong, and who inculcates that sense of fear of the subject so cogently analyzed by Buxton (1981) is conveying a set of values as powerfully as the teacher who identifies the specific errors in pupils' work, who patiently encourages those who find the subject difficult, and who deliberately sets out to make mathematics lessons enjoyable.

Aims of Mathematics Education

Just as the values on which a school community is based are expressed through the school's purposes (implicit or explicit), so with the individual subjects in its curriculum. Let us therefore consider the purposes of studying mathematics, as expressed by various influential bodies in recent years. The Dainton Report (1968) provided statistical evidence of a swing away from science and mathematics in the choices made by sixth-form students in Britain during the 1960s. It suggested that a contributory cause was that, for many young people, science, engineering and technology seemed impersonal and dangerous, and out of touch with human and social concerns. Because of the strong curriculum link in school, mathematics tended to suffer in the same way. Against this value-laden background, the Report gave four reasons for studying mathematics:

1 Mathematical language is an important means of communication.
2 Studying mathematics is a good training for the mind.
3 Mathematics is a crucial tool for other subjects.
4 The discipline of the study required is beneficial in itself.

Newsletter 55 of the Mathematical Association (1982) listed seven aims:

1 The acquisition of certain basic skills and knowledge necessary for everyday life.
2 The acquisition of further knowledge and skills pertinent to particular courses and careers.
3 An appreciation of the formulation of a problem in mathematical terms (i.e. a 'mathematical model') and hence of the role that mathematics can play in a wide variety of other disciplines.
4 Mathematics as 'Queen and Servant', a tool in man's control of his environment and an intellectual activity and human achievement involving pattern and structure.
5 Mathematics as a social activity, in its existence, its conduct, and its applications, with a concurrent emphasis on communication skills — verbal, graphical and written.
6 Mathematics as a language.
7 An appreciation of the problem-solving powers of mathematics through personal experience of investigation and open-ended situations.

Although the Report of the Committee of Inquiry into the Teaching of Mathematics in Schools (Cockcroft, 1982) does not set out any specific list of aims for an education in mathematics, four general reasons can be distilled from it. These are the acquisition of facts and skills, and the appreciation of conceptual structures and general strategies. Even such a very generalized analysis points to a balance that is not always apparent in practice in mathematics classrooms.

For the primary school level, the Cockcroft Report commends the list of aims contained in *Mathematics 5–11: a handbook of suggestions*. These are 'to develop:

(i) a positive attitude to mathematics as an interesting and attractive subject;
(ii) an appreciation of the creative aspects of the subject and an awareness of its aesthetic appeal;
(iii) an ability to think clearly and logically in mathematics with confidence, independence of thought and flexibility of mind;

(iv) an understanding of mathematics through a process of enquiry and experiment;
(v) an appreciation of the nature of numbers and of space, leading to an awareness of the basis structure of mathematics;
(vi) an appreciation of mathematical pattern and the ability to identify relationships;
(vii) mathematical skills and knowledge accompanied by the quick recall of basic facts;
(viii) an awareness of the uses of mathematics in the world beyond the classroom. Children should learn that mathematics will frequently help them to solve problems they meet in everyday life or understand better many of the things they see, and provide opportunities for them to satisfy their curiosity and to use their creative abilities;
(ix) persistence through sustained work in mathematics which requires some perseverance over a period of time.

Finally, there is the overriding aim to maintain and increase confidence in mathematics, shown by the ability to express ideas fluently, to talk about the subject with assurance and to use the language of mathematics.'

These aims are expressed in terms of mathematical 'objectives' in an appendix to the handbook.

In considering these various sets of aims, it is interesting to note that it is in this last one, specifically concerned with the primary level, that values are most clearly discernible. Many of these aims are affective, concerned with the attitudes of children and even with character development (for example, (ix)). Reading through them, one has the picture of a particular kind of classroom atmosphere, a place of activity and of creativity with children taking at least a measure of responsibility for their own learning. It is a place where mathematical initiative and exploration is encouraged, and where authority lies in the subject rather than simply in the teacher. This is an issue which will be explored later in this chapter.

During the past fifteen years, many Local Education Authorities in England have issued their own 'guidelines' for primary mathematics. In his analysis of these, Wilson (1982, and 1984) noted that, of the documents studied from sixty-seven LEAs, twenty-six explicitly listed aims for mathematics at primary level. Of these, twenty-two included affective aims. That one-third of LEAs should do so indicates a widespread belief that mathematics education, at least in its early years, is concerned with the development of children's attitudes and values, and not solely with inculcating conceptual understanding and technical skills within mathematics itself. Indeed, it is likely that many in the two-thirds of Authorities who regard the reasons for teaching mathematics in primary schools as so obvious that no statement of aims is necessary would, if pressed, concur with this view.

Upon what kind of value-related attitudes, therefore, can mathematics education be expected to impinge?

A Respect for Truth

Firstly, it should foster *a respect for truth*. The earliest memories of mathematics for many people are indelibly linked with ticks and crosses, with 'right' and 'wrong'. It is strange that a subject whose learning is characterized by such words should be thought by many to have nothing to do with values. Truth and falsehood are more easily demonstrated in mathematics than in any other school subject. Elsewhere in the curriculum, one may study source material and weigh evidence, but, eventually individual judgment and opinion must play a part; one can never be certain that Hamlet was schizophrenic — or even whether Shakespeare meant him to be. Even in science, pupils learn that observations affect the phenomena observed, that there is such a thing as 'experimental error', and that theories are only capable of disproof, never of proof. Nor is all this mere nit-picking. Within these disciplines, scholars argue over such basic issues as to whether Shakespeare actually wrote the plays at all, while controversy rages on both sides of the Atlantic, as well as among scientists in many developing countries, over such fundamentals as the evolutionary theory of biological change.

Only in mathematics, it seems, is it possible to demonstrate truth. Although in recent years the place of formal proof has been reduced in many school syllabuses, the idea is implicit whenever a child is doing mathematics. Certainly pupils are encouraged to explore mathematical situations, to make guesses, to 'try things', but those trials are then subjected to testing against further examples, and eventually reasons are sought. Only when a proof, valid at the learner's own level, has been found will he be satisfied. Although traditional methods of teaching mathematics often stressed the right/wrong dichotomy too strongly, the idea itself is basic to mathematics.

Bryan Wilson

Authority in Mathematical Learning

Another way of considering this is in terms of the source of authority in learning. For the young child, authority lies in the teacher, often indeed at the expense of the parent. 'My teacher said so!' is a devastating assertion to a parent who wishes neither to undermine that teacher's relationship with the child, nor to allow the child to believe untruths.

Yet in mathematics, even the young child instinctively realizes that authority lies within the subject itself. A teacher can tell a child that the Battle of Hastings took place in 1166, and the child will believe him; but if he tells the child that two and four make seven, there will be an argument. Children can find out for themselves whether their work is correct, by checking it, by working backwards, by applying their results to new cases. The whole philosophy of discovery-learning in mathematics rests on the subject's intrinsic authority and consistency.

It is this reliability of mathematics that enables it to have such a powerful impact on children's attitudes. If used threateningly by the teacher, it can generate the feelings of antipathy, of fear and even of guilt described by Buxton (1981). On the other hand, in the words of Edith Biggs, HMI:

> We can say, with complete assurance, every teacher who embarks on a programme which will enable children to make their own discoveries in mathematics will share to the utmost their children's enjoyment of mathematics and their increasing confidence in their own powers (Schools Council, 1965).

In an age where traditional sources of authority have largely been eroded, mathematics remains as an important element in a child's experience, as something stable, consistent, reliable, an area of life in which you can have certainty. For some children in the Western world it may, alas, be the only one.

At a higher level, of course, it can be argued that the authority of mathematics is illusory. Far from being 'true', it is merely 'consistent', all its results following from axioms which are themselves arbitrary. The view was succinctly expressed by Bertrand Russell in his famous dictum 'Mathematics is the discipline in which we do not know what we are talking about, and do not care whether what we say about it is true.' Indeed, even the possibility of consistency has been undermined by the work of mathematical logicians during the present century.

All this is a far cry, however, from mathematics as perceived by a pupil in school, or indeed by others concerned with mathematics education at school level. To them, mathematics retains an absolute

Values in Mathematics Education

quality which the exercises in arithmetic and in algebra, and the diagrams in geometry, constantly reinforce. Many mathematicians in the past have shared this sense of the 'absoluteness' of mathematics, from Plato's 'God is a Geometer' to Kepler's 'O God, I am thinking Thy thoughts after Thee'.

Mathematics and Islamic Values

Although it would now be unusual in the West to link the learning of mathematics with religion, this is not the case in the Islamic world. The Second World Conference on Muslim Education, held in Islamabad, Pakistan, in March 1980, made a number of wide-raging recommendations for restructuring school education. Educational patterns had been inherited from the 'secular' West, and its basic principles needed to be re-examined. Knowledge is of two kinds:

> In view of the fact that though all knowledge belongs to Allah and is granted by him to mankind, some knowledge is revealed to man through his chosen people, the Prophets, and some is granted to man when he strives with his mind and soul, the former therefore has the status of absolute truth and the latter of tentative truth, always to be judged with reference to the former (*Times Educational Supplement*, 1980).

Interestingly, mathematics belongs to the second category, that of tentative truth. Nevertheless, its study at school can lead directly to a greater appreciation of absolute truth. At the primary level, the purposes of mathematics teaching are described as follows:

> To be taught at first through games and puzzles, and later on through sums. By the time a student finishes the primary stage he should be able to handle algebraic symbols and geometric figures with confidence in addition to arithmetic numbers. The objective is to make students implicitly able to formulate and understand abstractions and be steeped in the area of symbols. It is good training for the mind so that they may move from the concrete to the abstract, from sense experience to ideation and from matter-of-factness to symbolization. It makes them prepare for a much better understanding of how the Universe, which appears to be concrete and matter of fact, is actually *ayatullah*: signs of God — a symbol of reality. (*Times Educational Supplement*, 1980).

Bryan Wilson

It is instructive to compare this important international statement with the various lists of aims of mathematics education in Britain, already quoted. It may well be thought that it contains a confidence and a coherence which many educators in the West, while not wishing to emulate, may nevertheless envy.

Content or Methodology?

Given that mathematics education can serve as a vehicle for the transmission of values, in what ways can it do this? It is doubtful whether selection of syllabus content can play much part. Transformation geometry may be marginally more relevant to a range of employment opportunities than was Euclidean geometry, but neither seems to correlate with any particular set of social, political or moral values. It is in terms of methodology, rather than of content, that mathematics education is value-laden.

Construction of Examples

One of the most obvious aspects of value-related methodology is in the choice of textbook examples. A few illustrations will make this clear. In *Socialist Mathematics Education* (Swetz, 1978), mathematics education is described in detail in seven socialist countries. The only way in which specifically socialist values come across, however, is in the contexts invented for the mathematical exercises to turn them into 'problems'. For example, from Tanzania we have:

> In an Ujamaa village, it is decided during one of the meetings to build a village library. The model of the simple library building is as shown below (figure provided). Draw a plan and the front and side elevations of the building so that the village masons can get down to work. (p. 320).

More aggressively, from China in the 1950s:

> To liberate Formosa, the liberating aircraft searching in the air is 12 miles away from the liberation gunboat and 16 miles from the American Imperialist fleet, the angle A is 60° (referring to a given diagram). What is the distance between the gunboat and the fleet? (p. 149).

Values in Mathematics Education

Later, the thrust of politico-mathematical exercises was modified to emphasize the exploitation and hardships that existed before the revolution in China:

> When worker Tung was six years old, his family was poverty-stricken and starving. They were compelled to borrow five dou of maize from a landlord. The wolfish landlord used this chance to demand the usurious compound interest of 50 per cent for three years. Please calculate how much grain the landlord demanded from the Tung family at the end of the third year. (p. 171).

It is not difficult to see how values are being conveyed through such examples. Howson (1980) however argues that there is no such thing as socialist mathematics education *per se*; dressing up examples in social or political garb is merely superficial. It has been going on for a long time, in capitalist as well as in socialist societies. A British textbook until very recently still on sale in a landlocked country of Southern Africa includes such gems as:

> A merchant fits out three ships in succession to run the American blockade, he reckons the total outlay on each ship after the first to be 25 per cent more than on the one that preceded it. The first and third get into port, and he gains 160 per cent on their cost, the second is taken. Find his loss or gain per cent on the whole.

Different values are conveyed through other examples in the same book, such as:

> A publician sells beer at 2d a glass to university men, and 1½d a glass to townsmen: an undergraduate by not wearing his gown passes with the publican for a townman; but, being caught by the proctors at the end of thirty-two days, he finds his savings in beer will just pay his fine of 6s. 8d.; how much beer did he drink per evening?

What an African child is expected to make of the values of the society depicted is not, however, clear.

More recently, the chapter on 'Stocks and Shares' that was normal in secondary mathematics textbooks, at least until the 1960s, was only relevant to a small and privileged minority of the population. Nevertheless, it carried the message, no less powerful for being unstated, that capitalism and the profit motive were Good Things.

Mathematics in Society

Another way in which mathematics education can convey values to children is through relating mathematics to society in a more comprehensive way than simply through individual examples or themes. This is being done for science education through a variety of projects, such as Science in Society, and Science in a Social Context (SISCON). Mathematics has been slower to adopt this approach. However, it is the basis of a recent international project, the Mathematics in Society Project (MISP). The instigators of the project had all been actively involved in the curriculum movement in school mathematics during the 1960s and 1970s, but felt that past work had suffered from too limited a view of the nature and role of the subject. They believed that such a limited view of what mathematics is, and how it functions in society, has been a root cause of the very disturbing negative attitude that so many people, both adults and pupils, have towards it.

Rogerson (1983) describes the strategy of MISP as teaching mathematics through its role in society. A central issue faced by the team of authors, and still unresolved at the time of writing, concerns whether the view of society conveyed should be neutral, simply describing things as they are, or biased, in the sense of adopting a particular set of social values and objectives. The outcome will be of particular interest to readers of this chapter.

Methodology and Values

It has already been suggested that values are transmitted to pupils by the mathematics teacher's methodology. The Cockcroft Report (1982) in its best-known paragraph (243) listed six elements that need to be present in successful mathematics teaching to pupils of all ages. There should be opportunities for:

— exposition by the teacher;
— discussion between teacher and pupils, and between pupils themselves;
— appropriate practical work;
— consolidation and practice of fundamental skills and routines;
— problem solving, including the application of mathematics to everyday situations;
— investigational work.

While the balance between these methods will vary with the social

Values in Mathematics Education

setting, the age and aptitude of the pupils, the experience and personality of the teacher, the mathematical content and the ethos of the school, all should be present in some measure. It is significant that the particular balance will to a considerable extent reflect the value-system of the society, the school and the teacher. Heavy reliance on teacher exposition and pupil practice usually occurs where there is an emphasis on the authority of the system and of the teacher, where discipline is seen as an important aspect of a pupil's upbringing, and where the school — rather than the individual learner — takes responsibility for pupils' progress. Marks and form-orders commonly characterize such schools.

Where discussion is encouraged rather than suppressed in mathematics lessons, where cooperation between pupils in solving problems is regarded as a virtue rather than as cheating, and where pupils are given freedom to pursue mathematical investigations that had not been pre-planned by the teacher, a different set of values is being conveyed. These have to do with the value of the learner's own judgment, even if he is still below the statutory school-leaving age. They imply a respect for his intellectual autonomy. Mathematics is being taught in accordance with a view of society as essentially cooperative rather than competitive. Marks, even in such a mark-prone subject as mathematics, will not play a dominant part in such a teaching strategy.

Competition or Cooperation?

The way in which the clash between cooperative and competitive social values is focussed in the teaching of mathematics is powerfully expounded by Henry (1963). In his chapter 'Golden Rule Days: American Schoolrooms' he sees in the competitive ethos of the classroom a reflection of a basic dilemma of American society in which competition is 'a pivot of action'. People who love one another cannot compete effectively in such a society, and so schools have to teach children how to hate, yet without appearing to do so since such an overt objective would be socially unacceptable. Schools resolve this ambiguity by encouraging competition among pupils, creating an artificial situation in which the price of one person's success is another's failure. Games contribute to this, and parents collude in it. Mathematics is a particularly effective vehicle for such competition, since it provides a constant succession of right/wrong alternatives. This viewpoint is a powerful explanation of why mathematics is the most disliked and feared of all school subjects.

Henry's thesis also shows why a competitive style of mathematics teaching is relatively ineffective in cultures which are based on cooperation rather than on competition, for example American Indians, and many African and Asian societies. In her work in the South Pacific region, Whippy (personal communication) observed that students from many of the islands readily took to group work in learning mathematics, whereas forbidding them to cooperate in the solution of a problem left them bemused. On investigating the social background she discovered that they came from communities where much manual and technical work, such as agriculture, boat building and house construction, is undertaken communally. Collaborative methods of learning mathematics reinforced those social values, whereas enforcing individual learning ran counter to them. It was ineffective as a learning strategy, not only through unfamiliarity but because it implied on outlook on life with which students did not wish to identify.

Social Convention

Every society has a set of attitudes which are acceptable, and other which are not. These may be only a matter of convention, but they are nevertheless powerful determinants of social interaction. Mathematical ability provides an interesting example in Britain. Respect, almost amounting to awe, is popularly accorded to people who are 'good at maths'. This is different from, for example, history; many people think that they could have become competent historians had they decided to put their minds to it instead of doing something else. So far is mathematics set apart from other disciplines that it is socially acceptable to admit, even to claim, that one is no good at maths; it carries a cachet that it is impossible to imagine ever being attached to an admission of illiteracy.

Priorities in Planning

Within a school, the hierarchical nature of mathematics means that pupil achievement covers a wider range than in any other subject apart from the fine arts. This means that curriculum planning has to face up to questions of making different provision for different groups of pupils in a particularly acute way within a mathematics department, an issue which is fundamental to any discussion of a strategy for mathematics teaching in a comprehensive school.

Which groups of children should have their needs considered as of highest priority? The values of the school community, and more specifically of the mathematics staff, will determine the answer.

What usually happens is that the highest attainers, particularly those in public examination forms, are catered for first in terms of staff allocation, the provision of rooms and resources, and so on. Then come the top sets/streams lower down the school, and lastly the non-examination and lower-achieving groups. This order is mirrored in mathematics curricula, which have developed, in the words of the Cockcroft Report, from the top downwards. All too often the mathematics taught to the lowest achievers is a severely diluted CSE course. CSE courses are themselves in the main watered-down 'O' level courses, which in turn are designed as preparation for 'A' level, which is prerequisite work for university mathematics. Cockcroft (para 442) asserts that 80 per cent of 11-16 pupils in England now follow courses based on concepts which, twenty years ago, were studied by only 25 per cent of the population.

The Cockcroft Report (para 450) proposes that curriculum development should proceed 'from the bottom upwards' by considering the range of work which is appropriate for lower-attaining pupils and extending this range as the level of attainment of pupils increases. Priority would thus be given to the needs of the mathematically weakest, and this could be paralleled by their needs similarly being considered first in the allocation of staff and material resources at school level.

Is it fanciful to suggest that such a reordering of priorities by mathematics educators would accord with a Christian framework of values? Christians have always to give special care to the poor, usually taken to mean the poor in wealth. In modern western society, the poor in mathematics and the poor in wealth are frequently the same; certainly few who are mathematically able need be financially embarrassed or unemployed. In today's schools, the poor in mathematics rapidly become the poor in spirit, and an education based on Christian values would give their needs priority over the needs of their more able contemporaries.

Conclusion

The inscription over the door of Plato's Academy was 'Let no-one ignorant of mathematics enter here'. The central position of mathematics in education is unchallenged. What is in question is whether its teaching is, or can be, as value-free as is commonly thought.

References

Buxton, L. (1981) *Do You Panic about Maths?*, London, Heinemann Educational.
Castme (1983) *Caribbean Regional Seminar*, London, The British Council, for the Commonwealth Association of Science, Technology and Mathematics Educators.
Cockcroft, W.H. (1982) *Mathematics Counts*, Report of the Committee of Inquiry into the Teaching of Mathematics in Schools, Chairman: W.H. Cockcroft (The Cockcroft Committee), London, HMSO.
Dainton, F.S. (1968) *Enquiry into the Flow of Candidates in Science and Technology into Higher Education* (the Dainton Report), London, HMSO.
Henry, J. (1963) *Culture Against Man*, New York, Random House.
HMI (1979) *Mathematics 5–11: A handbook of suggestions*, Matters for discussion series, 9, London, HMSO.
Howson, A.G. (1980) 'Socialist mathematics education — does it exist? *Educational Studies in Mathematics*, 11, 3, August, pp. 285–99.
Mathematical Association (1982) *Newsletter 55*, Leicester, The Mathematical Association.
Rogerson, A. (1983) *Mathematics in Society: the real way to apply mathematics?*, Victoria, Australia, Mathematics in Society Project.
Schools Council (1965) *Curriculum Bulletin No 1: Mathematics in Primary Schools*, London, HMSO.
Swetz, F.J. (Ed.) (1978) *Socialist Mathematics Education*, Southampton, PA, USA, Burgundy Press.
Times Educational Supplement (1980) *Recommendations of Second Conference* (on Islamic Education), 5 September, p. IV of inset.
Wilson, B. (1981) *Cultural Contexts of Science and Mathematics Education, A bibliographic guide*, Leeds, Centre for Studies in Science Education, University of Leeds.
Wilson, B. (1982) 'Primary Guidelines', *Mathematics in School*, 11, 5, November, pp. 13–18.
Wilson, B. (1984) 'Primary guidelines updated', *Mathematics in School*, 13, 2, March, pp. 6–8.

Use or Ornament? Values in the Teaching and Learning of Modern Languages

Nicholas Beattie

Teachers of modern languages in British schools talk quite frequently about methods, but rarely about values. This is not surprising if one considers the social character of any subject in a curriculum.

> Subjects provide teachers with a personal anchorage, a sense of who they are and what they stand for. Their attachment to their subject is nurtured through subject organizations; and teachers in schools, and particularly in universities, may even feel that their first loyalty is to their subject rather than to the organization which employs them.[1]

The social cohesiveness of language teachers is reinforced by the predominance of graduates in this area, by the experience which most of those graduates share of a period spent abroad, and by the supposedly esoteric nature of their skills.

This self-sufficiency within a defined subject area means that teachers are rarely called upon to justify their subject or explain why it should be in the curriculum. For themselves, they 'feel' its value and importance (the verb is taken from the above quotation); but when faced by questioning from outsiders, they tend to react defensively by asserting the self-evident worth of their area rather than by arguing a case. As in many areas of life, practitioners rarely bring to consciousness the values which underlie what they do, and have therefore little skill in defending those values, still less in clarifying them or increasing their success in teaching them. Presumably the attempt to contribute to that wider process of discussion is the justification for this essay and this book.

The reluctance to be explicit means that it is difficult to unearth statements of the values underlying language teaching which have any assured claim to be representative of what 'modern linguists' (the phrase usually means 'teachers of modern languages') think. Such statements tend to be made not by teachers but by experts as they interact like diplomats with external forces impinging upon 'their' subject. Hence the statements are often defensive, rhetorical or polemical in character, and may relate more to the preoccupations of 'subject diplomats' than to those of teachers, still less those of children. In addition, the references to values are often tangential or unclear — for example, appeals to vague consensual beliefs which all educationalists are supposed to hold. These problems must be borne in mind in considering the various statements of aims which will in due course be presented.

To stress the social character of modern languages as a subject is another way of saying that to make sense of its actual and potential contribution to schools and schoolchildren in the 1980s, some historical perspective is imperative. The very phrase 'modern languages' is a curriculum term. In what sense is a language 'modern'? Clearly, in the sense that it is not 'ancient'. The phrase that is now unthinkingly used in many schools where no ancient language is taught survives from the period in the latter part of the nineteenth century, when French and German were fighting hard to establish themselves in a secondary school curriculum which was dominated by Latin and Greek.

From its formation in 1892, the Modern Language Association campaigned energetically and effectively for the inclusion of foreign languages in the secondary curriculum.[2] By the early part of this century, the battle was won to the extent that French, at least, seemed a necessary part of the new grammar schools founded in the wake of the 1902 Act. But the battle had been won at a price. The prestige of the classics, themselves reformed and rethought in the mid-nineteenth century, was so great that modern languages found themselves fighting on two fronts. The arguments which distinguished them from the classics were usefulness and relevance. The teaching of French in schools could be justified partly on commercial and vocational grounds, and also as bringing into schools a more accurate picture of the contemporary world — a world which was not monoglot and insular, but polyglot and cosmopolitan. However, such arguments could rebound in a world where the dominance of the British Empire and the English language seemed total, and where many people despised vocational education: the Cambridge Modern and Medieval Languages Tripos, introduced in 1886, was known slightingly to some as 'the courier Tripos'.[3] Hence, modern languages tended to be 'sold' not as making a different contribution from that of Latin and Greek, but as being capable of the same sorts of effect. French literature was, it was argued, as extensive and as revealing of the human condition as that of Greece and Rome — and therefore as worthy of dominating a school curriculum. French was as difficult as Latin — or if, because of its relative lack of inflections, it seemed easier, it could be made more difficult by stressing historical philology, which became a part of most university courses in languages. French could be taught and assessed in the same ways as Latin, with a heavy stress on translation and on the written word, and a correlative neglect of oral and aural skills. These arguments between 'reformers' and 'translators' can be traced through the early numbers of *Modern Language Teaching* and *Modern Languages*.[4] Although the reformers seemed to carry the intellectual argument it seems that the translators came to dominate school practice. No doubt this was partly a result of the natural inertia of schools as social institutions and of a continuing problem of finding a sufficiency of adequately qualified and trained language teachers. No doubt also that preference of the written over the spoken was reinforced by the growing importance of public examinations, for whatever the undesirable backwash effects on teaching, it is generally easier and cheaper to test language skills in writing. However, the result of these developments was that from the very moment that modern languages became embedded in the secondary curriculum, they suffered from a split personality. On the one hand, the leaders of the language teaching profession proclaimed views and opinions which even today seem progressive; on the other the experience of many school pupils was of learning a living language taught as though it was a dead one, and passing examinations which certified an ability to translate literary texts rather than communicate with foreigners. This jaundiced view is evidenced by the reiterated complaints of leading modern linguists over the next sixty or seventy years about the dullness of so much practice in schools, by the unchanging character of the examination requirements, and by the style and content of so many of the textbooks used.

The years from 1900 to about 1965 saw the consolidation of the base on which current British language teaching has been built. Perhaps the most authoritative and intelligent statement of 'the value of modern studies' was formulated by the Leathes Committee, which in 1918 reported to the Prime Minister on 'the position of modern languages in the educational system of Great Britain'.[5] Their report spelt out the practical and cultural advantages of the wider and more effective teaching of foreign languages.

> Modern studies subserve the purpose of industry and commerce; they are needed for scientific instruction and information, by them alone can be gathered and disseminated that more

intimate knowledge of foreign countries which is necessary for the wise conduct of its affairs by a democratic people: they are required for the public service of the country at home as well as abroad; through and by them our people can learn what is best and highest in their countries ...[6]

The Report subsequently elaborated somewhat on the 'best and highest':

> All study has some moral value; modern studies are the study of man in all his higher activities, and thus may have a special moral value; but we need say no more of that. We are, and must be, concerned with modern studies as an instrument of culture; and by culture we mean that training which tends to develop the higher faculties, the imagination, the sense of beauty, and the intellectual comprehension.[7]

As authoritative statements of aims, these quotations are sufficiently explicit to begin breaking down aims into objectives ('imagination ... sense of beauty ... comprehension'). From the point of view of schools, however, their very explicitness throws up certain problems.

Firstly, the practical aims ('industry and commerce', etc.) are very difficult to apply to most work in schools. This is partly because the Leathes Committee clearly had in mind a quite small elite of business leaders and empire-builders ('Lord Cromer ... had no doubt that the conduct of public affairs in Egypt was constantly hampered' by British ignorance of foreign languages 'especially of French'[8]). But it is more generally true that general secondary schools cannot teach languages in a directly vocational way, becaue it is impossible to predict which languages will be needed in subsequent years by which children; also because in practice, no school can provide a sufficient range of languages. Thus the vocational argument has to be 'learning a language in order to learn how to learn languages'. For the purpose of this argument, it is almost irrelevant what language is chosen — in discussing the needs of the Egyptian Civil Service Leathes suggests that all that is required is that *a* language should have been learnt 'well before the age of 22'.[9]

If any language will do, then the language chosen might as well be one which brings with it a high degree of 'culture' in the sense of the second quotation. The clustering of values round this term is, of course, exceptionally dense. Over the period we are describing, it is mainly restricted to high culture, often to literary culture.[10] An appreciation of such culture is certainly not incompatible with a respect for more

Values in the Teaching and Learning of Modern Languages

directly practical skills and vocations: for example, the Leathes Report maintains the balance very wisely. However, a preoccupation with high culture can become exclusive. As T.S. Eliot remarks, 'It is commonly assumed that there is culture, but that it is the property of a small section of society'.[11] Although modern languages as a subject has always had its utilitarian aspect, it has by no means always resisted the temptation of intellectual snobbery. Consider this declaration from a well-known handbook on language teaching, published as recently as 1967:

> It is the task of the school to keep the pupil free of commercial considerations until he shall have chosen his career in accordance with his interests. This task is proving itself impossible of fulfilment at the present time: the rewards offered in industry to boys whose real bent is literary are a tempting bait.... Fortunately there are young persons who do not measure the value of their chosen career from its earning power alone; and that is why we continue to have our artists, musicians and actors. These supporters of the spirit in a material world are those who derive the greatest benefit from the study of modern languages.[12]

This vision of modern linguists as Bedes or Alcuins maintaining the flickering flame of civilization in a new Dark Age makes certain presuppositions about language learning and teaching. It assumes that the actual learning of a language is a preliminary to serious study, rather than having much value in its own right: in school terms it places a low value on most of what is learnt by most students up to the age of 16 and sees the 11–16 phase mainly as an anteroom to the stage that really matters: the modern languages sixth.[13] It is also non-developmental: it has difficulties in seeing that access to Racine, Cervantes or Goethe may be facilitated by delaying their presentation to younger learners and concentrating on contemporary France, Spain or Germany instead. Such views may seem antediluvian, and certainly few would now assent to them in the extreme form quoted above; yet they are still reflected in the so far almost unbroken dominance of literature in the A-level examination, in textbooks surviving from the past, and in the attitudes of a proportion of language teachers.

Such statements are rhetorical indications of attitudes of mind in both writers and readers, and should not perhaps be examined too solemnly. Nevertheless they are a useful reminder of the continuing gap between what experts said and what teachers did. Language teaching in British grammar schools by the end of the 1950s was engaged in two quite distinct tasks.[14] Firstly, it was putting over to a minority of pupils a particular set of beliefs about and attitudes towards a highly selective view of a few European cultures; secondly, it was teaching certain elementary language skills to a majority of the grammar school population (who were, of course, a minority of the total school population). The first of these tasks was more or less taken for granted, and fed pupils smoothly through into literature-oriented university language departments. The second had been the subject of unresolved dispute over method since the end of the previous century, and was widely criticized as uninspired, mechanical, dominated by translation and by external examinations, etc. The link between the two tasks was hardly glimpsed and there seemed little understanding that if, as the progressives argued, the oral was to be given much greater value in examinations, this might undermine the now traditional sixth-form curriculum.

In the sixties, this repetitive discussion, which never came to a conclusion because of resistance from many language teachers, and from the examination boards and the universities, was suddenly pushed to one side by two innovations. Both came from outside the traditional language-teaching profession in Britain. One was the introduction of audio-visual methods; the other was the move away from selective education.

Perhaps it would not be unfair to say that in the quotations cited so far, the learner has seemed distinctly marginal. He or she disappears behind social needs ('the purpose of industry and commerce ... scientific instruction and information ...' etc.) or appears as a 'supporter of the spirit in a material world'. Success in learning these values is presumably judged by the extent to which the learner becomes more like the teacher. The actual characteristics of the learner are extremely shadowy.

The importance of the audio-visual method was that it forced the majority of the British language teaching profession to consider the learner much more seriously than before. The method derived from services language courses: the first audio-visual course to be used in British schools was the Tavor course, which had originally been developed to enable NATO personnel to communicate among themselves. It therefore sidestepped the cultural preoccupations of school language teaching and restricted its criteria of success to skills which could be more or less objectively assessed — namely, how effectively students could understand, speak, read and write a foreign language: the first two skills were seen as having precedence over the second two, in a direct reversal of the traditional weighting of skills. The method relied on behaviourist principles, with language patterns overlearned by repetition: this approach was facilitated by rapid improvements in the technology of magnetic tape recording, and found its characteristic expression in the language laboratory drill.

Culture could not, of course, be entirely dispensed with, but it became in a sense, subordinate to language, and was redefined in terms more anthropological than literary. A well-known American handbook, originally published in 1960, devotes 167 pages to the teaching of various aspects of language, and two to 'the cultural and literary context'. The author's main message is:

> Unless we understand the cultural situation in which an utterance is made, we may miss its full implication or meaning ... A student who reads about a Frenchman going to a *pharmacie* and pictures him going to an American drugstore, is not getting the full meaning of what he is reading.[15]

What impact did this definition of culture have on the learner? Politzer's formulation was in a sense value-free: learning a language meant learning skills, the skills necessary to communicate effectively. The prior educational questions — why should these skills be of sufficient value to justify their place in a curriculum? — were not posed. Five years after Politzer, Edgerton was beginning to draw out some of the value implications.

> When men talk about fostering 'better international understanding' (and other similar notions) what must be meant in practical terms ... is first a preliminary willingness to accept the existence and validity of other ways of selecting and organising expertise — other 'realities' — and secondly the deliberate pursuit of intimate, sympathetic knowledge of such other realities. *A foreign language must be learned not as a more or less satisfactory set of labels for an objective, known, unique reality, but rather as the expression of a collectively subjective reality which can only be discovered by means of its expression* ...[16]

This experience should affect the learner's own value system quite profoundly:

> The student of a foreign lanugage must 'repackage' phenomena as he learns that language, and most importantly, he must acknowledge the arbitrary character of the packages into which he has learned to group selected phenomena in the process of acquiring his own mother tongue. It is precisely this realization that constitutes the intellectual justification of the study of a foreign language for the non-specialist ...[17]

This formulation might be regarded as a pedagogical restatement of the Sapir-Whorf hypothesis, which suggested that our perceptions of reality were strongly affected by the language forms we habitually use.[18]

However, in practice, the new audio-visual courses appearing in schools from the mid-sixties onwards, paid only lip-service (if that) to insights of this sort. The visible change in the perception of culture was a down-grading, even a disappearance of the high culture, with its bias towards literature, and its replacement by a stress on aspects of contemporary life. Fairly soon these 'aspects' gelled into a conventional syllabus of situations and information which will be recognized by generations of pupils brought up on *Longman's Audio-visual French Course*, *Sprich mal deutsch!*, etc. The foreign scene was usually presented through the medium of a fictional family, who would go through the rituals of greeting each other, ordering food in restaurants, celebrating Christmas and birthdays, and indulging in other activities designed partly to incorporate language patterns, but partly also to highlight minor cultural differences. To some British teachers reared in the older tradition, such an interpretation of culture seemed superficial and even trivial. However, the tension between this view of what was to be taught and the traditional 'A' level syllabus was to some extent lessened by the continuing split between pre- and post-16+ language teaching, and was in any case eclipsed by the urgent problems posed by the switch to comprehensive education.

Those problems were being grappled with for at least a decade after the Labour government's 1965 circular (10/65) which requested local authorities to prepare plans for non-selective secondary schools — a period which coincided with the rise and decline of the audio-visual method.

The consequences of 'going comprehensive' were deeply disturbing to the language teaching profession as it existed in the mid-sixties. It is, of course, true that many language teachers welcomed the comprehensive school, and that many of them met the resultant problems optimistically and creatively. Nevertheless, the word 'trauma' would not be too strong to describe the collective experience of 'going comprehensive'.[19] The problems soon became evident. A foreign language (almost invariably French) became part of the core curriculum for all pupils. Language teachers normally had little or no experience of teaching pupils outside the top 20–25 per cent they had encountered in selective schools. Still less had they any experience of teaching widely differing abilities within a single class. Their problems were exacerbated by a failure to train sufficient numbers of new teachers to cope adequately with the large numbers of new learners. The examinations in terms of which they, their colleagues, parents and pupils judged success were still the old grammar school examinations. Pressure for good results in the new schools was considerable, and competition for able pupils was sharpened by the widespread introduction of systems of free choice of options at 14+. In this competition, modern languages options showed up badly. To many, it seemed to be a chronically unsuccessful part of the new comprehensive curriculum. By 1983, the DES could state as a self-evident truth that 'The results of foreign language teaching in the schools in England and Wales do not ... match up to the substantial effort devoted to that important subject'.[20] Modern linguists tended, naturally enough, to react to new pressures by insisting on doing what they knew how to do — for example, by preferring homogeneous ability groups and by excluding the less able from more advanced language classes, sometimes substituting 'European studies' or 'background studies' conducted in English. Language departments in some comprehensive schools tended to become a sort of enclave of grammar school attitudes and practices. This position was reinforced by the virtual demise of Latin so that in an odd way 'modern languages' stepped in to the curriculum slot held half a century before by the ancient languages.[21]

This summary account is, of course, a caricature of what really happened in thousands of schools, and does scant justice to the struggles of committed and enterprising language teachers. Nonetheless, it is necessary to grasp something of this historical shift within the curriculum, and its deep effects on the attitudes of teachers, if the present value-orientations of the subject are to be understood or evaluated. It must be appreciated that in modern languages we are considering an area of great complexity of purpose and practice, and that that complexity is inevitably reflected in confusion and conflict about values.

What this chapters has so far attempted is to place a number of general statements about aims in the context of their time and of the evolution of the social group 'modern linguists'. The approach has necessarily been impressionistic rather than properly historical, but it is only on the basis of some 'feel' for the general background evolving over time that we can now move to discuss the current scene, and tease out some general observations about values in the teaching and learning of modern languages.

This enterprise is rather like studying an iceberg. We shall first survey the bits we see (the sort of explicit statements already sampled) then consider the bits that are invisible (the omissions and silences).

The overt justifications for the presence of modern languages in the school curriculum fall broadly into four clusters, which can be crudely labelled as follows:

Utilitarian

Modern languages are taught in schools because a knowledge of languages will at some future time be useful to the learner, or to the state, or to both. In broad terms, there is some truth in this, but the argument is leaky when applied to schools. Surveys of the vocational applications of languages[22] suggest that a quite high degree of competence is required before jobs (which normally combine languages with other skills) open up. In any case; schools have the perennial problem that they can teach only two or three languages (usually the most obvious European ones) and that it is impossible to predict the languages which will be useful to an individual in ten or twenty years.

The more tenable or diluted version of the utilitarian arguments comes in the form of 'learning a language in order to learn how to learn languages'. Success in one language promotes confidence in learning another and the strategies useful for learning one can to some extent be applied in learning another, at least if the second language is structurally and lexically allied to the first. In the last few years, efforts have been made to teach 'awareness of language' courses, and the first textbooks have begun to appear. The idea is in part to give children the conceptual tools they need to see how languages work. This should allow them to make the generalizations which will ease the learning of many discrete items which is what language learning means in the early stages.[23]

The utilitarian arguments enjoyed a brief revival at the time of Britain's joining the the EEC in 1973. In school terms they seemed rather insubstantial: the connection between French irregular verbs and becoming a long-distance lorry driver are easier for teachers to make than, say, 12-year-olds. However, there is a sense in which the utilitarian approach has been more deeply rooted in pedagogy with the appearance since the middle 1970s of courses structured on 'notional-functional' or 'communicative' principles.[24] Such courses are organized not around the traditional list of grammar points based ultimately on written usage, but on the uses of language: for example, the ability to indicate time relations (past, present, future), to persuade (warn, direct, invite) or to express personal emotions like pleasure. This has tended to provide courses based on situations in which language is deployed to achieve certain objectives useful to people visiting foreign countries: ordering meals in restaurants, making appointments by telephone, reading warning notices etc. While this has in some ways been an interesting and productive way of teaching, it suffers from similar problems to the lorry-driver argument: for example, younger children often cannot realistically imagine ordering meals in restaurants, especially if they neither do this themselves in England nor ever see their parents doing it.

Perceptual

In these arguments it is suggested that the real value of learning a foreign language is that it makes you think differently. This is roughly the pedagogical version of the Sapir-Whorf hypothesis expounded by Edgerton. The attractiveness of these arguments is that unlike the other three 'clusters' they do relate to the teaching and learning of language *per se*, not as a mere preliminary to or vehicle of something else, and they do have something to say about the very early stages of language learning. For an 11-year-old brought up in a restricted monoglot environment, the most elementary language exchange really can open a window by showing through experience that it is possible to cross the divide between 'us' and 'them'. The learner may even discover, in due course, that to 'them' 'we' are 'them'. Thus, even in the early stages, it is argued, modern languages can contribute to the lessening of prejudice and the growth of tolerance and to greater awareness of the complexity of human groups and the variability of custom. Modern languages can be a powerful form of political and social education: consider, for example, the depth and variety of attitude change which may flow from a well-conducted school visit to France, with children staying with French families.

The new 'awareness of language' courses are designed in part to bring prejudices to light, at least in so far as they attach to attitudes to language use, dialect, etc.

One problem with the perceptual arguments is that if pushed to an extreme, they suggest that it might be more educationally sound to learn languages which differ sharply from English in phonology, structure and lexis. Sapir and Whorf regarded all Indo-European languages as conceptually very similar, and lumped them together as SAE (Standard Average European): for really instructive psychological differences, Navaho or Chinese should be tackled. Sometimes one hears French teachers saying things like 'We say "I *am* cold" but the French say "I *have* cold"'. Whether such trivial surface differences have any bearing on 'the repackaging of phenomena' seems dubious. It may be that the perceptual impact of learning a language in the early stages lies less in the actual differences perceived than in the sheer experiential awareness of beginning to function in another medium.[25] A musical parallel might be the excitement of embarking on the flute after learning the piano: the impact on the learner is not so much rationalizing about what the flute can do that the piano can't, and vice-versa, as actually beginning to produce qualitatively different sounds and fit them together into musical patterns. The learner may soon stop learning the flute, but the experience of having started is a permanent enrichment of his or her internalized picture of music.

Sociopolitical

This label is perhaps less appropriate than the others, but has the merit of brevity. These arguments grow out of the perceptual ones, which assert that attitude changes may flow from the mere process of learning a language. But languages are not neutral communication systems. They are the expressions of 'language communities' and, in the European context, of nations. Hence, it is a natural extension of the perceptual arguments to attempt to present some of the contemporary reality of the relevant community: how people live and govern themselves, their family life, what sort of newspapers they read, etc. The list is potentially infinite:

> The reader must remind himself ... of how much is embraced by the term *culture*. It includes all the characteristic activities and interests of a people: Derby Day, Henley Regatta, Cowes, the 12th of August, a cup final, the dog races, the pin tables, the dartboard, Wensleydale cheese, boiled cabbage cut into sections, beetroot in vinegar, nineteenth-century Gothic churches and the music of Elgar.[26]

Potentially infinite lists tend to be skewed: for example Eliot's supposedly heterogeneous list is restricted almost entirely to leisure activities. Pedagogical attempts to select the most relevant information about modern France or Germany or Spain have produced some rather odd assemblages of data, with a tendency to stress consumption of wine and food, folklore and tourism. European studies (or background studies, or French studies, etc.) is an attempt to highlight the 'sociopolitical' aspect, sometimes excluding language teaching altogether and producing what one headteacher described to me as 'non-French'.[27] While this new subject has undoubtedly suffered from being restricted

Values in the Teaching and Learning of Modern Languages

to the less academic and from syllabuses sometimes devised by people with little expertise in either curriculum development or contemporary European institutions, the basic idea is rational enough. This 'sociopolitical' area spans the divide between language teaching and other subjects such as geography and history. It should contribute to values of tolerance, etc., by spreading information about other peoples.

The dangers and the potential of this whole area can be suggested by asking whether any late twentieth-century young person who leaves school without some knowledge and awareness of events in Germany from 1933 to 1945 can be regarded as morally and politically educated.[28]

Cultural

From one point of view, high culture is simply part of culture at large: thus Eliot included Elgar alongside boiled cabbage, and might have included the novels of Dickens. However, because high culture, especially literary culture, has played such an important part in the traditional rationales for modern languages, it seemed preferable to separate it out from other aspects of foreign cultures. That is certainly how British language teachers see it, drawing a sharp distinction between 'literature' on the one hand, and 'background' or *'civilisation'*[29] on the other.

Cultural arguments state that a central reason for including modern languages in the school curriculum is to give learners first-hand access to the summits of the European cultural achievement — or, if that sounds over-ambitious, to introduce them at first hand to literary insights into man, life and society.[30]

The high culture presented is predominantly literary. This is understandable in the light of what schools are traditionally supposed to be, of the obvious centrality of language to 'modern languages', and of the cheapness and accessibility of books as cultural artefacts. It is perhaps less justifiable in a world where film, television, slides, records, tapes, etc. make other cultural media more accessible than twenty or thirty years ago. Even in literature, it is not clear that the sort of literary and human insights derived from limping through a Balzac novel in the original French will necessarily be lessened if the book is read in translation.

These four categories give a crude map of the overt rationales for modern languages in the school curriculum. The map contains several blank spaces — matters which the overt rationales omit or neglect. Those blanks relate for the most part, to the crucial area of *learning*.

121

The utilitarian, sociopolitical and cultural clusters are essentially *adult* constructs. They presuppose that a reasonable level of language competence will already have been attained. As traditionally formulated, their relevance to the average learner in a school is therefore limited. Only the perceptual cluster seems directly applicable to this category of pupil.

There are perhaps three areas or problems, which the traditional formulations of objectives largely overlook.

The Nature of Learning and Teaching a Foreign Language in the Early Stages

Languages are in a sense arbitrary systems. Reasoning in the sense of describing structural patterns or outlining the historical reasons for apparent inconsistencies of spelling, may be increasingly helpful as the learner knows more and becomes more sophisticated. In the early stages, however, the learner has simply to accept most of what the teacher presents. Modern languages are a part of the curriculum which rely quite heavily on teacher authority and more or less mechanical modes of learning. They do not fit easily into curricula dominated by 'progressive' notions such as discovery learning, pupil autonomy, etc. Equally, the 'irrational' or 'prerational' aspects of language learning are ignored by many traditional justifications of their value which depend heavily on the reasoned presentation and absorption of information about foreign cultures.

Developmental Factors

Most statements of the values of language learning overlook the limited experience of young learners and the difficulties they have in understanding abstractions. For example, simplified accounts of the West German constitution may be meaningless to pupils who have no daily experience of the country, and therefore no need to ask even simple question like 'Why is it *federal* post?' This problem is exacerbated with learners (probably in the majority in secondary schools) who have no grasp of the workings of the United Kingdom. This failure to appreciate the developmental nature of political and social education has perhaps been the greatest weakness of European studies. It cannot be solved by modern linguists on their own, but only in the context of a much more thoughtfully conceived curriculum-wide programme of social and political education.

The Average Pace of Learning

The traditional way of justifying modern languages in the curriculum presupposes rapid sucess in the early stages on the basis of which the learner can proceed to 'the interesting stuff'. When language learning is spread right across the ability range, a high proportion of learners never gets to that point. From the point of view of some teachers, their daily work is a constant painful reminder of John Webster's criticism of language teaching without content, expressed in 1654:

> ... Now for a carpenter to spend seven years' time about the sharpening and preparing of his interests and then have no further skill how to employ them were ridiculous, so for the scholar to spend divers years for some small scantling and smattering in the tongues, having for the most part got no further knowledge, but like parrots to babble and prattle, whereby the intellect is in no way enriched, is but toilsome and almost lost labour.[31]

In terms of the practice in schools, the problem with the four 'clusters' of justification we have identified is not just that they ignore important areas of learning, but also that they are translated into pedagogical reality in a patchy and incoherent way. To list those clusters baldly is to realize that there is some relationship between them which can be expressed in a pedagogically ordered way. The 'perceptual' insights acquired even in the early stages of learning a language can to some extent be formulated in language awareness terms and thus contribute to some 'utilitarian' objectives (learning how to learn languages); they lead naturally on to a consideration of the society or societies in which the language is spoken, and thus eventually to 'high culture' as one important expression of a language community's ethos and ideals. The four areas ought to overlap and reinforce each other, yet teachers quite often see them as being in conflict or competition: 'literature' versus 'background', 'language' versus 'literature', 'language awareness' versus 'language learning', 'use' versus 'ornament'. Yet it should not be impossible to work out from the aims an ordered array of objectives suitable for the comprehensive schools of the 1990s.

In the final section of this essay, recent attempts to start on this task will be briefly described. Before then, however, it may be useful to mention two other broad areas in which the subject intersects with values.

Nicholas Beattie

Values Inherent in Particular Languages

The Leathes Report was written in the later years of the First World War, at a time when German in the curriculum was suffering because of national prejudice against anything connected with Germany. Presumably the more recent failure to implant Russian in the secondary curriculum in spite of a powerful central initiative and the allocation of quite generous resources reflects in part a certain prejudice against the USSR[32]. Many of the statements about the deep values supposedly enshrined in particular languages (for example, the clarity of mind to be derived from learning French) seem remarkably silly.[33] Nonetheless, nations, and therefore their languages, certainly have images. Again in the area of tolerance, one of the tasks of language teaching is to expose those images to the light of day and show how often they are based on false or partial information, and how they vary from one historical era to another.

Values Incidental to Language Teaching and Learning

All parts of the curriculum reflect the value preoccupations of the society in which they are placed, and modern languages is no exception. In some ways, it is more susceptible than some subjects to becoming the unwitting vehicle of unquestioned assumptions, because of its skill orientation. If the content of reading passages etc. is chosen primarily to exemplify linguistic points, then the content may receive little attention. There is ample evidence that language courses (many of them based on the formula of an anodyne middle-class family engaged in various stereotyped activities) are a repository of attitudes to sex, class and race which are now widely questioned.[34] No doubt it will take many years before all language teachers become sensitive to such matters, and textbooks incorporating out-dated attitudes linger on in schools for many years after they first appear. Nonetheless, it should not in principle be difficult to rethink courses to take greater account of contemporary beliefs, by showing women at work outside the kitchen, by covering a wider range of social situations, by including material about immigrant labour in Europe, and about French- and Spanish-speaking areas in the Third World, etc. This trend has been helped by greater emphasis on early exposure of learners to authentic texts (newspaper articles, advertisements, television programmes, etc.) which should fuel more considered discussions of topical questions with value implications. The decline in the central importance of the course-book may make it easier to adjust to future changes in the value positions held in society.

An allied criticism of modern languages in the school curriculum is that it is 'Eurocentric'. In practice, this is certainly so, as the languages actually taught in British schools rarely go beyond French, German and Spanish. The pressure to include Gujerati, Urdu, Arabic, etc. has come in the first instance from areas with large minorities of recent immigration from these non-European language communities. Its aims are mainly the strengthening of cultural identity in the second generation.[35] Clearly, though, arguments about tolerance and freedom from prejudice which are deployed to justify European languages apply with even greater force to non-European ones, so there is certainly a case for teaching such languages to native speakers of English. The practical problems (shortage of teachers, textbooks, etc.) are formidable. It should be pointed out, however, that 'competition' between European and non-European languages, and the emotions raised in that conflict, would be lessened if a curriculum-wide policy incorporating both could be spelt out. In such a policy, the European languages actually taught in most schools would form part of a concerted and acknowledged drive to break down parochialism and prejudice. To learn a European language is surely not *per se* Eurocentric: it becomes so only if no attempt is made to view Europe in a world context. There is a pedagogical logic in proceeding from the home community to nearby communities with similar cultural backgrounds in continental Europe, and to use that springboard to consider the wider linkages between Europe and the rest of the world. This is a task which can be done in a particularly vivid way through French and Spanish, because those metropolitan languages have become *lingue franche* for large areas of the Third World. But this is a task which can sensibly be undertaken only within a curriculum-wide policy, with the language teacher reinforcing from a different angle and through different modes of experience, the work of his or her colleagues in geography, history, English, etc.

Let me now turn to review critically some recent attempts to state or restate the aims of language teaching, highlighting as far as possible the value aspects, whether implicit or explicit. For coherence and brevity, these will grouped under three heads:

Collective Statements

The crisis in modern languages has naturally produced a variety of reports, discussion papers, etc. These typically begin with a statement of aims. The most recent is a DES consultative paper on 'Foreign languages in the school curriculum',[36] which because it is recent and authoritative, can to some extent be taken as representative of other similar formulations. The section on 'the goals of foreign language teaching' cites five aims devised by a Council of Europe conference in 1966: four of them are statements of languages skills (understanding, speaking, reading, writing); the fifth is 'to give them a knowledge of the foreign country and an insight into its civilization and culture'.[37] In other words, aims are really left unformulated and the discussion focusses almost entirely on ways and means of teaching language skills more effectively. Even the fifth 'goal', formulated in terms of the provision of information, is hardly mentioned in the text — what sort of information? about what? how presented? — and, most importantly of all, to what end?

Eric Garner, in a useful paper on 'Aims and objectives' in a recent collection,[38] goes rather further. He quotes two aims originally formulated by the Scottish Central Committee in 1977.

> Aim 1: To develop in children an understanding of an interest in, and a respect for the way of life in a society other than their own, thus adding to their understanding of themselves and their own society.
>
> Aim 2: To sensitize pupils to the nature and the functions of language.[39]

To these he adds a third aim, which he characterizes as 'subject — specific' and subordinate to the other two:

> Aim 3: To promote an active command over selected aspects of the foreign language as a basis for communication by developing proficiency in the four major skill areas according to pupils' capacities.[40]

In fact, most of Garner's subsequent discussion about translating aims into achievable objectives relates to this third aim:

> ... the accent would fall on immediate, short-term success ... During the continuation phase, the main emphasis would fall on the further development of performance skills ... although the wider linguistic and cultural aims would not be sacrificed.[41]

This preoccupations with measurable language skills, and the accompanying consignment of attitude-changing activities to subordinate 'although' clauses, is entirely proper and right in terms of the practical priorities of the 1980s — i.e. the situation created by previous events and attitudes as sketched in in the first part of this chapter. As Garner points out, modern languages will become 'a truly liberating experience for pupils across the whole ability range' only 'if we review our ultimate objectives and genuinely fit courses to children, abandoning the procrustean tendencies of the past'.[42] It is difficult to question thoughtful documents like Garner's paper, or some HMI reports, without sounding as though one thinks that the authors are idiots. Nonetheless, the questions so often sidestepped or ignored remain. Has the moment in the evolution of the subject not come to 'review' the 'ultimate objective' of tolerance and the overcoming of prejudice? How can that aim be built into the teaching by the side of, and through the means of, the four skills?

A recent article by Rebecca Ullmann suggests 'a multidimensional curriculum framework which expands the view of curriculum content for second languages beyond the linguistic focus'.[43] Her approach adds to the usual categories of skills and information ('proficiency' and 'knowledge' in her terminology) the more elusive areas of 'affect' ('positive attitudes towards the L2 and towards learning the second language') and 'transfer' ('general knowledge about language and language learning, the ability to apply L2 learning strategies in new settings, and the ability to apply knowledge, attitudes and skills learned in the L2 setting to other subject areas of the curriculum'.[44]) This interesting attempt to integrate the aims which are usually banished to 'although' clauses, as in the above quotation from Garner, should be looked at in depth by anyone seeking to rethink the value aspects of foreign language teaching and to place the subject in the context of the whole curriculum.[45]

Attempts at Curriculum Change

Practical answers to those questions have begun to emerge, albeit partially and tentatively and sometimes unsuccessfully, in European and background studies, and in discussions of the 'A' level syllabus.

European studies has already been briefly discussed. Many language teachers consider it a passing fad, and in its mid-seventies form that may be so. Yet the movement poses real questions for mainstream modern languages — questions with value implications: what are we trying to do? what attitudes are we trying to affect? what is the most effective way of setting about that exercise? If European Studies has been a failure, the reasons for its failure (which are various) deserve sober study and discussion.

The potential of 'A' level as the vehicle of a wider engagement with culture than the traditional four or five set books was explored in depth as long ago as 1970.[46] However, it is only quite recently that substantial moves towards reform have been made.[47] They have provoked some opposition from teachers. However, a reformulation in practical teaching terms of the 'sociopolitical' and 'cultural' content of post- 16+ work seems likely and as it is implemented, it will certainly produce backwash effects on the 11–16 curriculum. It may even begin to erode the split between pre- and post- 16+ work which has for so long distorted discussions of values in language teaching.

Individual Reformulations

I will cite just two authors, to give a taste of the debate which may now be opening up.

Eric Hawkins' 1981 exploration of *Modern Languages in the Curriculum* is, in many ways, the culmination of a lifetime's reflection and practice. He is one of the few thinkers in this area who seems able to resolve the tension between general educational aims and the internal preoccupations of the subject, and should certainly be turned to by any reader of this chapter who wants to pursue the issues more deeply. He advances the view that:

> Schools at their best are refuges within which freedom from outside pressures is guaranteed and within which the values, skills and *apprenticeship* in citizenship which are required in a democracy can be learnt. (p. 30)

Within that context, he then explores how language learning can contribute to 'lighting fires about the polyglot world which will blaze throughout adult life' (p. 57) and to 'linguistic awareness'. He places these broad aims against a historical background, and discusses in detail ways of implementing them through the organization and teaching of foreign languages. In another fifty years some of his solutions may seem outdated or impracticable, but at least he engages openly with the question: What's it all *for*? He also attempts to fill the gap identified earlier in this paper relative to the learning of a language in its early stages.

In a provocative paper published in 1981[48], Werner Hüllen also attempts to fill that gap. He attacks head-on the problem evaded by

Values in the Teaching and Learning of Modern Languages

almost all thinkers in this area: the artificial, teacher-dominated character of so much language learning. Recent theorists who have addressed the issue[49] have to some extent evaded it by advocating a degree of 'individualized learning' which is unlikely to be implemented in the average British secondary school, and which seems generally more appropriate to adult learners than to school children in groups. Hüllen, on the other hand, points out that the sort of playful activity required in the early stages of language learning may have its own values. Although teachers go to great lengths to engineer realistic communication they never succeed because 'the exchange of information and ideas in the foreign language remains a *simulation* of reality'.[50] Yet maybe the ability to collaborate in such simulations is very useful.

> All the members of one communicative society live in a language community whose frames of reference can themselves be negotiated. A constituent of the process is the ability to shift perspective which allows the individual to develop, stabilize or alter his own behaviour, with constant reference to that of others. From this it will be obvious that the introductory association with literature and historical information, as is normally to be found in even the most rudimentary educational system, serves a valuable purpose and, indeed, is not only justified by efforts to teach knowledge, as such, or by tradition. Attempting to place oneself in a world existing only figuratively and fictitiously is of great value in developing the ability for social interaction.[51]

This line of thought, though only sketchily developed by Hüllen, has great potential in evolving a more coherent and unified statement of the values underlying the confused surface manifestations of language teaching and learning.

What, in summary, does this rather messy and incomplete survey of the value implications of one subject tell us about values in general, as they impinge upon the school curriculum? It reminds us that, as social constructs, values tend to be enunciated in more or less partial or distorted ways in response to the pressures exerted on the social groups which formulated them and act by them. It reminds us that in a curriculum, individual subjects reflect or exemplify three distinct categories of value: those specific to the subject, those relating to the subject's place within the general curriculum or the school system, and those incidental to the subject, which simply use it as a temporary resting place or exponent. Finally, it reminds us that in the last resort no subject can put its own house in order, but that a coherent view of how any subject should affect the developing value systems of children can be evolved only by open discussion across the whole curriculum.

Notes

1. Musgrove, F.W. (1968), 'The contribution of sociology to the study of the curriculum', in Kerr, J.F. (Ed.) *Changing the Curriculum*, London, University of London Press, pp. 96–109; here, p. 102.
2. For a detailed account of this phase, see Gilbert, M., (1953–55). 'The origins of the reform movement in modern language teaching in England', *Durham Research Review*, 1, 4, pp. 1–9; 1, 5, pp. 9–18, 1, 6, pp. 1–10.
3. Committee to enquire into the position of modern languages in the educational system of Great Britain (Chairman: M. Stanley Leathes) (1918), *Report*, London, HMSO, para, 11.
4. See for example, Kirkman, F.B. (1908), 'The place of translation in the teaching of modern languages', *Modern Language Teaching*, 4, 2, pp. 44–58: this includes a verbatim report of the debate on Kirkman's paper.
5. Committee to enquire ... , *op. cit.*
6. *Ibid.*, para. 30.
7. *Ibid.*, para. 54.
8. *Ibid.*, para. 42.
9. *Ibid.*, para. 42.
10. Claims are sometimes made in relation to particular languages (for example, Italian) that to know the language will assist an appreciation of architecture, painting, etc. Individual teachers may give emphasis to these non-literary aspects of high culture, but the 'A' level examinations have remained predominantly literary.
11. Eliot, T.S. (1948), *Notes Towards the Definition of Culture*, London, Faber, p. 32.
12. Incorporated Association of Assistant Masters in Secondary Schools, (1967), *The Teaching of Modern Languages*, London, University of London Press. p. 4. This is the fourth edition of a standard work first issued in 1949 and 'completely rewritten' between 1962 and 1967.
13. 'It is the atmosphere of the sixth form which transforms the tempestuous and resistant schoolboy into the purposeful student', IAAM (1967), *op. cit.*, p. 6.
14. The early pages of Incorporated Association of Headmasters (1963), *Modern Languages in the Grammar School*, London, IAHM, provide a revealing description of the state of affairs as seen by a group of 'progressives' at the beginning of the sixties.
15. Politzer, R.L. (1965), *Teaching French, An Introduction to Applied Linguistics*, Waltham, Mass., Blaisdell, 2nd edn, p. 169.
16. Edgerton, M. (1965), 'The study of languages; a point of view', *Liberal Education*, 51, 4, pp. 517–25; here p. 521 (his italics).

17 *Ibid.*, p. 522.
18 WHORF, B.L. (1956), *Language, Thought and Reality*, Boston, Mass., Technology Press of Massachusetts Institute of Technology.
19 For a well-documented general account, see HAWKINS, E. (1981), *Modern Languages in the Curriculum*, Cambridge, Cambridge University Press, Chapter 1, pp. 3–26.
20 Department of Education and Science and Welsh Office (1983), *Foreign Languages in the School Curriculum, A Consultative Paper*, London DES/Welsh Office, para. 2.
21 Another very complicated problem which is presumably related in some way to the value connotations of modern languages is the increasing female predominance in the subject: why are girls attracted to it, and in some ways more successful at it? The answer may lie in some conjunction between modern languages' placing in the whole curriculum, and changes in school organization (decline of single-sex schools), but it has also been argued that there are innate differences between the sexes in language learning ability. (POWELL, R.C. (1979), 'Sex differences and languages learning', *Audio-Visual Language Journal*, 17, 1, pp. 19–24.)
22 For example, EMMANS, K.A. *et. al.* (1974), *Foreign Languages in Industry and Commerce*, York, Language Teaching Centre, University of York.
23 HAWKINS (1981), *op. cit.* provides a useful description and discussion on pp. 228–39.
24 See WILKINS, D.A. (1976), *Notional Syllabuses*, Oxford, Oxford University Press; BRUMFIT, C.J. and JOHNSON, K. (Eds.) (1979), *The Communicative Approach to Language Teaching*, Oxford, Oxford University Press; LITTLEWOOD, W. (1981), *Communicative Language Teaching, An Introduction*, Cambridge, Cambridge University Press.
25 The stress on experience is important, and is one answer to White's argument that languages should not form part of a core curriculum because one can understand what it means to speak a foreign language without actually doing it oneself. This seems dubious for adults, and doubly dubious for children. (WHITE, J.P. (1973), *Towards a Compulsory Curriculum*, London, Routledge and Kegan Paul.)
26 ELIOT, T.S. (1948) *op. cit.*, p. 31.
27 The most considered exposition is WILLIAMS, M. (1977), *Teaching European Studies*, London, Heinemann. Williams, incidentally, is a geographer, and sees language as having no special part to play.
28 It is an interesting comment on the separateness of language teachers that the School Council's *Working Paper on the Whole Curriculum* not only ignores language teachers, but also in discussing an interdisciplinary project on the rise of Nazi Germany assumes it will be dealt with by the history, geography and RE departments. (Schools Council (1975), *The Whole Curriculum 13–16*, Schools Council Working Paper 53, London, Evans/Methuen Educational, p. 45.)
29 Modern linguists pronounce *civilisation* in French and mean by it any

aspect of background which is not literary. The German phrase *Landeskunde* is similar.

30 I cannot resist quoting the Secretary-General of the *Alliance Française*, writing a preface to a language course published in 1964: 'We at the *Alliance Française* believe we know why the citizens of the French Community and foreign elites study French. It is not in order to conduct rudimentary communication between themselves. Nor is it for the convenience of their touristic pleasures. It is in the first place, to come into contact with one of the richest civilisations of the modern world, to cultivate and embellish their minds by studying a splendid literature, and to become in truth, *des personnes distinguées* ...' (in MAUGER, G. (1964), *Cours de langue et de civilisation françaises*, Vol. I. Paris, Hachette, p. vi.)

31 Quoted in WATSON, F. (1909), *The Beginnings of the Teaching of Modern Subjects in England*, London, Pitman, p. 423.

32 The Annan Report of 1962 (Ministry of Education and Scottish Education Department, (1962), *The Teaching of Russian*, London, HMSO), outlined practical measures to implant Russian in the education system. Many of the language teachers retrained to teach Russian in special post-Annan crash courses are now in schools teaching French and other subjects.

33 See, for example, Chesterton's vigorously nonsensical essay on 'Our Latin relations' (in CHESTERTON, G.K. (1949), *Selected Essays*, London, Methuen, or CAMPOS, C. (1965), *The View of France: From Arnold to Bloomsbury*, London, Oxford University Press.

34 See, for example, FREUDENSTEIN, R. (1978), *The Role of Women in Foreign Language Textbooks: a collection of essays*, Paris, AIMAV/Didier; WILLEKE, A.B. and SANDERS, R.H. (1978), 'Walter ist intelligent und Brigitte ist blond: dealing with sex bias in language texts', *Unterrichtspraxis*, 11, 2, pp. 60–5; FOLSOM, M.H. (1979), 'Equality of the sexes in German grammar', *Unterrichtspraxis*, 12, 2, p. 78; GAFF, R. (1982), 'Sex-stereotyping in modern language teaching: an aspect of the hidden curriculum', *British Journal of Language Teaching*, 20, 2, pp. 71–8; CLAUSEN, J. (1982), 'Texbooks and (in-)equality: a survey of literary readers for elementary and intermediate German', *Unterrichtspraxis*, 15, 2, pp. 244–53.

35 For a useful recent summary see MILLER, J. (1983), *Many Voices: Bilingualism, Culture and Education*, London, Routledge and Kegan Paul. Most of the attempts to reconsider the curricular implications of bilingualism (as opposed to treating it as a separate problem) come from Inner London: for example, North Westminster School.

36 Department of Education and Science and Welsh Office (1983), *op. cit.*

37 *Ibid.*, para. 21.

38 GARNER, E., (1981) 'Aims and objectives', in SMITH, D.G. (Ed.) *Teaching Languages in Today's Schools*, London, Centre for Information on Language Teaching and Research, pp. 20–31.

39 *Ibid.*, p. 24.

40 *Ibid.*, p. 25.

41 *Ibid.*, p. 25.
42 *Ibid.*, p. 30.
43 ULLMAN, R. (1982), 'A broadened curriculum framework for second languages', *ELT Journal*, 36, 4, pp. 255–62; here, p. 255.
44 *Ibid.*, p. 256.
45 In these matters we are still at a primitive stage. For similar groupings in another subject, see PORTAL, C. (1983), 'Empathy as an aim for curriculum', *Journal of Curriculum Studies*, 15, 3, pp. 303–10.
46 Schools Council (1970), *New Patterns of Sixth-form Modern Languages Studies* (Working paper 28), London, Evans/Methuen Educational.
47 Several examination boards have recently made, or are about to make, changes. For a general introduction see French 16–19 Study Group (1981), *French 16–19: A New Perspective*, London, Hodder and Stoughton.
48 HÜLLEN, W., (1981), 'Pedagogical considerations in teaching foreign languages at school', in JUNG, UDO, O.H. (Ed.), *Reading: A Symposium*, Oxford, Pergamon, pp. 199–205.
49 STRASHEIM, L.A. (1970), 'A rationale for the individualization and personalization of foreign-language instruction', in LANGE, D.L. (Ed.), *Britannica Review of Foreign Language Education*, Vol. 2, Chicago, Encyclopedia Britannica Inc., pp. 15–34; ALTMAN, H.B. (Ed.), (1972), *Individualizing the Foreign Language Classroom*, Rowley, Mass., Newbury House; ALTMAN, H.B. and VAUGHAN JAMES, C. (Eds.) (1980), *Foreign Language Teaching: Meeting Individual Needs*, Oxford, Pergamon.
50 HÜLLEN, W., *op. cit.*, p. 202.
51 *Ibid.*, pp. 203–4.

Values in Physical Education

Jim Parry

Introduction

It should be said at the outset that the subject-matter itself will probably not be the most important determinant of values presented to children in schools, although it is obviously the main vehicle. Of much greater significance will be the views held or practices adopted by staff in relation to a very wide range of educational questions which are logically prior to a consideration of which subjects (or at least which parts or which conceptions of those subjects) are to be represented on the school curriculum.

There is as great a diversity in view and in practice within physical education on these matters as there is in education generally. Differing educational ideologies tend not only to suggest differing methods of teaching physical education, but often suggest a different content, too. For example, whilst 'traditionally' the subject had been seen mainly in terms of teaching children how to engage in various sporting and athletic activities (such as track and field, gymnastics and certain team games), 'progressivism' permitted and encouraged the growth of the 'Movement' movement, and a new content was introduced under the headings of movement, modern educational dance, modern educational gymnastics, and so on. Recently, a behaviourist emphasis on rational curriculum planning and taxonomical objectives has paralleled an emphasis in physical education on skills learning and psycho-motor development, and even more recently the economically determined 'Education for Leisure' bandwagon has carried with it those in physical education who argue for greater relevance, more choice of activities and community involvement. Now, this is obviously a very crude and incomplete characterization, meant only to illustrate a point, but even so, it must not be assumed that such differing views are necessarily incompatible. Each approach might rather best be seen as most appropriate to a particular subject-matter or age-range, so that a teacher might embrace a range of perspectives during his/her teaching day. Be that as it may, it must continually be held in mind that it is theoretical movements which generate subject-matter and approaches to the teaching of it, as the history of 'physical education' in British schools amply demonstrates: from the days of marching and drill, through PT and games, to PE and human movement studies (see Clegg, 1976).

So, whilst this is not the place to examine in detail those wider considerations which will inevitably influence conceptions of and developments within physical education, the reader will doubtless perceive their shadows constantly in the background.

On Physical Education

Secondly, then, I should say something about what 'physical education' (PE henceforth) means and has meant. It might be thought that, since this book is about values, I ought not to take too much time over conceptual preliminaries. However, this would be to misinterpret the way in which values enter into the picture. It is not as though we could get the definitions smartly out of the way so as to proceed to the 'real' task of hunting out the values. For, as we have seen, our values enter into our definitions, our definitions prescribe content and method, and our practies and procedures encapsulate our aims. In PE (as in much else) everything depends on the the overall evaluative position(s) taken (explicitly or not) by individual teachers and the school as a whole.

I shall try to illustrate this in two ways.

Of, Through and About

It is a commonplace to distinguish three views of PE:

(a) Education *of* the physical (the development of health, strength, endurance, skill, etc. through physical training, exercise and practice).

(b) Education *through* the physical (the development of desirable characteristics of personality and mind through physical activity).

(c) Education *about* the physical (the development of rationality and understanding in the forms of knowledge which constitute the field of human movement studies).

Jim Parry

Besides quite neatly encapsulating three very different sets of claims regarding what PE is and how it is to be justified on a school curriculum, it must be noted that the three slogans obscure under the same sign three very different conceptions of education:

(a) refers to physical *training*;
(b) attempts to ally the aims of physical education with the aims of 'general education', for which I think we may read '*schooling*';
(c) refers to some such cognitive model as that advanced by Hirst and Peters (1970, Chapter 2), which we may, perhaps tendentiously, call *education*.

This account yields two related observations. Firstly, it cannot be said too often that the very term 'physical education' constitutes a claim: namely, that the specified physical activity *is* educative (Renshaw, 1972, p. 62; Morgan, 1979, pp. 11–12). Secondly, to show that physical activity *develops* people in various ways is not the same as to show that it *educates* people. As Barrow (1982) remarks, beginning a section ominously titled '*Primary and Physical Instruction*':

> Two of the largest groups in the teaching fraternity, primary or junior school teachers and physical education instructors, are in the interesting position of being only marginally related to education. (p. 60).

This fact, he thinks, should not worry either group, since they are, nevertheless, engaged in important work. The health and fitness of children are important enough as aims of *schooling*, without the need for spurious argumentation to support the undignified scramble towards 'cognitive' (and, hence, 'educational') status. However, Barrow's concession (that there are other legitimate personal and social goods than educational ones which justifiably form part of a child's schooling, cf. Wilson, 1972, pp. 2–4) is unlikely to cut much ice with those who would see it as a confirmation of second-class citizenship in the teaching profession. This is a curiously British phenomenon: firstly, in the way in which physical activity is undervalued in the system as a whole; and secondly, in the strategy adopted by physical educators to improve their status. In, for example, America, Russia or the Germanys, physical activity is not so undervalued, and (therefore?) physical educators gain status from the demonstration of high standards intrinsic to their activities, rather than trying to show that they contribute to an intellectual/academic conception of education.

Even at this very general level, then, our conceptions of PE and its rationale present quite clearly to students our views as to what sorts of activity are legitimate and what value it might have in in their schooling.

The Aesthetic, Movement, Leisure, Skill, Understanding and Human Movement Studies

Another way of proceeding would be to identify a range of physical education 'ideologies' which might be seen as underpinning a certain content or approach (following Yates, 1977). For illustrative purposes I have chosen six which take varying stances towards the traditional and dominant emphasis on participation in competitive team games.

The Aesthetic Dimension

As Carlisle asserted (1969, p. 18): 'Physical education is concerned with activities which are best conceived of as aesthetic activities'. This approach has three seeming virtues: firstly, it assembles disparate activities under a unifying concept; secondly, it advocates a 'form of knowledge' or 'mode of awareness' as particularly appropriate to a consideration of PE activities, thus directing us to a route towards curricular justification; thirdly, it provides an antidote to the emphasis on violence, aggression and competition.

Brief comments are: firstly, since *anything* may be viewed aesthetically (from a Rembrandt to a bat's toenail) the supposed noteworthy unity here is illusory; secondly, this limits the range of application of the supposed justificatory criterion, for surely it is *artistic* activity which is the paradigm here, and not *all* PE activity; thirdly, we should note that violence and aggression are not antithetical to an aesthetic interest, and that competitions whose standards of judgment are aesthetic are not unknown.

The 'Movement' Movement

Sometimes closely related to the above, this approach suggests that, underlying all of the 'movement forms' which constitute PE there is a general movement capacity which is significantly educable. There is sometimes also the claim that the experience of moving constitutes a special source of knowledge. Against these suggestions it has been held that movement capacities are activity-related rather than generalizable, and that any general capacity is either trivial in application or not significantly educable; and that the *context* of a movement is the source of its significance, rather than the brute *experience* of it.

Leisure and Recreation

The emphasis here is on preparation for a leisured post-school life, together with a prescription as to what people should be doing during it: more physical activity. Critics of the movement see in it a sort of paternalism or social control, together with a relationship with 'Leis Rec Biz' which is far too cosy. Advocates discern a concern for the expansion of the horizons and opportunities of those who, only a few years ago, would never have dreamed that such leisure possibilities would be open to them. They would stress the increased range of choice whilst critics would question the value of 'suck it and see' option courses.

The Science of Skill

Yates (1977, p. 11) traces the source of this ideology in Britain to the 'skill/Whiting/Leeds' syndrome, which emphasized the scientific analysis of sport skills so as to improve individual performance, especially in athletic events and ball skills, which are the most amenable to the information-processing research paradigm in psychology. This approach is potentially very powerful in directing teachers to better methods of skill teaching, and especially in the coaching of elite performers, which is its major application at the moment. The British systems of education and coaching have barely begun to exploit the possible benefits for all of scientific research (especially in psychology and biomechanics) and should take the lead of the Eastern bloc here. The main value presented to a student by a teacher operating on this approach is an interest in and care for an improvement in his skill level or personal performance. There is also, in the willingness to go to the expense and trouble of applying science to sport, the suggestion that sporting excellences are worth developing — a certain seriousness of purpose is conveyed. On the other hand, this does direct our attention to the elite performer and the competition element and away from day-to-day concerns of the PE teacher.

The 'Understanding' Approach

Recently developed at Loughborough (see Bunker and Thorpe, 1982) this approach sees itself as a response to the highly structured teaching of techniques and skills to large groups, and to the all too frequent passive supervision of activity periods. It begins with a game (or *some* form of it) and its rules, so structured as to allow maximum participation and successful maintenance of activity. From the start, then, students are engaged in tactical and strategic thinking regardless of their skill level, so that they come to see the need for particular techniques in order to achieve their desired ends.

As with many new-fangled ideas, this one seems to me to seize upon and develop a good old one. Good teachers have always perceived the motivational point of 'getting a game going' without bothering too much about the niceties of adult rule structures, and then introducing the teaching of techniques by way of improving game performance. It is one way of indicating to students that it is their learning about the game that is important, rather than my presenting my carefully graded and sequenced lesson plans. But a *most* important emphasis in the approach as recently presented is its overt championing of sports appreciation. Some of us will doubtless go on to play some sport and games after school, but many more of us will *consume* many more sports and games, and this fact requires acknowledgement.

Human Movement Studies
Since the inception of the BEd degree and the inclusion of human movement studies (HMS) as a way of increasing the academic content of teacher training courses in PE, there has been a trickle-down effect on schools. The argument has been of a 'liberal' kind: education is to do with cognitive goods, i.e. initiation into forms of knowledge. HMS is a field of knowledge with a focus on the physical, and since this is justifiable in a way that physical activities are not, HMS can increase the status of the subject in schools. There are two problems with this line of argumentation: firstly, although forms of knowledge are self-justifying (as constituent features of rationality) fields are not (see Morgan, 1975, on coffee studies); secondly, even if the field were justifiable on other grounds there would still be the question of whether it should be included on the school curriculum, since the curriculum is a *selection* from justifiable items, many of which may not find a place on practical grounds, or because there are other activities which are more central or important representatives of a discipline. Given that science is a form of knowledge and should be represented on the curriculum, for example, is there any good reason why science should be exemplified as sport science? (This is a problem, too, for dance. Given that children should be introduced to art, and that we could not possibly introduce them adequately to all its forms, why should balletic dance be selected over painting, sculpture, drama, photography, etc.?).

I do not myself think that there is a good argument for HMS in schools. The basic motivation seems to be a misplaced ambition for academic respectability and peer-group regard amongst some PE teachers, who wish to conform to a reputable view of what education is about. In my view they should have trained as biologists, physicists, sociologists or historians, all of which are already represented in their first-hand forms in schools. Apart from legitimizing the introduction of the apparatus of 'O' and 'A' level examinations into PE, thus reinforcing the dominant values of schooling, the main objection to HMS in schools is that its focus and interest is the professional preparation of teachers, coaches, sports medics, etc. If so, then this is also an argument for its postponement until that level.

As I have suggested already, I am leaving the reader to pursue such connections as there may be with the above ideologies and more general educational ideologies. What I hope to have done is to give some idea of the vast range of co-existing and competing positions which it is possible for a PE teacher to take with regard to some part of his/her job. I have also included some observations and criticisms which, doubtless, reflect my own positions on these matters.

Now we should go on to look at the content of PE — the specific activities engaged in — but first I should say a very brief word regarding the key concepts of this volume's title.

On 'Values' and 'Curriculum'

If one takes a 'liberal' view of the concept of education, it carries with it a certain view of what values may properly be seen as 'educational' ones. Moral education, for example, may be seen as the development of autonomy and rationality, and whatever does not conduce to that end may safely be passed over. For our present purposes, though, such a definition would rule out consideration of many aims and practices which should not go unexamined. By 'values', then, I shall mean whatever is presented to students by teachers and schools which affects or intends to affect their ways of behaving, thinking and decision-making in regard to their conduct and attitudes towards themselves, other people, and the communities they inhabit. (Whether such values are properly to be considered moral, social, political, prudential, ideological or cultural would be the subject of another essay). In addition, I shall be referring to other values which might best be called the values *of* physical education activities, which are a subset of the values *in* physical education.

I shall take a similarly cavalier attitude towards 'curriculum'. Clearly, to encompass the activities of a subject such as PE, which includes work at lunchtime, after school, weekends, residential stays and vacation trips as well as timetable time, a less than generous conception of curriculum would be unduly restrictive. Paradoxically, then, my idea of curriculum will include the extra-curricular.

Some General Features of PE in Schools

Before getting down to a discussion of sets of particular activities, I should make mention of fairly obvious general features which, nevertheless, exert a great influence on the values presented to children by the subject-matter and by teachers. Those features relate to gender, popular culture, examinations, 'difference' and compulsion.

PE is profoundly atypical in the differential presentation of the subject to boys and girls. As in many other subjects, this often boils down to the expertise or predilection of individual teachers, heads of department or headteachers, but there is more to it than that. The majority of PE teachers working in British schools have themselves been trained in single-sex institutions or departments, and in turn teach only boys or girls. Although there have been recent changes in this pattern, with the demise of the old colleges, such a startling segregation cannot be expected to have been without some influence.

Some PE activities (I am thinking mainly of 'sport' here) are directly related to popular culture in a way that many other school subjects are not. It therefore bears a certain relevance to the non-school life of a large number of students and, correspondingly, is the main site within school for the importation of 'external' values and attitudes. We cannot ignore the social nature of sport and the impact that that has on school PE, and especially we should take note of those critiques of modern sport which emphasize its role in the maintenance of racism, sexism, nationalism and conservatism.

In most schools PE is not an examinable subject, although 'O' and 'A' level examinations are now offered by certain boards, and the Schools Council has produced a special Bulletin on the matter (1977). There are those who believe that this trend will result in a second-rate academicism in PE at the expense of its chief value: the presentation to students of excellences *other* than academic ones. Hargreaves (1982), for example, says,

> PE teachers should revel and rejoice in their non-academicism; they should see this as a way of raising their standing and reject the strategy of striving for a pale imitation of academic subjects. (p. 6).

There is another important way in which PE is 'different'. Students change their clothing, are active, make noise, are perhaps subject to a change of disciplinary regime, and so on. In Willis's analysis of the school behaviour of 'the lads' (1977, pp. 29 ff.), 'having a laff' is posited as a central motivator. In another study, Madness (1981) report:

> Oh what fun we had
> And did it really turn out bad?
> Finding different ways
> To make a difference to the days.

PE periods may provide a space in which the 'laff' is tolerated, and which provides a legitimate source of 'difference'.

Finally, there is the matter of compulsion. Although there is a sense in which all schooling is compulsory, there is a compulsion to *participate* in PE activities. Given low post-school participation rates and the suspicion that a large proportion of students would choose not to participate if there were an option, the simple fact of compulsion (especially if unsupported by an argument such as White's — see 1973, pp. 27–8) undercuts many of the values claimed for the activities and brings into question the validity of stated aims.

On PE Activities

As well as looking at overall evaluative positions, ideologies and some general features, we need to look at the various kinds of specific content. Rather than offering an argument at this point, I shall simply assume that the following list of six areas of activity is representative of nearly all that goes on in schools under the general heading of PE: sport (competitive games and athletics), swimming and life-saving, dance, gymnastics, outdoor pursuits and fitness training. Let us consider them in that order.

Sport

To begin with there is the problem of *which* sports are to be offered. Some are not represented in schools on moral grounds: boxing because it is one of the few sports whose explicit aim is the infliction of injury on another; blood sports because they involve gratuitous and ritual cruelty to animals; snooker and darts because (I suppose) they are signs of a misspent adolescence, and so on. Some are often excluded on practical grounds such as expense (polo, rowing), lack of specialized facilities (pursuit cycling, high-board diving), inadequate teacher knowledge, inappropriate weather conditions (ski-ing, skating, surfing) and so on. Of those not so excluded a selection must be made, and criteria are hard to come by. The choice, however, will ally the school with certain attitudes, interests and values expressed in and through the sports.

Values in Physical Education

They will form part of the school's representation of its aims and character to its constituency and to itself, and its constituency may be seen in community or class terms — but more of this later.

Although there is perhaps a distinction to be drawn between recreative and competitive sport (see Parry, 1978), it is the latter with which we are here concerned, and its defining feature has been seen as raising problems of value. Bailey (1975) has argued that since competitive games are necessarily competitive they are merely ways of beating other people, and education has nothing to do with the demonstration of superiority over others. I have two observations: firstly, although competitive games *are* ways of testing one's abilities against another's, they are not *merely* that; and secondly, education *is* about standards of performance, even if those standards are not necessarily contested between individuals. Bailey does not tell us *why* there should be no competition in education, whether or not the subject-matter entails it.

Bailey also argues against the traditional view that games provide a secure avenue to values education — that games are in some sense character-building. His view that it is possible to play games effectively either morally or not is surely incontrovertible. Aspin's (1975) counter-arguments that the constitutive rules of games enshrine moral values, and that games are collaborative enterprises which *ipso facto* entail moral considerations, lie behind Meakin's assertions (1981 and 1982) that sport offers opportunities for learning about values. It seems to me that everyone is right here. Games are, in part, constructed out of values, but this does not guarantee that they will be played morally. Bailey's further assertion that moral values cannot be learned through games participation seems to me unfounded, for his concession that games can (only) be played morally if a player's morality is imported from without entails that games are the site of moral behaviour. He does not explain why a site of moral and immoral behaviour may not be a site of moral learning. It seems to me quite clear that it may, and so I am with Meakin: games provide *opportunities* for the presentation of values.

At this stage it might be objected that *any* collaborative human practice could be the subject of moral reasoning, so that to show that moral dilemmas arise in games is to show very little. In such cases, the game would be only the contingent *occasion* for a moral *discussion*, and any contribution to moral education should be credited to the discussion, not to the game. However, this would be to ignore the more important point made above: it is the constitutive rules and the intrinsic features of games and athletics which are necessarily presented to a participant, and it is these which require recurrent elucidation.

It is true that competitive games are contests, which entails competition with a view to establishing a winner and loser (i.e. superiority in respect of the game's required abilities — see Fraleigh, 1984, pp. 41–6). But this does not entail that we have to have winning as our overriding concern: rather, one can play to win, valuing the opportunity to exercise speed, strength and skill (see Reddiford, 1982, pp. 114–5). For a good sport contest, though, there are certain prerequisites. Firstly, there is a presupposition of *equality of opportunity* to contest (equality under the rules), without which the game could not take place. Superiority in respect of a certain range of abilities could not be demonstrated unless all other variables are strictly controlled. Secondly, no contest could exist without the opponent, which would seem to require at least the minimum *respect* due to a facilitator — to one whose own level of performance is a major contributor to the very possibilities for excellence open to oneself in that category of endeavour chosen by both. Thirdly, although it is clearly possible to break the rules, to do so alters the conditions of the contest, so that a range of abilities *not* specified by the rules comes into play. A good contest will maintain the framework which secures the integrity of the contest, and this requires *rules adherence* and *fair play* (see Fraleigh, 1984, *passim*; and McIntosh, 1979, pp. 81–4). Fourthly, there is a *knowledge of relative abilities* which is a necessary outcome. Bailey sees this as a form of braggadocio, but Reddiford (1982) reminds us that 'you win some, you lose some' and so to make the game the occasion for 'marking up superiorities and inferiorities' is a short-term and self-defeating attitude. We play

> to produce an outcome favourable to (our)selves but do not allow the actual outcome to be of persisting importance. (p. 115).

Humility and generosity are at least as likely an accompaniment to a demonstration of one's relative abilities as overweening pride and conceit.

Fifthly, in games, there is a simple right and wrong, easily enforceable by a clearly identified authority. At the same time, there is some possibility of differing interpretation and judgment. In playing games, students learn how to follow explicit rules, how to bend them and evade them, and how to operate within a system of penalties and consequences, both official and unofficial. Games are *laboratories for value experiments*. Students are put in the position of having to act, time and time again, sometimes in haste, under pressure or provocation, either to prevent something or to achieve something, under a structure of rules. The settled dispositions which it is claimed emerge from such a crucible of value-related behaviour are those which were consciously cultivated through games in the public schools in the last century. These days there is still the expectation that games will contribute to an elementary socialization function, even if no more than that.

As mentioned earlier, we should also take note of the important role played by sport in popular culture. Some critics assert that such deeply embedded social practices as sport are likely to be infused with the beliefs, ideals and values of the dominant class — in brief, that sport functions as an expression of bourgeois ideology all the more powerful for its implicit character. The way in which this ideology is able to present itself as commonsensical or natural in people's experience of the social world (for example, in sport) is evidence of its powerful hold upon us (see Parry, 1984, p. 76).

As Hoberman (1984) suggests:

> ... fascist, liberal-democratic and Communist societies have distinct political anthropologies or idealized models of the exemplary citizen which constitute complex answers to the fundamental question of philosophical anthropology: 'What is a human being?' (p. 2).

In participating in sport, we are being invited to assent to a political anthropology, and possibly to certain views on nation, class, gender, race and the value of commercialism. Sport may therefore present an ideal opportunity to interrogate the lived experience of students and teachers for its ideological content.

Swimming and Life-saving Instruction

This should be a part of every child's schooling. It directs our attention to the most basic of values: the preservation of our own (and others') lives. No other subject on the school curriculum has such a direct and dramatic relationship to the most fundamental of values, and it is important to notice that the *necessary* requirement here is the performance of the *skill*. Here we have the classic example of the exemplification of a value simply by the performance of a skill.

In addition, if PE took seriously its claims to advance the health of its students through exercise (rather than simply assuming that being fit enough to pursue sometimes hazardous sports is the same thing as being 'healthy') it would take greater pains to encourage students to make regular exercise part of their daily routines. I am thinking here

Jim Parry

particularly of walking and swimming, the two most beneficial forms of exercise in terms of long-term overall fitness and health.

I have not discussed competitive swimming or water polo, since they would come under sport, nor diving and synchronized swimming, for they may be seen as forms of gymnastic activity.

Dance

This is a difficult area to deal with, not least because some of its practitioners would prefer it not to be regarded as a PE activity at all, but either as a discipline on its own or as a member of an arts department. I am sympathetic to both alternative suggestions, and nothing that I shall go on to say would controvert either arrangement. It is rather like the argument about whether or not a whale is to be considered a fish — it depends upon the circumstances and your reasons, and is ultimately a matter of decision, not logical necessity. So, without making any further claims, I am simply acknowledging, in what follows, the fact that some dance does take place in schools under the umbrella of PE, and that the PE world has been extremely influential in the development of dance in schools in this country. My final preliminary observation is that it seems to me dishonest of those who disparage and disvalue PE in its aspects other than dance, or who do not regard dance as part of PE, to continue happily to accept PE time on the curriculum. Perhaps they should take a firm grasp of their principles and take their chances in competition with other disciplines on the arts curriculum.

For myself, I would be happy to see balletic dance either in an arts department or in a PE department. (I would, for example, be far happier in regarding a dancer as a sort of athlete than a footballer as a sort of artist). As a contributor to the PE curriculum, dance as an art form would contribute immensely to our ability and willingness to adopt an aesthetic attitude in our appraisals of other PE activities, and this can only extend and deepen our understanding of the values which are presented in them. It will be useful for this section and the next to set out two distinctions made by Best (1978, pp. 101–5). Firstly, we should distinguish purposive from aesthetic sports on the ground that means and ends are separable in the former and not the latter. *What* I do (score a goal) can be specified independently of *how* I do it, so long as it is within the rules — but you couldn't explain what a barani is without explaining how to do one. Secondly, we should distinguish the artistic from the aesthetic. The aesthetic is an interest which may be taken in anything at all, whereas the artistic is that which has been created for the purpose of aesthetic appraisal. So: a sunset is not a work of art, whilst a painting of a sunset may be — but it is possible to take an aesthetic interest in both. So: purposive sports are not art, although they may be appraised in aesthetic terms; aesthetic sports seem to share with balletic dance the feature of being created for aesthetic appraisal, but the sports do not have the capacity for commenting on life issues, which Best identifies as a further feature of art. We thus arrive at a threefold classification: purposive sports, aesthetic sports, and art.

Now, with balletic dance we are clearly dealing with an art form, and it will clearly share those values and justifications which are generalizable across all art forms, to do with creativity, expression, emotion, imagination, and the illumination of the human condition. At least, it will share in these values so long as it is taught and presented as a performance art, and not as a series of techniques, skills and themes which do not issue in (or confront) performances (or productions). A further value of dance is that it is *another way* of being creative/expressive/imaginitive. Each art form provides a different medium of engagement, and it would seem important that students are put in the way of as many of them as possible, for this one might be *the* form which initiates a student into the values of art in general.

The status of national, country, folk or social dance is more problematic, but they are likely to be more of cultural and historical than artistic significance. This is not to denigrate them. They may perform some similar ideological functions to sport, and they may be a primary occasion for personal engagement with one's own living culture and history — the effect striven for by museums, pageantry and ceremonial occasions. More 'recent' forms of social and popular dance bear the same relationship to students' out-of-school life as do some sports. They therefore share the opportunity for bridge-building between education and 'life', the school and the community.

Gymnastics

The various forms of gymnastic activity (Olympic, rhythmic, educational, tumbling, diving, trampolining, etc.) are aesthetic sports. That is to say, their ends cannot be specified independently of their means, so that to assess the *way* in which a movement is performed *is* to assess the movement. The intention is to create movement patterns for the purpose of their aesthetic appraisal, although sheer complexity and difficulty are also valued.

Jim Parry

In formal, Olympic, gymnastics, the composition and performance of gymnastic routines involves a combination of value components: the whole must sustain a convincing aesthetic unity, demonstrating line, flow, grace and effortlessness; it must also encompass athletic qualities such as strength, power, flexibility, agility and stamina; and it must include a variety of acrobatic 'tricks' which demonstrate a high level of skill and difficulty.

Educational gymnastics, the other most popular form in British schools, is a child of the progressive movement in primary education and has captured the attention of those working in middle schools and the younger sectors of secondary schools. Given its background it is not surprising to find that child-centred values are enshrined in it. Students are set tasks which they must answer in their own way, thus enjoying a measure of freedom and autonomy. The emphasis is on exploration of movement possibilities and discovery of personal capacities. Individual creativity and imagination is encouraged at the expense of pre-determined outcomes.

Outdoor Education

Outdoor Education is a general term which refers simply to location — it is education out of doors. But this does not get us very far, so let us distinguish outdoor studies (for example, a geography field trip, an art landscape class, an environmental studies nature walk, a land survey, or a day visit to the coast to collect and study samples for marine biology) from outdoor pursuits and residential stays.

Outdoor pursuits are physical activities which typically involve a journey through the natural environment where some danger or risk to safety is accepted (for example, rock climbing, mountaineering, caving, potholing, ski-ing, surfing, sailing, hang-gliding). Central to these activities are the values of adventure, challenge, exploration, awareness and appreciation of the environment, self-reliance and self-discovery. They may also, for practical reasons, carry with them some sort of residential stay (for example, camping, bivouacking, staying at a local authority centre or mountain hut or youth hostel, going away on expedition or holiday) and this in itself may be influential in promoting social education, independence and friendship. Students are placed in a situation which takes them away from their families and which generates possibilities for social interaction quite different from those in the context of their everyday experience of their fellows. They are thrown on to their own resources in ways which challenge their personal

Values in Physical Education

organization, ability to negotiate understandings with others, sensitivity to and ability to cope with the weaknesses of self and others, sharing responsibility and leadership, and other co-operative skills.

Fitness Training

Under this heading I include weight training, circuit training, training for a particular sport, or any other regular activity whose aim is general or specific fitness.

As with swimming, these activities have been vastly underrated as regards their contribution to basic values, such as staying alive. A sensible diet and regular exercise have dramatically reduced the proportion of early deaths from heart attacks in the USA over the past ten years or so, although no similar pattern has yet emerged in Britain. A settled disposition to consider and care for one's bodily condition, and to take personal responsibility for preventive health measures are virtues which are advocated by a 'health-related fitness' emphasis in PE. There is also a concern for the aesthetic dimension of self-presentation — what used to be called deportment, but in present times has changed in emphasis to be referred to colloquially as 'looking fit' — which has a dangerous propensity to topple over into narcissism.

On Method

All teachers are teachers of values, since whatever content they present to students will have value presuppositions, and so will whatever methods they use — there is no escape from responsibility in these matters. As Peters (1959) argues:

> Values are involved in education not so much as end-products, but as principles implicit in different manners of proceeding ...
> (p. 87)

Also, teachers of varying subjects will draw on a common fund of ideas and practices when considering how to approach their teaching task. There is a finite number of teaching 'styles' taken for granted in the literature for purposes of classification. Both Kane (1974) and Hendry (1977) identify five styles (direct, guided discovery, problem-solving, creative and individual programmes) which they use to structure their empirical enquiries regarding the PE curriculum. But it is clear to see that these same five styles could be applied to an analysis of all the teaching of any subject, so that PE will have no special claim here. Doubtless we could find examples within PE of these styles in operation, as did Hendry, and we would also doubtless find that the first three were often used and last two seldom used by both men and women. The important question to be asked, though, is *why* a particular method is being used on a particular occasion, and what values will be presented to students because of the teacher's choice. Direct teaching, for example, might carry with it some of the following values and suggestions: knowledge is something which is transmitted from knower to recipient, a student's task is to be a passive recipient of knowledge (for later recall?), recall is the most valued intellectual ability, learning occurs under conditions controlled by an authority, and so on. The 'creative' style, on the other hand, under which the pupil selects the problem and proposes solutions, would seem rather to suggest that knowledge is something to be discovered (whether by teacher or by student), that a student will be active in this endeavour, that questioning and enquiry will be necessary, that learning can be autonomous, and so on.

Now, these two examples are meant simply to demonstrate that the methods used by teachers of all subjects are likely to have value presuppositions. Indeed, in the present case, the examples are expressive of two quite clear educational ideologies. PE teachers will have choices to make here, and they will be important ones, but in this they are no different from all other teachers. A similar consideration applies to Meakin's analysis (1982, p. 80). He places great emphasis on methodology, claiming that whilst PE offers *opportunity* for values education, much (if not all) depends on the teacher's methods. He/she should, above all, engage in informal discussion of values issues, should commend good behaviour, be a model of good behaviour him/herself, and exhibit his/her values in his/her attitudes towards students and his/her style of communicating with them. The value of gymnastics and dance, he thinks, resides largely in the opportunities presented in those activities for partner and group work, which may lead to the development of desirable personal qualities.

All this may be true, but my point is that all of the above could be said of the teaching of drama, chemistry or woodwork as well as PE. I think that there are two sorts of special claim that can be made regarding PE, in addition to the more general points listed above. Firstly, there is again the matter of 'difference': it is possible to demonstrate the depth and consistency of our commitment to fundamental values by showing how they spill over from classroom to corridor to laboratory to playing-field, gymasium and countryside. PE provides *another* — different —

context in which these values may be articulated and illustrated, the more so that they may begin to infuse the whole life of the student. This is one way, I would suggest, to tackle the vexed problem of the 'transfer' of desirable behaviour from one context to another. Secondly, a central concern of PE has always been for quality of athletic movement. PE teachers have always been committed to teaching practical skills and competences, and may be especially knowledgeable about the methods for teaching skills. Now, it seems to me that there is room for development in this area — that many teachers are now taking up an interest in a 'skills' approach to the teaching of their subject. (One example is in philosophy of education, where Straughan and Wilson (1983) are described as offering 'a unique new approach' which presents 'philosophical skills and techniques', chapter by chapter, for the student to learn, use and practice). An underlying value here might be autonomy (or possibly 'empowerment'), since to teach someone a skill is to render the student independent of the teacher and able to act in the world. If PE teachers have some principles of skill teaching which could profitably be generalized, here indeed would be a contribution.

Aims and Practices

So far I have tried to provide an overall picture of the values to be found in PE by examining some PE ideologies, some general features of PE in schools, its typical content and some methods. It is now time to try to bring together some of the emphases and insights in this complex and confusing picture by turning our attention to the way in which the values identified may or may not find expression as overt aims or a hidden agenda.

Perhaps the best way to begin is to record a list of overt aims which have been compiled by others who have taken the trouble to summarize some of the literature. Renshaw (1972) lists:

— physical fitness and health
— neuro-muscular skills
— motor sensitivity and competence (for communication and expression)
— social adjustment through group activities
— moral socialization
— emotional stability
— positive attitudes towards physical activity (and future leisure use)

Jim Parry

— aesthetic appreciation of movement

Hendry's list (1977) adds nothing to this, but Kane's (1974) is different in some respects:

- motor skills
- self-realization
- leisure
- emotional stability
- moral development
- social competence
- organic development
- cognitive development
- aesthetic appreciation

(Incidentally, this is the *rank order* of teaching objectives for a sample of 888 men and women PE teachers).

Now, Meakin makes the point (1982, p. 69) that such research as Kane's and Hendry's imposes a list of aims upon teachers, who are then asked to rank order them. The origin of this list is previous academic publications, and not the teachers' own experience in schools or perceptions of their job, which may result in a misrepresentation of PE teachers' aims. For example, it seems odd to me, from what I see going on in schools, that neither list has included the aims of enjoyment, play, recreation and fun. Nor do we find mention of simple activity as an aim (getting them out of the classroom, letting off steam — cp. Williams' work on primary teachers, 1980, p. 101) nor is there pot-hunting. This may be for the reason that they are not overt aims at all, but part of the hidden agenda. However, I tend to the view that many PE teachers would cheerfully admit to chasing trophies for themselves or their headteachers, and would see nothing wrong in saying 'We'll just have a game today' or 'They're rather rowdy today, so I'll keep them really busy.' Here are some more aims which might have seen the light of day if teachers' responses had not been so tightly pre-programmed:

- learning games rules
- survival skills in water and the outdoors
- producing élite performers and good teams
- satisfaction in the display of skill
- developing of informed and appreciative spectatorship
- excitement, challenge and adventure
- initiating students into the cultural significance of sport
- heightened sensory experience
- non-verbal communication

Values in Physical Education

— an alternative avenue to status and success
— to develop community links

and so on. Some of these, of course, may not be overt aims, but all of them *could* be. Let me now add a short list of possible candidates for the hidden agenda, which might be worth considering if only to bring them to mind. They are potentially at least as powerful influences as anyone's list of overt aims:

— perpetuation of racist attitudes (sport as a sidetrack for blacks)
— reinforcement of gender stereotypes
— collusion with commercial interests (sport consumerism)
— bias towards competitive and aggressive activities
— authoritarian and paternalistic attitudes
— greater attention given to good performers
— anti-intellectualism
— compulsion, coercion and corporal punishment

Opportunities

I would like to conclude on a positive note by outlining what seem to me to be opportunities for PE to become a more self-reflective and educative enterprise. I would share Hargreaves' (1982) view that secondary education needs an urgent and drastic overhaul, and that PE should become an important element in a core curriculum. He says:

> ... in arguing for more PE I am not assuming that all is well in the world of PE ... If I want more PE, then I also want a rather different PE. (p. 5)

My suggestions for a rather different PE are as follows:

(i) PE should stand out anew for a conception of education which does not over-emphasize the academic/intellectual function, but which presents us, in its ideal product, with a philosophical anthropology — an answer to the question: What is a human being? Recent definitions have begun with the concept of 'education' or 'educated man'. I think we should begin again with the concept of 'human being' or 'person'.

(ii) Between now and the end of this century will be a time of increasing formal and actual equality. PE, given its present reactionary position, is ideally placed to take a lead by reforming its practices radically. It should combat sexism in this most sexually divisive of subjects by providing opportunities for boys and girls to participate together, by providing equal resources, and by re-examining the range of activities offered and the status accorded to them. It should similarly combat racism by providing equal opportunity, but also by guarding against the possibility that sport might act as a sidetrack from other avenues of achievement.

(iii) I believe that the interest of all forms of dance should be strongly promoted within PE, firstly because of the stimulus that they give to our willingness to make aesthetic appraisals throughout the discipline, and the contribution that they make to its breadth of interest and concern; and secondly, because of the obvious link between some forms of dance and other school departments which I believe would lead to fruitful collaboration for all concerned.

(iv) The cognitive emphasis in education has led to some interesting developments in PE, such as problem-solving approaches to, for example, gymnastics and the 'understanding' approach to games. But it has also led some to a willing acceptance of the primacy of propositional knowledge and hence examinations. Hendry (1977) reports that his teachers 'considered that the freedom within a non-examination subject ... was *the* most important factor influencing their work'. (p 179). I can only echo that sentiment. PE should develop its own strengths, not try to compete on foreign soil, at least in the first instance.

(v) I have already mentioned the special relationship of physical activities to popular culture, which makes possible a reciprocal influence between school and community. Many schools already open up their facilities to the local community and also use community facilities for their own PE programmes, especially during option periods for older pupils. The benefits of such links are very much underestimated in my view, and PE should be in the vanguard of subjects which attempt to utilize outside expertise to enrich their programmes, and which assist in the development of community structures into which they would then feed their school leavers. This would be community development and education for leisure rolled into one.

(vi) The benefits of a short residential stay or the adventure and challenge of outdoor pursuits are becoming increasingly recognized and appreciated, but in most schools this aspect of PE work stands out on a limb, not fully integrated (especially in conceptual terms) with whatever else is happening. We need a fresh look at the whole business of outdoor education, to see what it might be possible to develop on a systematic basis in schools. It seems to me an enormous source of potential benefit in terms of personal and social growth, and it has a large dose of 'difference' too.

(vii) There have been recent experiments in French and Canadian schools with daily physical education. I do not know what the value of this has been, but it does at least appear to be an attempt to take the aims of health and fitness seriously. Too often, it seems to me, we pay lip-service to these notions, but continue with the same activities regardless of the damage we cause ourselves. Some hospital departments are full not of sick people, but of broken-down joggers and footballers! PE should reassess its commitment to the notions of health and fitness, and should do its best to encourage sensible and regular exercise as part of a life routine.

(viii) Finally, PE teachers should be far more willing to consider for themselves, and discuss with students, values-related issues within the subject. Is excessive competitiveness stifling those humanitarian values which are written into the constitutive and regulative rule-structures of all sports? What are we to make of McEnroe's latest outburst? (And why is *that* shown on the news, and not the *tennis*?) Why has the government refused entry on this recent occasion to two North Korean gymnasts? What's brewing for 1988? Should we play with apartheid? Why do we do dance in the PE department? And outdoor pursuits? Why not darts and snooker? Do we *have* to do cross-country? Possibly the most important question that could be asked is: What is the place of physical activity in human life? The last word will be the answer of Jerome Bruner (1962, p. 102):

That PE for instance is pursued in accordance with a rational appraisal of the place and value of physical activities in human life, which we wish the pupils to aquire — that the activities themselves are viewed as those of a developing rational being not merely an animal, and that they therefore form part of the life of a rational person. (p. 102)

References

ASPIN, D.N. (1975) 'Games winning and education — some further comments', *Cambridge Journal of Education*, 5, 1, pp. 51–61.
BAILEY, C. (1975) 'Games, winning and education', *Cambridge Journal of Education*, 5, 1, pp. 40–50.
BARROW, R. (1982) *The Philosophy of Schooling*, Brighton, Wheatsheaf Books.
BEST, D. (1978) *Philosophy and Human Movement*, London, Allen and Unwin.
BRUNER, J. (1962) *Essays for the Left Hand*, Boston, Harvard University Press.
BUNKER, D., and THORPE, R. (1982) 'A model for the teaching of games in secondary schools', *Bulletin of Physical Education*, 18, 1 (see this issue *passim* re. 'Understanding games').
CARLISLE, R. (1969) 'The concept of physical education', *Proceedings of the PESGB*, 3, pp. 5–20.
CLEGG, A. (1976) Preface to FOSTER, R. *Knowing In My Bones*, London, A and C Black.
FRALEIGH, W. (1984) *Right Actions in Sport: Ethics for Contestants*, Champaign, Ill, Human Kinetics Publishers.
HARGREAVES, D., (1982) 'Ten proposals for the future of PE', *Bulletin of Physical Education*, 18, 3, pp. 5–10.
HENDRY, L.B., (1977) 'Conflicts in the curriculum: an example from PE', *Educational Research*, 20, 3, pp. 174–80.
HIRST, P. and PETERS, R.S. (1970) *The Logic of Education*, London, Routledge and Kegan Paul.
HOBERMAN, J.M. (1984) *Sport and Political Ideology*, London, Heinemann.
KANE, J.E. (1974) *Physical Education in Secondary Schools*, Schools Council Research Studies, London, Macmillan.
MADNESS, (1981) *Baggy Trousers* (popular song recorded on *Stiff*).
MCINTOSH, P. (1979) *Fair Play: Ethics in Sport and Education*, London, Heinemann.
MEAKIN, D.C. (1981) 'Physical education: an agency of moral education?', *Journal Philosophy of Education*, 15, 2, pp. 241–53.
MEAKIN, D.C. (1982) 'Moral values and physical education', *Physical Education Review*, 5, 1, pp. 62–82.
MORGAN, R.E. (1975) 'Coffee studies as a model for academic rigour in physical education', *The Times Higher Education Supplement*, 6 June.
MORGAN, R.E. (1979) 'Physical education — a traditionalist's view', *Bulletin of Physical Education*, 15, pp. 11–16.
PARRY, S.J. (1978) 'Competitive and recreative sport', *British Journal of Physical Education*, 9, 3, p. 68.
PARRY, S.J. (1984) 'Hegemony and sport', *Journal of Philosophy of Sport*, 10, pp. 71–83.
PETERS, R.S. (1959) 'Must an educator have an aim?', *Authority, Responsibility and Education*, London: Allen and Unwin, pp. 83–95.

REDDIFORD, G. (1982) 'Playing to win', *Physical Education Review*, 5, 2, pp. 107–15.
RENSHAW (1972) 'Physical education: the need for philosophical clarification', *Education for Teaching*, 87, pp. 60–8.
Schools Council (1977) 'Examinations in physical education', *Schools Council Bulletin*.
STRAUGHAN, R., and WILSON, J. (1983) *Philosophizing about Education*, London, Holt Rinehart and Winston.
WHITE, J.P. (1973) *Towards a Compulsory Curriculum*, London, Routledge and Kegan Paul.
WHITEHEAD, N.J. and HENDRY, L.B. (1976) *Teaching Physical Education in England — Description and Analysis*, London, Lepus Books.
WILLIAMS, A., (1980) 'Intention versus transaction: the junior school PE curriculum', *Physical Education Review* 3, 2, pp. 96–104.
WILLIS, P. (1977) *Learning to Labour*, Farnborough, Saxon House.
WILSON, J. (1972) *Philosophy and Educational Research*, Windsor, NFER.
YATES, J. (1977) 'Ideology in physical education', *Bulletin of Physical Education*, 13, 1, pp. 9–17.

Revaluing Science Education

David Layton

Is Science Neutral?

Like oil and water, science and values are commonly supposed not to mix. Certainly, scientific knowledge has frequently been claimed to be 'neutral' applicable equally to good or evil purposes, but itself 'value-free'. Science discloses; man disposes. 'As long as it limits itself to the descriptive study of the Laws of Nature', the Nobel Laureate Sir Ernst Chain asserted, in writing about social responsibility and the scientist, 'science has no moral or ethical quality'.[1]

The origin of this viewpoint on science can be traced back at least to the seventeenth century when 'the business and design of the Royal Society' was stated to exclude 'meddling with Divinity, Metaphysics, Morals, Politicks'.[2] The same considerations were prominent in the founding years of the British Association for the Advancement of Science, almost two centuries later. 'Statistics', for example, because it might be used to serve political ends, was not deemed by some to be a suitable subject for inclusion within the programme of the new body. The idea that papers should be read on statistical matters at the annual meetings of the Association was vehemently opposed, leading to a decision that reportage should be limited to neutered, non-interpretative accounts of 'facts and numerical results'. In this way it was hoped that the new 'Eden of Philosophy' would be protected from 'the foul demon of discord'.[3]

'Pure science', an activity insulated from society and associated with 'the disinterested pursuit of truth', became the dominant mode of science in the late nineteenth century. As Thomas Kuhn has pointed out, this freedom to work without regard for societal values enabled scientists to concentrate on problems of their own choosing, and ones they had good reason to believe they could solve.[4]

In saying this, however, one weakness in the position of those who assert the independence of science and values is exposed. Clearly there are internal, or constitutive, values which govern the ways in which scientists work and which are instrumental to the supreme goal of scientific activity, the advancement of knowledge about the natural world. Something of them is captured in Robert Oppenheimer's chilling description of research on the hydrogen bomb as 'technically sweet', a phrase which for him embraced considerations such as accuracy, precision, problem-solving capacity, breadth of scope, elegance and truth.

Much has been written about such normative constraints on scientific activity,[5] but it is not these that most proponents of value-free science have in mind. Rather, they contend that the activity of scientists is independent of personal, social and cultural values, hence scientific knowledge is uncontaminated by contextual preferences external to science.

Whether this proposition is regarded as tenable or not will depend, amongst other considerations, on the view taken of science. It will suffice here to recall that many who are termed scientists today work in industrial or military organizations; that policy on financial support for scientific research, a major determinant of the kinds of knowledge produced, is frequently influenced by economic and social considerations; and that studies of the generation of 'scientific facts' indicate that 'laboratory life' involves complex processes of intellectual negotiation and judgment which cannot be totally divorced from the religious, ethical, political and ideological standpoints of those taking part.[6] In short, the rhetoric of neutrality loses much of its force when the touch-stone of 'real life' is applied.

Science Education and Values

From an educational standpoint these considerations about science would matter less if it were not for the fact that curriculum endorsements of value-free science are common place. The aims predominantly associated with school science are cognitive ones such as knowledge and understanding of scientific laws, and skill in designing and carrying out experimental investigations.[7] Indeed, this emphasis on 'intellectual training', debasing science education to the acquisition of technique without regard for its human significance, was the principal source of opposition to science as a school subject in the nineteenth century. Unlike the study of literature, that of science was said not to bring students into contact with value issues; it was a dehumanizing activity and had no place in an education whose prime function was moral. The overall goals of education may have altered subsequently, but those of the science curriculum are little changed as a glance at the objectives associated with GCE and CSE examinations in science will confirm.

Apart from a reference to the part which scientific knowledge and experience might play in establishing a sense of personal and social identity for a student, the recent (1981) policy statement on the aims of science education by the influential Association for Science Education likewise contains little that could be said to be value-related.[8] In the words of a Canadian commentator, science teachers 'continue to allow students to learn most of their attitudes and values through the "hidden" ... curriculum'.[9] Explicit teaching of science for value outcomes is rare. Furthermore, opportunities to explore and develop the value-related aims of school science, where these exist, seem to be ignored or even officially discouraged. In its response to a question from the Committee of Inquiry into the Education of Children from Ethnic Minority Groups about 'the relevance of a multi-ethnic society to the teaching of science as a component of the curriculum', the Association for Science Education stated that 'science is regarded by the majority of its teachers as an international study, with no particular national bias, and with its own neutral terminology, which is also culture free'.[10] This might well be an accurate statement of the perceptions of many teachers, derived from their education in science, but it is also an extraordinary failure to recognize that curricula are inescapably linked to the cultural context of their origin and that 'political and economic pressures, social customs and expectations combine to set limits on what should be taught in schools, on what can be taught ..., and on the teaching methods to be used.'[11]

The reaction in 1983 of the Secretaries of State for Education and for Wales to proposals that science examination criteria should in fact embrace social and economic issues arising from the application of scientific knowledge illustrates both the limiting process in action and official unwillingness to depart from 'value-free' science curricula. Their opinion was that the inclusion of such issues 'might make it difficult to avoid tendentiousness in the teaching of science subjects', a risk which was 'best avoided'.[12] In passing it might be noted that the *Concise Oxford Dictionary* defines 'tendentious' as 'having an underlying purpose' or 'calculated to advance a cause'. The teaching of science in a manner which implies it is value-free escapes the stricture of tendentiousness, presumably because there is approval of the purpose it serves.

What Values are Learnt in Science Lessons?

Because explicit recognition is rarely given to value-outcomes in science education it does not follow that values are not being transmitted and learnt. Curriculum, pedagogy and evaluation represent three powerful, and often mutually reinforcing, message systems from which students 'pick up' values.

Curriculum

Consider first a curriculum example and the purported distinction between facts and values. As presented in chemistry textbooks, and as encountered in science lessons, the gas phase structure of a water molecule is 'an established objective fact'. The angle between the H-O bonds is the same whether measured in California, China or Chile. It is a result which is independent of the religious conviction, economic status, political affiliation and geographical location of the experimenter. What values, then, can possibly be learnt from this?

The answer, of course, is that there are many possible versions of 'the chemistry of water'. The generalized, theoretical account with a focus on bonding, energy and structure is a powerful version for understanding the chemical behaviour of water in relation to other group VIB hydrides. It is not necessarily the most useful account if the problem to be solved is the supply of potable water to an isolated rural community in an impoverished Third World country. In such a case, a greater emphasis on the practical techniques of chemical analysis and methods of removing impurities could be more helpful. By the selection of the former version priority is accorded to 'abstract science' and 'the disinterested pursuit of truth', as opposed to social utility. The particular selection of knowledge ('facts') which is included in the curriculum is reflective of this value position.

A second example will reinforce the point. The electrolysis of brine in the Kellner-Solvay cell to yield sodium hydroxide and chlorine is a familiar component of many introductory chemistry courses. The stan-

David Layton

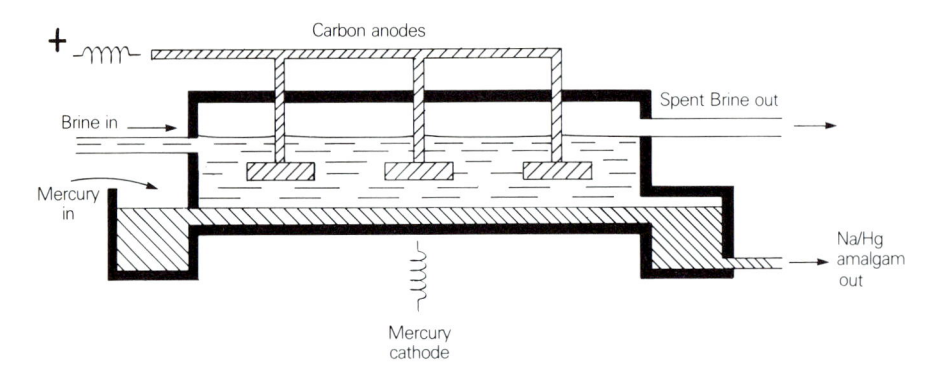

Figure 1. The Kellner-Solvay cell.

dardized treatment draws attention to the economy of the cell, the processes occurring at the electrodes, the preferential discharge of sodium ions at the mercury cathode and the decomposition of liquid sodium amalgam to yield sodium hydroxide. (Figure 1)

It can be argued that an arbitrary line has been drawn around this to define what constitutes a valid account of the electrolysis of brine. Certainly much interesting chemistry associated with the process is excluded from the standardized account above. Thus, there is no consideration of mercury losses in the spent brine, in the atmosphere, in the alkali product and in the anode sludge. Much less is there any mention of the impact of this 'lost mercury' on ecosystems, although quantitative data are available. If the priority is economic efficiency and skill in solving technical problems (for example, how to avoid hydrolysis of the chlorine by OH ions) then the standardized account serves well. If the priority is one which includes a concern for the environmental impact of industrial processes, then there is much to be added to the standardized account. Putting the matter another way, a shift in value position would necessitate a different account.

A difficulty in this area is that so-called 'objective scientific fact' is inescapably enmeshed in the language of its presentation and in the framework of explanation in terms of which it is interpreted. An interesting illustration involving different ways of presenting the same 'facts', is provided by the case of Linus Pauling and Edward Teller, two distinguished scientists in the USA, who each reported the same experimental results on the predicted effects of radioactive fall-out.[13] Pauling expressed his conclusion as the absolute number of deaths likely to occur. Teller, in contrast, gave the expected shortening of average life

Revaluing Science Education

expectancy compared to the shortening due to smoking. Each statement embodied a value judgment on the desirability of continued testing of nuclear weapons; indeed it would be difficult to think of a way of reporting in this case which was not similarly value-laden.

If further evidence was needed that 'facts' and 'values' are frequently intertwined, it could be drawn from a study of the processes by which safety threshhold limits are set for toxic materials. Here data interpretation is less than an objective exercise, experts can disagree violently, and the resolution of different positions is far from being a matter of collecting more experimental results. Argument surrounding the acceptable concentration of lead in blood is a case in point. Just as the concept of pollution entails a judgment as to whether there is a threat to some standard of purity, so also the concepts of risk and safety are social and political, as well as scientific. As Stephen Cotgrove has argued, 'Risk is not just a statistical calculation. It is also a moral judgment about defensible conduct. For the proponents of nuclear power, the overriding importance of wealth creation is sufficient moral justification for the risks involved. For the environmentalists, there is no such moral justification'.[14] Such differences now penetrate the classroom. So far as the nuclear debate is concerned, curriculum materials from the Ministry of Defence, such as its tape-slide sequence *A Better Road to Peace* and its film *The Peace Game*, are condemned by some teachers as 'dangerous, one-sided propaganda', needing to be counter-balanced by the unilateralist *The War Game* and other resources such as a projected CSE syllabus planned by Teachers for Peace, an offshoot of CND, in collaboration with Scientists Against Nuclear Arms (SANA).[15]

In a less emotive area, but making a similar point about the relationship between 'facts' and 'values', it is noteworthy that, at the end of an exhaustive analysis of the basis of recent estimates of the UK reserves of coal and spent fuel from nuclear reactors, the author of an article in the scientific journal *Nature* concluded: 'Statistics on fuel reserves do not constitute cold hard facts, they are judgments about the probable outcome of a series of events in space and time. One might even claim that they do not so much *form* government policy as *result from* such policy'.[16]

Summarizing to this point, then, the situation is one in which values indubitably are transmitted by means of science curricula, though the nature of these values is rarely made explicit, much less questioned. In a unique and systematic evaluation of science textbooks in terms of the value presuppositions they embody, two American researchers, Lance Factor and Robert Kooser, have identified a number of distinct value positions.[17] In one category of texts, which they describe as *skills and drills*, they point to the remarkable consensus which exists on what are 'the facts' of a particular science and 'the skills' in which the learner needs to be drilled. In general, such texts make little reference to applications of science, or to social and environmental issues. Moral and political considerations, where mention is inescapable, are truncated and quickly passed over. The emphasis is on the standardized versions of scientific knowledge which have become collegially acceptable substitutes for the contextualized and judgmental reports in which the knowledge was first generated. The impression conveyed is that the nature of scientific activity and communication at the research front is identical to the form and style of the textbook. The notion of controversy between scientists is incompatible with this portrayal of science, the knowledge produced by scientists being represented as certain, and an undisputed contribution to progress. Science education is, quite simply, as Thomas Kuhn described it — again with reference to the important role of textbooks — 'a relatively dogmatic initiation into a pre-established problem-solving tradition that the student is neither invited nor equipped to evaluate'. Furthermore, in so far as *skills and drills* texts allude to technology, it is undistinguished from science, as if all practitioners shared a common set of values. The slogan 'Better Living Through Chemistry' is an expression both of the ethos of 'truth and progress' associated with pure research and of the economic and material benefits of chemical technology.

Another category of textbook identified by Factor and Kooser is designated *Science and Society*, the term being used to cover works which stress the relation of science to the understanding of social issues such as policy on nuclear energy, or personal issues such as drug abuse. Here they contrast a number of different value positions. One well-defined position is codified as the *truth and progress* approach. It projects a view of the scientist as a disinterested truth seeker, readily accepting material sacrifices for the sake of higher goals. Its classic exposition in the English educational context, was Sir Richard Gregory's book, *Discovery, or the Spirit and Service of Science*.[18] Published in 1916 at a time when science was staking a claim for prominence in the blue-print for the School Certificate Examination, Gregory's hagiography associated science with values such as the disinterested pursuit of truth, a disregard for personal profit, internationalism, courage and humility. Far from being 'a callous necromancer', lacking the 'compassionate heart of a full life', the scientist was projected as a selfless quester after objective knowledge, freely bestowing his gifts upon the world, an emissary of light leading mankind along the road to progress.

Among other value positions exemplified by *Science and Society* texts, Factor and Kooser designated one *naturalist* because it used ecological principles as a means of organizing scientific knowledge. What it was possible to challenge here, although only one representative text was found, was the quality of the relationship between man and nature, the dominant, exploitive role of man implicit in many texts being contrasted with a view of man as the caretaker or steward of a natural world, of which he himself was a part.

More radical critiques of the central cluster of values which characterize 'main-stream' science textbooks were not apparent in the large sample of North American 'non-major' science textbooks which Factor and Kooser reviewed. No comparable study of value presuppositions in secondary school science textbooks in Britain has been undertaken, but recent criticisms of the published materials of the ASE sponsored *Science in Society* project, as well as advocacy of an alternative, also ASE sponsored, *Science in a Social Context* project have centred very much on the value issues involved.[19]

Pedagogy and Evaluation

It is well known that more things are learnt in school than are taught. The organization of science lessons, including the nature of the interactions between students and teachers, and the ways in which students' learning of science is evaluated, constitute further sources of value messages. Much has been written about these aspects of the 'hidden curriculum' and considerations which apply to the curriculum generally will not be dwelt on here.[20] A number of points, specific to science education, are worth brief mention however.

Science exists in a large number of curriculum versions; it appears in timetables as single subject science (principally biology, chemistry and physics), as combined or integrated science, and as applied science (for example, rural science, domestic science, technology, electronics). The management of these varieties and the ways in which they are offered to students is indicative of judgments about worth. A familiar pattern of organization is one in which pure, single subject sciences are available to able GCE 'O' level students, with some form of integrated and/or applied science course for CSE and non-examination students. Such differentiation reinforces a view of the superiority of pure over applied science, and of single subject sciences over integrated courses. This is not to say that their valuations have their origin in the organization of a school's curriculum; merely that they reflect the ways in which status has been allocated to different organizations of scientific knowledge by social mechanisms which have operated in the wider community outside the school.

Moving from curriculum management to the teaching of science in classrooms and laboratories, it is perhaps more difficult in science than in some other areas of the curriculum to convey the impression that the personal opinion of students is valid and worthwhile. After all, where is the room for debate about the structure and function of the mammalian heart or the inverse square law in relation to the force between electric charges? A well-authenticated and mainly unproblematic account has been long agreed by scientists, 'learning science' being interpreted as acquiring an understanding and mastery of this. One consequence of this view is that the 'right answer syndrome' afflicts science education severely. Its manifestations as far as student behaviour is concerned are well-known and seem conducive to acute value conflict. It is difficult to reconcile the application of 'Cook's Law' and the massaging of experimental data to ensure conformity with the result that is 'in the book' with value assertions about the need for 'intellectual honesty', 'regard for data' and a willingness 'to slay a beautiful hypothesis with an ugly fact' on the part of good scientists. Talk about the essential corrigibility of scientific theory is largely misplaced in the context of a pedagogy and evaluation system which reinforces a view of scientific knowledge as certain and uncontestable.

Other aspects of 'the hidden curriculum' include the seating arrangements for boys and girls in mixed science classes, the respective roles of boys and girls in shared practical science assignments and the distribution of teachers' questions across the sexes. Each of these factors has been suggested as contributory to an explanation of the under-achievement and under-representation of girls in science. Clearly that problem is of a magnitude and complexity that requires more embracing solutions than shifts in the conduct of science lessons, but it would appear that sex-stereotypes are maintained and reinforced by unthinking actions in classrooms and laboratories.[21]

A more general point relates to a unique feature of the English tradition of science teaching, the emphasis on individual practical work by students.[22] This same emphasis is not found in science teaching in all other countries, where lecture demonstration experiments and group practical assignments can play a much more significant role. The origins of the English predilection for educational individualism, and its manifestation in the science curriculum, notably in the long standing advocacy of heuristic methods of teaching science, lie deep rooted in the political, economic and religious dispositions of the nation. The realization of individual potential through self-development, comprising what

Steven Lukes has termed one of the 'unit-ideas of individualism',[23] has been reflected in the broad purpose of English education since its systematization in the late nineteenth century. The school science curriculum was developed in and adapted to an educational context which reflected such values. Knowing nothing else, it is easy to accept familiar science classroom and laboratory practices as 'the only possible way'; in reality, they are value-laden procedures conveying tacit messages the nature of which becomes more evident once comparison is made with science teaching in educational systems elsewhere.[24]

What Values Might be Taught in Science Lessons?

From what has gone before it will be clear that:
(i)   present day science teaching in England rarely aims to teach values in any direct or explicit sense;
even so,
(ii) values are inescapably transmitted in science lessons.

A number of questions arise. Should science teachers make more deliberate efforts to include value outcomes in their objectives, and should they teach consciously to these ends? If so, what are the possibilities in terms of value outcomes to be included, and what teaching and learning problems arise from an extension of science education into these new realms? The kind of response which can be given to these general questions might be better informed by a preliminary examination of some specific instances: two have been selected for inclusion here.

Science and Multi-cultural Education

The School Curriculum (1981), published by the Department of Education and Science as guidance to local authorities and schools in England and Wales on how the school curriculum could be further improved, identified the multi-cultural character of our society as an issue deserving special mention. More specific proposals for the adaptation of the curriculum to the needs of a multi-cultural society were made in the *Interim Report* of the Rampton (Swann) Committee of Inquiry into the education of children from ethnic minority groups (1981); in the Schools Council publication *Multi-ethnic Education: the way forward* (1981); and in the fifth report of the Home Affairs Committee, *Racial Disadvantage* (HMSO, August 1981). In practical terms, and in the words of a working party of teachers in a multiracial school, one central question is: 'To what extent does the content of my subject involve cultural attitudes and assumptions? Am I consciously or unconsciously projecting certain values? Are they likely to seem difficult or strange to some pupils?'[25]

Here, then, is a dimension of science education which offers opportunities for re-examination in terms of value outcomes. As has been mentioned above, the reported reaction of members of the Association for Science Education has been, broadly, that no problem existed: in general they did not see the need to consider the appropriateness of curriculum materials for a multi-ethnic society, nor the relevance of a multi-ethnic society to the teaching of science, because science itself transcended national and cultural divisions.

It has been argued here, however, that the schools science curriculum, as we know it in English schools, has developed in a way which is reflective of particular Anglo-Saxon predilections and of its specific historical context. Might it not be that some of the tacit value positions, intrinsic in curricula, are more challenging, perhaps alienating, even threatening, to children from ethnic minority families than they are to children from other homes? At the most superficial level, the impression that all 'great scientists' have been, and hence need to be, white European or American males can be corrected, or at least qualified. Perhaps the models of 'great scientists' on which we draw could be broadened to include those who have applied scientific knowledge or used engineering capabilities in the service of man in a wide range of situations, including Third World, as opposed to mainly those who have contributed to the conceptual framework of science. The history of science, engineering and medicine could be 'raided' for examples of effective international/intercultural cooperation, and the contribution of migrant groups and individuals.

At a different level, the methodology of science teaching, with its messages about the questioning of 'authority' and an overriding reliance on empirical evidence, may conflict with general attitudes to authority fostered in some children outside school. The difficulty of transplanting Nuffield-style inquiry learning into an educational context where there is a strong reluctance to question teacher-exposition and the prevalence of rote-learning is well known. The teacher-student relationship which is socially approved in some cultural contexts may be inimical to any style of discovery learning in science. Heurism is as inappropriate in the Punjab as it is in Japan, where, despite a long history of 'borrowing', it was never been properly assimilated into Japanese science teaching.[26]

Specific value conflicts can arise in connection with the teaching of certain topics in science lessons, notably human reproduction and the

theory of evolution. The problems here are not unique to multi-cultural education, although their manifestation in this context can be acute. In relation to the former topic, protest has been engendered because:
(i) unacceptable values have been deliberately incorporated, or insinuated, into an account of the biology of reproduction, notably in connection with contraception and abortion;
or, alternatively, because
(ii) sex education has been limited to the biological aspects of sexual intercourse and the reproductive cycle without the inclusion of moral and ethical considerations in relation to, for example, behaviour outside marriage, respect for persons, loving and caring.

It would seem that the unfortunate science teacher, whether he incorporates values or not in a programme of sex education, is likely to draw criticism from some quarter. Organizations like the North American *Council on National Righteousness* do not as yet have politically effective and vocal counterparts in the UK; their attack on 'dirt, sex and drugs' in science lessons has led the National Science Teachers' Association in the USA to publish a guide for teachers, *Sex Education in the Science Classroom*, defending the inclusion of sex education in the school curriculum and including a position statement by the NSTA supporting the efforts of all teachers to provide 'appropriate family life education'.[27]

A similar NSTA position statement was recently formulated in relation to the second topic, the theory of evolution. Here the opposition groups included a demand that the 'creationist' account of the origin of species should receive equal time to that allocated to the teaching of evolution in science lessons. Such opposition to the teaching of the theory of evolution is by no means confined to Christian fundamentalists; other religous groups such as Muslims find the scientific view unacceptable on its own.

For the National Science Teachers Association the issue became one of whether a 'theory' was scientific or not, the 'true test' of a theory in science being said to be '(i) its ability to explain what has been observed; (ii) its ability to predict what has not yet been observed; and (iii) its ability to be tested by further experimentation and to be modified as required by the acquisition of new data'.

All measures to incorporate in science teaching a theory that failed to meet the three-fold criteria above were to be opposed. In these terms 'creationism' was not 'science', but 'religion'. If it was to be included in the school curriculum, the place for it was in lessons on religious education, not science education. Value conflict was to be avoided by establishing a separation of territories, one province for science and another for religion, on the principle that 'Good fences make good neighbours'.[28]

From the standpoint of multi-cultural education in England and Wales the significance of the attack on the teaching of evolution is that the rational-empirical foundations of scientific belief are not ones which all cultural (and religious) groups are ready to accept without challenge, especially when a scientific theory appears to run counter to belief which is sanctioned in other ways. The demand on science teachers here is not for some dramatic recasting of material or syllabus reconstruction. Rather the need is for an extension and sharpening of existing sensitivities to the range of value positions in any classroom and the fostering of styles of teaching which convey respect for them.

Science, Technology and Society Courses

'How can we prepare students to make the decisions which they will face in the future?' This question, from an advertising leaflet describing the *Science in Society* course sponsored by the Association for Science Education and directed by John L Lewis, is reflective of a widespread concern about the impact of science and technology on society. Pursuing the theme of decision-making, one of the aims of this course is stated to be 'to lead students to recognize that making decisions may involve moral considerations'. Here, then, is a second aspect of science education where values might be introduced.[29]

Public concern about the effects of science and technology has grown appreciably in recent years, being centred largely around:

(i) fears about potential health and environmental risks; for example, lead in petrol;

(ii) fears about mis-use of science, research findings being used for pernicious ends; for example, foetal research;

(iii) fears that science and technology may change, or threaten, cherished beliefs and values; for example, 'creationist' opposition to the theory of evolution;

(iv) fears about the effects of science and technology on political choice and democratic principles; for example, the rise of scientific 'mandarins' and the exclusion of the public from decision making.[30]

Concomitantly, in a period of economic recession, there has been general recognition that pure science courses characterized by 'science for the inquiring mind,' were not orientating students sufficiently to the contributions which technology and engineering might make to industrial recovery and to the occupational opportunities and requirements ahead.

One aspect of the school curriculum response to these concerns has been the development of course materials designed to foster awareness of science, technology and society issues and to encourage students to begin to grapple with the complex arguments — scientific, economic, political, religious and moral — which often are associated with proposals for the social use of science and technology. The *Science in Society* project includes decision-making simulation exercises on a variety of topics including the establishment of a health service in a fictitious African Country; the fluorination of public water supplies; and the siting of, and choice of fuel for, a new power station. Other courses have units on computers and privacy; social and technological aspects of human reproduction; biomedical technology; the atomic bomb; and technology, invention and industry.[31] Common to all these teaching materials is the association of 'values education' with 'science education', a development which takes teachers and students of science into new areas of learning.

It is perhaps necessary at this point to indicate in a little more detail what is meant by 'values education'. Amongst a number of broad approaches which have been identified are:

(i) inculcation — in which certain desired values are instilled in students by processes such as repeated exemplification, and reinforcement;

(ii) moral development — in which students are helped to develop more complex moral reasoning patterns, often by the use of moral dilemma episodes, with structured small group discussion. (This approach draws on the work of Lawrence Kohlberg and his attempt to establish hierarchical stages of moral development, ranging from actions based on the avoidance of punishment and on self-benefit, to actions based on values shared with others or on conscience based on self selected ethical principles).

(iii) clarification — in which students are helped to become aware of, and to identify, their own values and those of others, techniques such as simulations and self-analysis exercises being employed to assist students to use both rational thought and emotional awareness in the examination of their values.

Unfortunately, in the field of science education there is little in the way of 'case law', let alone well-founded empirical evidence, to guide teachers in the choice of approach and of appropriate student activities for effective values education. What can be said is that the problems of implementing inter-disciplinary science, technology and society courses are formidable and the demands on science teachers, in terms of pedagogical skills, severe. Certainly, most of the issues that arise for discussion are cognitively complex, not only in relation to their science and technology components, but also in relation to understanding of 'society'. A student with a friend or family member on dialysis might well be interested in kidney machines, but a cost-benefit analysis of specific medical advances involves abstract thought which goes beyond the cognitive capabilities and interests of the majority. Furthermore the interaction of technical knowledge and personal values to yield a clear position on a particular issue is undoubtedly a process whose complexity taxes many adults. A scientist who has studied deeply the social consequences of producing and using the herbicide 2, 4, 5-T may nevertheless — or possibly in consequence — have great difficulty in coming to an opinion on the correctness of a government decision to use the herbicide. Notorious for its effects as Agent Orange, sprayed to defoliate trees in Vietnam, and also in the Seveso disaster, because of its dioxin contaminant, the chemical can contribute notably to agricultural productivity. In reaching their decision to approve or ban 2, 4, 5, -T, government regulatory authorities in different countries have all reviewed the same scientific literature, yet Sweden and Italy conclude the herbicide is too dangerous to use, the USA permits restricted use, whilst Britain approves it as a domestic weed killer to be used in accordance with instructions. At an individual level there is some indication that 'the more profound the understanding of the scientific and technical evidence, the greater the probability of ambivalence and political paralysis'![32] In such circumstances the science contribution to decision making can be ineffective and other considerations — economic, social, moral — override to determine the outcome. Possibly recognition of this 'fact of life' alone, would be a salutory outcome if it could be achieved by science, technology and society courses.

There are, however, powerful arguments why anything that is achieved in the years of compulsory schooling needs supplementing by additional education at adult level. Indeed the closer association of science education with values education provides one of the strongest arguments for transforming the slogan 'life long science education' into a reality. There is first the consideration, already mentioned, about the cognitive complexity of the issues. Second, it is adults who are 'the voters' and in a position to influence directly decisions on science, technology and society questions. Third, no matter what is achieved in the years of formal schooling, the rate of technological advance is so great that it would be impossible to prepare adequately for every future contingency. Would awareness and understanding of the scientific and moral issues associated with amniocentesis and fluorination be a sufficient preparation for subsequent participation in debates about computer privacy and the mining of uranium ore? Not only do the problem specifics change, but their contexts also. In short, serious attention to preparing citizens to make decisions on these issues requires not only curriculum change, but also structural change with appropriate new institutional provisions for the consideration of interactions of science and values at adult level.[33]

Possibilities and Problems

The formal disengagement of science, and science education, from values external to science was a deliberate step taken by scientists in the interests of the advancement of science. The re-engagement with values, what might be termed 'the revaluing of science education', could clearly produce some tension between different purposes of science teaching. Recognition of this is inherent in recent proposals that consideration of science, technology and society issues should be limited to 10 per cent of the available time for school science.[34]

However, it is important to recognize that science education could be 'revalued' in a number of different senses. First, there is the possibility of a more explicit recognition of the internal, constitutive values of science itself as objectives of science education. 'Curiosity', 'open-mindedness', 'a willingness to suspend judgment' and similar outcomes might be given greater prominence in lists of objectives and in assessment schemes. One difficulty here, however, is the problem of achieving agreement on what these constitutive values are. A listing such as:

> longing to know and to understand;
> questioning of all things;
> search for data and their meaning;
> demand for verification;
> respect for logic;
> consideration of premises;
> consideration of consequences[35]

is open to a number of objections. It could be argued that there is nothing here which is associated uniquely with science, as against any other area of rational inquiry, such as history. Furthermore, the actual practices of 'successful' scientists have not always been in accordance with such 'values' or 'virtues'. Judgment can be exercised as to when virtue is to be flouted, the end justifying the means. As for prescriptions about 'what works', or what is necessary 'to do science', these range from anarchistic exhortations (for example, Bridgeman's 'doing ones damnedest with one's mind, no holds barred') to Merton's institutional imperatives of 'communality, universalism, disinterestedness, and organized scepticism', to precise logical formulations of 'scientific method'. Perhaps, following J.R. Ravetz, what is needed here is a return to the point of origin of scientific knowledge in research schools where the craft character of scientific work is recognized. As Ravetz emphasises 'the work of scientific inquiry requires knowledge which is learned only through precept and experience in a multitude of particular cases.'[36] In particular, the learning of 'method' takes place 'almost entirely within the interpersonal channel, requiring personal contact, and a measure of personal sympathy between the parties. What is transmitted will be partly explicit, but partly tacit; principle, precept, and example are all mixed together'.[37] It would seem to follow that if an attempt is to be made to teach the constitutive values of science, then teachers must learn to practise the craft of genuine scientific inquiry, with students as their apprentices, learning by inculcation, reinforcement, guided practice and modelling. The practical problems of providing the experiences and personal contacts to make this a realistic possibility are equalled in difficulty only by those of assessing the outcomes in this domain of values education.

A second sense in which science education could be 'revalued' would be by achieving a greater awareness of what values are in fact being transmitted as part of the hidden curriculum of present-day science teaching. Making explicit these values, as illustrated above (pp. 163–5), would not necessarily lead to changes in practice, although it could. The prime effect would be to transform a perception of science classrooms and laboratories as value-free places, where consideration of gender, ethnicity, religion and politics are irrelevant, to one which acknowledges that value interactions can take place either to the detriment or the enhancement of learning.

The third sense in which school science education could be 'revalued' would be by making it serve new purposes such as 'the development and formulation of reasoned responses on science, technology and society issues'. Change in this direction is being advocated in many countries throughout the world, though the extent to which secondary school science teaching should adapt to the new goal of assisting decision-making on science-related controversial issues is a point of dispute. For some, the new goal should dominate all pre-professional science education. For others, any significant weakening of the effort to initiate students into the conceptual structures which scientists have constructed to interpret the natural world would disadvantage them, by reducing their competence to use science in the world of work. But even a modest step in the new direction will call into play classroom strategies which are unfamiliar to most teachers and students of science. The gathering of a balanced supply of information on some value-laden issues can be difficult and, of course, on many issues the prospect of achieving consensus will be as remote as in the adult world. The establishment and management of active and involved student groups and the promotion of purposeful discussion become of central importance. New competencies will have to be acquired by science teachers especially if charges of tendentiousness and indoctrination are to be avoided. Recognizing this, one Australian attempt to encourage the examination of science, technology and society issues in science lessons offered a set of guidelines:

'The teacher's role is to
(a) keep the discussion on target;
(b) allow groups to develop leadership, cooperation and critical evaluation;
(c) help students to avoid becoming set in their ideas before adequately exploring alternatives;
(d) help students to see other points of view and alternative explanations;
(e) help resolve (but not necessarily avoid) conflict within and between groups; and
(f) seek understanding and consensus rather than the making of ill-considered decisions or totally suppressing minority views.

Some means of helping to achieve these goals include:
(a) setting clearly defined tasks;
(b) setting tasks meaningful to the groups
(c) allowing groups a degree of self-selection so as to enhance cooperation and trust;
(d) not expecting results immediately, especially if groups have not worked together before;
(e) valuing all group members (but not necessarily their contributions); and

(f) valuing the group conclusions and decisions so as to foster continued involvement and cooperation'.[38]

Not all of these guidelines would be endorsed by those experienced in the practice of values education, but consideration of their application in the context of specific issues under discussion with particular groups of children might make one useful starting point for the in-service education of science teachers embarking on work in this field.

Revaluing science education in this third sense of linking it instrumentally to the development or clarification of student values on science-related issues might be interpreted as science education at long last coming of age and fulfilling its educational potential. Maturity, however, brings increased responsibilities. The demands of the innovation on teachers and students are at least as severe — it could be argued considerably more severe — than anything previously attempted in the reform of science teaching since the curriculum projects of the Sputnik era. It behoves us not to set unrealistic goals in this field.

Notes

1 CHAIN, PROFESSOR SIR ERNST (1970) 'Social responsibility and the scientist', *New Scientist*, 22 October, p. 166.
2 The words are Robert Hooke's, cited in MASON, S.F. (1953) *A History of the Sciences*, Routledge and Kegan Paul, p. 207.
3 MORRELL, J. and THACKRAY, A. (1981) *Gentlemen of Science*, Oxford, Clarendon Press, pp. 291–6.
4 KUHN, T.S. (1970) *The Structure of Scientific Revolutions*, (2nd. edn) Chicago, University of Chicago Press, p. 164.
5 See for example, RAVETZ, J.R. (1973) *Scientific Knowledge and its Social Problems*, Penguin Books, pp. 289–313.
6 LATOUR, B. and WOOLGAR, S. (1979) *Laboratory Life: The Social Construction of Scientific Facts*, London, Sage Publications.
7 It is true that some curriculum projects have included amongst their aims such outcomes as 'intellectual honesty', 'open-mindedness' and 'critical-mindedness', and attempts have been made to analyze the components of an affective domain; see for example KLOPFER, L.E. (1976) 'A structure for the affective domain in relation to science education', *Science Education*, 60, 3, pp. 299–312. The fact remains that such aims do not influence the practice of science teaching to any great extent, the emphasis being heavily on cognitive outcomes, for example, the science activity categories employed in the national monitoring of science attainments by the Assessment of Performance Unit of the DES (see for example Assessment of Perform-

ance Unit, Summary Report No. 12., (1982) *First Age 15 Science Survey*, London, DES p. 2.)
For a review of problems in measuring 'scientific attitudes' see GOULD, C.F. and HUKINS, A.A., (1980) 'Scientific attitudes: a review', *Studies in Science Education*, 7, pp. 129-61.
8 The Association for Science Education, (1981) *Education through Science: Policy Statement*, Hatfield, pp. 11-12.
9 BINNIE, H.H., (1978) Identifying affective goals in science education', *The Science Teacher*, 45, p. 29.
10 The Association for Science Education, Response by the Association for Science Education to the Committee of Inquiry into the Education of Children from Ethnic Minority Groups, 1982.
11 WILSON, B. (1981) *Cultural Contexts of Science and Mathematics Education: A Bibliographic Guide*, Centre for Studies in Science Education, University of Leeds, p. vii.
12 Annex to letter dated 8 March 1983 from Sir Keith Joseph, Secretary of State for Education and Science, to Miss I. Whittaker, Joint Chairman, Joint Council of GCE and CSE Boards, p. 2. Interestingly, whilst apparently insisting on the 'neutrality' of physics teaching, the Secretary of State required the study of history to promote 'the shared values which are a distinctive feature of British society and culture'. *The Times Educational Supplement*, 15 April 1983.
13 GILPIN, R. (1962) *American Scientists and Nuclear Weapons Policy*, Princeton University Press, p. 167.
14 COTGROVE, S. (1981) 'Risk, value, conflict and political legitimacy', in GRIFFITHS, R.F., *Dealing With Risk*. Manchester University Press, pp. 124-5.
15 See for example *Education*, 14 January 1983, p. 25; *The Times Educational Supplement*, 8 April 1983, p. 15, 11 March 1983, p. 1 and 27 May 1983, p. 16.
16 OLBY, R. (1982) 'Britain's resources of coal and spent uranium fuel', *Nature*, Vol. 296, 29 April, p. 801 (my emphasis)
17 FACTOR, L. and KOOSER, R. (1981) *Value Presuppositions in Science Textbooks: A Critical Bibliography*, Knox College, Galesburg, Illinois, USA.
18 GREGORY, R.A. (1916) *Discovery, or the Spirit and Service of Science*, London, pp. v-vii.
19 See for example PREECE, P. (1981) 'Uneven course', *The Guardian*, 24 March; LANCASTER-GAYE, R. *et. al*. 'Used or abused', *The Times Educational Supplement*, 13 March, p. 36.
20 See for example various papers on 'The politics of the hidden curriculum' in WHITTY, G. and YOUNG, M.F.D. (Eds.) (1976) *Exploration in the Politics of School Knowledge*, Nafferton Books. Also HARGREAVES, D. (1978) 'Power and the curriculum', in RICHARDS, C. (Ed.), *Power and the Curriculum*, Nafferton Books, pp. 97-108.

21 Research on girls and science education is summarized in KAMINSKI, D.M. (1982) 'Girls and mathematics and science: an annotated bibliography of British work, 1970–1981, *Studies in Science Education*, 9, pp. 81–108.
22 Ministry of Education. (1960) *Science in Secondary Schools*. Pamphlet No. 38. London, HMSO, pp. 26–7.
23 LUKES, S. (1973) *Individualism*, Oxford, Basil Blackwell.
24 See Bryan Wilson, *op. cit.*
25 WILLEY, R. (1982) *Teaching in Multicultural Britain*, Longman, for Schools Council, p. 21.
26 GHUMAN, P.A.S. (1978) 'Nature of intellectual development of Punjabi children', *International Journal of Psychology*, 13–14, pp. 281–94; TERAKAWA, T. and BROCK, W.H. (1978) 'The introduction of heurism into Japan, *History of Education*, 7, 1, pp. 35–44.
27 STRONCK, D.R. (1982) 'Sex education for science teachers', *The British Columbia Science Teacher*, 23, 3, spring, pp. 11–12.
28 *The British Columbia Science Teacher*, 23, 3, spring 1982, p. 5. The 'good fences make good neighbours' solution was endorsed by the Arkansas judgment on creationism in schools: see *Science*, 215, No. 4535, 19 February 1982, p. 942.
29 Heinemann Educational Books and the Association for Science Education, *Science in Society*, advertising leaflet, stating the aims of the course.
30 See for example NELKIN, D. (1982) 'Science and technology policy and the democratic process', *Studies in Science Education*, 9, pp. 47–64.
31 Biological Sciences Curriculum Study Project, *Innovations: The Social Consequences of Science and Technology*. SOLOMON, J. (1983) *Science in a Social Context*, Basil Blackwell and the Association for Science Education.
32 TRACHTMAN, L.A. (1981) 'The public understanding of science effort: a critique', *Science, Technology and Human Values*, 36, summer, pp. 10–15.
33 LAYTON, D. (1982) 'Science education and values education — an essential tension?' in HEAD, J. (Ed.) *Science for the Citizen*, London, The British Council, pp. 101–8.
34 International Council of Scientific Unions, (1980) *Newsletter from the Committee on the Teaching of Science*, Number 5, July, p. 4.
35 Educational Policies Commission, (1966) *Education and the Spirit of Science*, National Education Association, Washington, D.C., pp. 15–27.
36 RAVETZ, J.R. (1973) *Scientific Knowledge and its Social Problems*, Penguin Books, p. 101.
37 *Ibid.* p. 177.
38 HALL, W. *et. al.* (1983) *Teaching Science, Technology and Society in the Junior High School*, Brisbane College of Advanced Education, pp. 36–7.

2
Values Across The Curriculum-General Issues

Aims, Problems and Curriculum Contexts

Richard Pring

Education and Values

The introduction of pupils to a set of values is an inescapable task of education. This is partly a logical point, about education, partly a political point about the social consequences of education, and partly a sociological point about the present day demands upon the education system.

First, the logical point. R.S. Peters (1966) argues that education is an initiation into worthwhile activities. 'Education' is essentially an evaluative term. To refer to someone as an *educated* person would be to approve of what that person has accomplished in certain respects. What we would be picking out as valuable are certain qualities, namely, certain powers of the mind — the ability to reflect, to argue, to grasp difficult points, to appreciate, to understand, to reason. This is, of course, a much more complex thesis than I have time to elaborate on here, and it has been subjected to a great deal of refinement and criticism. But the main thrust of the analysis is surely correct, namely, that the *educational* activities promoted by any society are intimately connected with what that society believes to be a valuable form of life. Furthermore, the particular values embodied in what is designated to be educational will be about the kind of *persons* that the society wishes its young people to grow up into — the kind of sensitivities, mental powers, basic skills and knowledge, that are embodied in the traditions and the aspirations of that society. An educated person in Great Britain will need to read and write, to have grasped basic scientific and technological concepts, to have an historical perspective, to be acquainted with a literary tradition, and to have an appreciation of the arts.

What I am *not* saying is that by philosophical analysis one can arrive at those substantive values that educational activities ought to be promoting. Far from it. Different societies will emphasize different values. Social, economic and technological circumstances change so that there will be a changing list, as it were, of the virtues and qualities that we associate with the educated person. Even within any one relatively cohesive society there will be differences in what is valued which will be reflected in differences over what counts as educational. For example, within our own society there are different educational traditions reflecting significant disagreements about what are worthwhile forms of life and these are at the base of current educational controversy. I am thinking particularly of the recent emphasis upon the practical and upon vocational orientation — a concern for relevance to adult life as that is understood in a fairly utilitarian and pragmatic sense. Such a view of the educated person would contrast sharply with those values which stress learning for its own sake, a distancing from the immediate concerns of the society, a disdain for the practical and the relevant. My main point is that to educate someone does logically entail the introduction to a valued form of life but that what counts as a valued form of life is essentially a matter for moral debate. And teachers, insofar as they see themselves to be educating children rather than simply child-minding or training, are implicitly engaged in a moral enterprise — promoting a form of life as an intrinsically worthwhile one.

Secondly, the political point. Education is about the development of persons — about the initiation of young persons into a form of life which affects the sort of person they are going to be. Certain forms of education, for example, stress competitive, individualized learning. It is part of the educational system that pupils compete for a limited number of rewards and that they are judged in relationship to each other. Other forms of education stress cooperation, team work, interdependence. These are different personal values, but they both reflect and affect the form of society the young people are entering into. The ethos of any society is developed through various forces and will no doubt reflect the dominant economic form of life. Individuals born into and educated within that society will imbue those prevailing values. But the process must not be seen as one way and deterministic. An education that stresses rationality, critical examination of received assumptions, a wider historical and philosophical perspective will form the sort of person that in turn will affect the social ethos — possibly engaging in activities that challenge social values and social institutions. There is a social price to pay for encouraging children to think.

It is for this reason that different societies have, in different degrees, endeavoured to exercise political control over what happens in schools. How and what children think can always be evaluated in a political sense. This indeed underlies the hidden conflicts in current educational developments that Her Majesty's Inspectorate points out in *Curriculum 11 to 16* (1977)

> the educational system is charged by society ... with equipping young people to take their place as citizens and workers in adult life ... Secondly there is the responsibility for educating the 'autonomous citizen', a person able to think and act for herself or himself, to resist exploitation, to innovate and to be vigilant in the defence of liberty. These two functions do not always fit easily together. (p. 9)

There are several recent instances of the political significance of the values inherent within educational activities. Firstly, the attempt of the Assessment of Performance Unit to monitor pupils' performance in the area of personal and social development (central to the avowed aims of most schools) was quashed by the force of union and other opinions because of its political significance — the probing into the moral and political values and behaviours of pupils. The members of the working party were referred to as Nazis in the press and by a member of the Consultative Committee. Secondly, some submissions by subject panels of suggested syllabuses and assessment criteria for the new 16+ examination were rejected by the Secretary of State for their political implications (for example, the social questions raised about technological development in the sciences and the more global concerns of history). Thirdly, recent pre-vocational and vocational developments in full-time as well as in off-the-job education have placed emphasis upon wider social awareness, in particular an understanding of the situation in which young people find themselves. Such developments have, however, met with hostility on the part of some politicians and MSC officials, who have said that certain courses will close if such controversial areas are not omitted.

In short, educating young people is essentially political in that it is an imparting of knowledge, understanding, and values which may be the basis for critical examination of the values and institutions which make our society the kind of society it is.

Thirdly, the sociological point about current pressures upon schools to take on responsibility for promoting values. This is apparent from many recent documents. The Green Paper — *Education in Schools: a consultative document* listed the aims of schooling that, it was thought, the majority of people would agree with. The aims included

Richard Pring

(ii) to instil respect for moral values, for other people and for oneself, and tolerance of other races, religions, and ways of life.

This theme was developed further in the DES documents *A Framework for the School Curriculum* (1980) and *The School Curriculum* (1981). The latter develops what it means by the aim quoted above.

> There are also some essential constituents of the school curriculum which are often identified as subjects but which are as likely to feature in a variety of courses and programmes and may be more effectively covered if they are distributed across the curriculum. These concern personal and social development and can conveniently be grouped under the headings of moral education, health education (including sex education) and preparation for parenthood and family life.

The (now) explicit concern for personal and social education in 'official' curriculum documents needs, of course, to be translated into practical policy at the local level. And indeed this is what is happening. Devon LEA, for instance, produced its own discussion document that governing bodies of its secondary schools were asked to consider and to respond to, detailing the curriculum policy of their respective schools (see Devon County Council, 1982). And this is by no means untypical. A great number of schools now have some written policy on personal and social education, and have developed programmes accordingly.

Possibly the most significant changes in the educational system are occurring at the post 16 level — firstly, with the development of full-time pre-vocational courses and secondly, with the growth of MSC funded youth training programmes. The most significant document in the pre-vocational developments is the Mansell Report *A Basis for Choice* (FEU, 1979). This has become the basis of the City & Guilds of London Institute 365 courses (now available to schools pre-16), the Royal Society of Arts vocational preparation courses, and now the Certificate of Pre-vocational Education. The distinguishing feature of the pre-vocational courses outlined in ABC is the core curriculum, centred not on a range of discrete subjects, but on personal development and preparation for adult life. Such development and preparation will of course require some concentration upon curriculum areas that bear some relation to traditional subjects — communication skills, numeracy, political and economic literacy, for example. But of the twelve aims of the core, two relate directly to the major theme of this book.

Aim 4: To bring about an ability to develop satisfactory personal relationships with others.

Aim 5: To provide a basis on which the young person acquires a set of moral values applicable to issues in contemporary society.

It is of course easy to write down aims — these are so often the rhetoric of curriculum which bears little relation to the underlying values of the curriculum. But there are changes taking place in the pre-vocational area that reflect a radical shift in curriculum thinking and that are, through CGLI 365 courses and through the Technical and Vocational Education Initiative, affecting the aims and content of schooling pre-16 — particularly in the significance of values education. From the fringe of school life, guidance and counselling, tutorial work concerned with personal development, the exploration of personal values *vis-à-vis* the adult world have been brought to the centre of the curriculum life of the schools.

To sum up this section: schools and colleges are involved in promoting values. This is an inescapable part of the educational task — the development of persons through the selection and promotion of significant learning experiences. Furthermore, it arises from the unavoidable political significance and function of schools, in assisting in the development of a certain kind of citizen — whether through tacit promotion of the compliant. obedient, unquestioning, respectful adolescent or whether through the encouragement of critical, socially aware, and questioning students. Finally, it arises from the quite explicit pressures, now put upon schools to have a policy for personal and social development.

There are problems for schools taking on this task, unavoidable though it is. These I shall briefly outline in the next section. Then in the following section I will suggest ways in which schools might develop a curriculum that is centrally concerned with values. This will have two sections — a curriculum policy that transcends subject boundaries (and that takes on board the hidden values of the school) and a curriculum policy that looks at the explicit contribution of different sections of the formal curriculum.

Problems

The problems to be encountered in promoting values across the curriculum have already been introduced, albeit implicitly. They are chiefly the following:

Richard Pring

Ethical

It is one of the paradoxes of the moral life that we cannot escape moral questions yet at the same time remain unclear about how, rationally, to resolve them. Promoting a worthwhile form of life is part of what is meant by educating young people, but it is not easy to reconcile conflicting views about what is a worthwhile form of life. Educational debate thus takes on the very issues that have always beset moral philosophers. In an atmosphere of ethical scepticism, it is difficult to argue for the promotion of one set of values rather than another.

There are indeed various ways of replying to ethical scepticism. One is to agree with the general position and to adopt a curriculum policy of values clarification (see Simon, 1972; and Raths, 1966), where, in acknowledgement of the 'equal validity' of different points of view, pupils are helped to clarify and to make up their own minds about what is important. Shades (but only shades) of such a philosophical position are reflected in the Humanities Curriculum Project in which, by the adoption of a position of neutrality, the teacher encourages the pupils to develop different points of view on matters of social controversy.

Ethical scepticism, manifested in an indifference to different moral positions, is not a position I share. I have argued briefly in a recent book (Pring 1984, chapter 4) for the central role of moral traditions to which pupils need to be introduced. But it is a difficult argument to pursue in depth. Let it suffice here to say that to place the total burden of values clarification and of 'inventing right and wrong' (to refer to the subtitle of Mackie's book on ethics — see Mackie, 1977) on the children is to ignore the significance of the moral struggle, the critical debate, the sense of obligation and of right which are part of the moral form of life.

A distinction can be made between the form and the content of value judgments (see Pring, 1984, p. 58). Certainly the content — the specific 'dos' and 'don'ts' — will change from group to group, and from age to age. But it can be argued that, firstly, what counts as, say, a moral principle and, secondly, what are the basic moral principles (respect for persons and their interests, concern for the truth, keeping promises, etc) are not so ephemeral. Even values clarification presupposes the moral value of respecting the rights of individuals to take on responsibility for their own moral life.

This is too big a philosophical issue to enter into here. The point is that, whilst admitting the large area of unresolved controversy in matters of value which must affect the confidence of teachers to promote one set of values rather than another, one need not remain totally sceptical. There remains a range of values that can and should be promoted in schools concerned with the promotion of respect and dignity of each person, with taking on responsibility for the consequences of one's action, for telling and pursuing the truth, and for doing what one has undertaken to do. Of course, such general aspirations will need to be translated into more specific rules of action if they are to be learnt.

Political

Little more needs to be said in addition to what I have already spoken of. The promotion of values of whatever kind has its political implication, and thus will be resisted by those who wish to control or influence the kind of society that is being shaped. There is considerable pressure, for instance, to stop peace studies in schools — peace studies, we are told, is politically partisan. The assumption is, however, that so much of what has been taught in history is not politically partisan — the selection of heroes, the focus upon particular eras and events, the interpretation of events through textbooks. To some extent (although thanks to the resilience of young people, only to *some* extent) the control of the curriculum is the control of young people's minds, and then the control over the future shape of society. Hence, there will always be political problems to face in promoting values in schools.

Conceptual

These problems relate particularly to the pressures upon schools to promote personal, social and moral education. When one looks at the details one sees that PSME covers a vast range of skills, qualities, values, and understandings. How can one make some conceptual sense of this? Is it possible to pick out certain central values which can be the focus of curriculum development across the subjects and across the different learning experiences?

There are, I believe, such general values. They are to be developed not only through the content of the curriculum but also through the methods of teaching and through the general ethos of the school. This is important to remember, for too often, in taking seriously its role in introducing pupils to a worthwhile form of life, a school cannot think beyond the content of discrete subjects. And yet it is so often in terms of the modes of learning, of the kinds of relationships, and of the respect for rules and for those who are authors of those rules that significant personal and social development takes place and values are absorbed by the pupil.

Brevity forces me to be dogmatic. But key values that are affected by schools and that in turn affect all else are

(i) *the respect for rule-governed behaviour, and for the authorities* that exert control within a rule-governed social life. Piaget (1932) talks of the important shift from a position of unilateral respect for authority to one of mutual respect. Indeed, the relation of the young person to those in authority would seem to be one of the most significant factors in a person's moral growth — the ability to live a principled moral life, to take on responsibility for one's own actions, to think through the consequences of one's actions, to develop a sufficiently stable yet flexible set of values as to be able to cope with a difficult and often unpredictable future.

(ii) *the respect for persons, whether oneself or others*, and the development of that feeling for others which we call empathy. Empathy is both a feeling and an awareness. It is something that can be developed through the encouragement of imaginative insight, through the attempt to see things from another's point of view, through the impartial consideration of reasons that others give for what they believe in and what they do.

(iii) *respect for the truth* in the sense not only of telling the truth, but also of respecting the force of argument, of evidence, and of enquiry. There are values intrinsic to any academic or intellectual enterprise. Not cooking the books is one. Openness to criticism and alternative viewpoints is another.

(iv) *trusting and unselfish relationships* with others — significant friendships, if you like, which go beyond respect and empathy referred to above. These are not easily formed by many young people, and it is not clear how one can directly help them be formed. But a school can promote the sense of community, of mutual concern and support that provides the system within which more trusting and tolerant relationships can be formed.

(v) *a sense of justice and fairness* such that maldistribution of scarce resources, or arbitrary creation and application of rules, or undeserved or disproportionate punishment for behaviour creates a sense of moral outrage.

These are general values which can be developed in schools that transcend particular moral disagreements and that seem intimately connected with the educational enterprise. How then might they be promoted across the curriculum?

Values Across the Curriculum

Curriculum Context

It would be wrong to translate the general concern for personal and social development, and for developing in particular a set of defensible values, into the content of specific subjects — or indeed into a new subject called 'active tutorial work' or 'health education' or 'moral education'. For that could be but a distraction from the more important questions that a school should be asking about the impact of the curriculum as a whole upon the values of individual pupils.

First Hargreaves (1982) argues that

> ... our present secondary school system, largely through the hidden curriculum, exerts on many pupils, particularly but by no means exclusively from the working class, a destruction of their dignity which is so massive and pervasive that few subsequently recover from it.

His is a devastating attack upon a system of schooling which, despite the claims for personal development and the many programmes to that end, destroys the sense of personal worth. It is destroyed through constant pupil failure and through a dismissal by the system of those values which, however open to critical examination, are what the pupils prize and bring with them to school.

If pupils are to develop self-respect then their achievements need to be recognized, and their failure minimized. An interesting feature of many pre-vocational developments lies precisely in the steps taken to ensure that this happens. And these are *curriculum* innovations. A more *negotiated* curriculum (such as is now developing in some TVEI programmes, CGLI courses, and MSC sponsored training schemes) with contracts undertaken and with an increased guidance role for the teacher, is both a reflection of, and a contribution to, the respect given to a pupil as someone who can take on responsibility for his or her own learning.

Secondly, Rutter *et al* (1979) was a study of twelve schools in Inner London Education Authority. The main question it raised was: do schools make a difference? To answer this question the study needed to identify outcomes that seemed to be significant indicators of the worthwhile differences that schools make — for example, examination results, pupil behaviour, and pupil attendance. Furthermore, it analyzed those factors which were closely related with these differences in outcomes. The results were quite startling. Schools that were roughly comparable in social and physical conditions produced very different results. Poor behaviour, for example, measured in terms of vandalism, graffiti, bullying, rudeness was significantly different in different schools where these differences could not be accounted for in terms of the values or behaviours or expectations that the pupils brought with them into the schools. The report correlated these outcomes not with any single factor but with clusters of factors. What above all seemed significant was the 'ethos' of the school.

To get at the ethos of the school, you need to examine the various stable procedures through which business is conducted towards individuals and their work, towards the commmunity as a whole, and towards those outside the school. And picking out these procedures is exactly what Rutter did. What correlated highly with approved behaviour were such procedures as displaying children's work on the wall, recognizing achievement through praise, preparing thoroughly for lessons, displaying as often as possible trust in pupils by giving them responsibility, turning up punctually for class. The account given on pages 182–98 of Rutter (1979) could be used by a school as a basis for examining its own particular 'ethos'.

Thirdly, we can attribute justice not only to individuals but also to communities. Indeed, the qualitative improvement in moral judgment — being able to handle moral issues in a mature and principled way — mapped out by both Piaget and Kohlberg required the right social conditions. And indeed it was this that Kohlberg (1982) tried to capture in his 'just community' schools

> In summary, the current demand for moral education is a demand that our society becomes more of a just community. If our society is to become a more just community, it needs democratic schools. This was the demand and dream of Dewey.

Kohlberg argues here and elsewhere that if you want the pupils to develop a more mature and responsible attitude towards adopting a set of defensible moral values, at the centre of which is a concern for justice and fairness, then you must also be concerned for the 'moral atmosphere', the ethos, of the school. If you want pupils to think and act fairly, then you must ensure that the institution they are in is an open and a fair one.

In an interesting piece of research Power and Reimer (1978)

describe their analysis of the moral atmosphere of the school based on transcripts of community meetings, interviews with individual students about the school, and observations of the interactions between students and teachers in different situations. The five questions they were investigating were:

(i) What are the collective normative values (for example, trusting implicitly in others' honesty) operating in the school?
(ii) How well established and how influential upon individuals are those normative values?
(iii) What sense of community has developed in the school?
(iv) How well established and influential upon individuals is the sense of community?
(v) At what stage of moral thinking are the students in their perceptions of, and talk about, these normative values and this sense of community?

Power and Reimer noted a developmental sequence in both the normative values within a group and in the sense of community. Furthermore, they noted that as these developed, so the individuals in their judgment and behaviour developed accordingly. The general point is that, contrary to so many attempts to explain moral development (in particular the development of persons within whom there is little or no conflict between higher levels of moral thinking and how they typically behave), the connection between thought and action depends upon the general atmosphere and expectations of the wider community. How individuals behave will so often depend upon the values that are operating in public life and upon the interaction between the individual and those values within a developed sense of community.

To conclude this section on curriculum context, I would emphasize the need, in values education, to examine the impact of the curriculum as a whole — the atmosphere of the school, the relationship between teacher and pupil, and the exercise of authority — upon the values that pupils develop. It is too easy to fob off to curriculum content, and to programmes of instruction, tasks which really require a more fundamental examination of the relationships within and structures of the institution.

There is clearly a need to examine the values which are often hidden in the unexamined methods of teaching, structures of authority, and modes of control, and yet which correlate so strongly with educational and behavioural outcomes. The moral atmosphere of the school or classroom seems to be the key element in translating thought into action and in ensuring the personal and moral growth of the individual pupil. In particular the classroom teacher might consider

(i) how he or she might encourage greater mutual respect between teacher and pupil and between pupil and pupil;
(ii) create a climate of caring and fairness;
(iii) ensure a sense of achievement rather than of failure and of personal worth;
(iv) develop a habit of deliberation and reflective learning;
(v) introduce systematic discussion of significant socio-moral issues;
(vi) approach learning cooperatively rather than competitively;
(vii) foster care for the group and eventually the wider community rather than for self-interest; and
(viii) increase group responsibility for decisions taken.

At a very general level it is a matter of respect for persons. But such a value needs to be translated into specific attitudes and procedures if the appropriate classroom ethos is to be achieved.

It would be wrong, however, if this concern for the context of the curriculum should be seen as an excuse for doing nothing about the formal, timetabled curriculum itself. To that we must now turn.

Curriculum Content

Each subject will, in its own way, contribute to the development of values — this is a logical point, as I explained earlier, about these subjects as *educational* activities. Each subject involves a selection of knowledge which in theory at least is thought to be valuable in the development of the mental powers and the sensitivities of young persons. They will involve, in theory at least, modes of enquiry that embody general principles of critical scrutiny, respect for evidence and the truth, respect for others as the source of criticism and of ideas. Each subject teacher will adopt teaching methods that will implicitly convey messages about personal relationships, the exercise of authority, the treatment of people as worthy of respect.

Nonetheless, it may be the case (and this is argued throughout the book) that each subject will have a distinctive contribution to make because of its own particular subject matter. It is not the aim of this paper to suggest what these distinctive contributions might be. Rather do I want to suggest a framework within which individual subjects might examine their contributions.

Aims, Problems and Curriculum Contexts

One needs to distinguish between the general values that I have, in passing, referred to — the respect for persons, whether oneself or others; the respect for truth (including evidence, argument, criticism); acceptance of responsibility for one's actions; a concern for justice and fairness — and the specific contexts and issues in which these more general values are seen to be relevant. It is wrong to think of values, and the promotion of values, as somehow abstracted from concrete situations, types of moral question, and particular choices. And these in turn will require specific kinds of knowledge and understanding that subjects will provide.

Each subject will need to ask therefore what contribution it makes (and how it makes it) to the range of values and value issues suggested in the following matrix. It is crude and simplistic, but no doubt each

Table 1

General Values	Curriculum Content	Teaching Methods
Respect for oneself as a person Respect for others as persons Respect for the truth (evidence etc) Concern for fairness Acceptance of responsibility for own actions 'Mutual respect' (rather than 'unilateral respect') for authority		

Specific issues to which these more general values are applied

	Knowledge	Cognitive Capacity	Attitude	Behaviour

Moral rules
Social issues
  race
  sexism
  nuclear war
  environment
Politics
  citizenship
  community
  rule of law
Place within society
  occupation
  status and class
  economic and social needs
Health
  physical
  mental
Ideals				

subject specialist will be able to adapt it to his or her own special needs or requirements.

It would be useful for different subjects to see whether and how they contribute to the development of the more general values and to an 'evaluative' appreciation of the more specific issues and contexts. There are three reasons for the utility of such a self-examination. First, there may be values and their application which by default, do not get developed because the right questions are not asked by someone who sees the impact of the curriculum as a whole. Secondly, it may be the case that a lot of what happens in the classroom might militate against the values which, at least in theory, the school is promoting. Thirdly, such an exercise is one way into raising the broader curriculum issues connected with values which so often are neglected.

References

Assessment of Performance Unit (1981), *Personal and Social Development*, London, DES.
DES (1977), *Education in Schools: a consultative document*, London, HMSO.
DES (1980), *A Framework for the School Curriculum*, London, HMSO.
DES (1981), *The School Curriculum*, London, HMSO.
DES/HMI (1977), *Curriculum 11 to 16*, London, DES.
Devon County Council (1982), *Personal, Social and Moral Education*, Exeter, Devon Education Department.
Further Education Unit (1979), *A Basis for Choice*, London, DES.
HARGREAVES, D. (1982), *The Challenge for the Comprehensive School*, London, Routledge and Kegan Paul.
KOHLBERG, L. (1982), 'Recent Work in Moral Education', in WARD, L.O., *The Ethical Dimension of the School Curriculum*, Swansea, Pineridge Press.
MACKIE, J.L. (1977), *Ethics: Inventing Right and Wrong*, Harmondsworth, Penguin.
PETERS, R.S. (1966), *Ethics and Education*, London, Allen and Unwin.
PIAGET, J. (1932), *The Moral Judgment of the Child*, London, Routledge and Kegan Paul.
POWER, C. and REIMER, J. (1978), 'Moral Atmosphere' in DAMON, W. *New Direction for Child Development and Moral Development*, San Francisco, Jossey-Bass.
PRING, R.A. (1984), *Personal and Social Education in the Curriculum*, London, Hodder and Stoughton.
RATH, L.E. (1966), *Values & Teaching*, Wembley, Merrill.
RUTTER, M. *et. al.* (1979), *15000 Hours*, London, Open Books.
SIMON, S.B. (1972), *Values Clarification: a handbook*, New York, Hart.

Values and the Social Organization of Schooling

Janet Strivens

No educational institution is value-neutral in terms of its social rganization. Implicitly or explicitly, values are reflected in the type of educational experience a society provides or permits for its young people. These are most easily recognized through studies of individual institutions where values are explicitly articulated (sometimes in opposition to the mainstream), but the values fostered and perpetuated by the system as a whole should not therefore be overlooked. This tends to happen when the educational system within a society has been established without major upheaval for some time, so that institutional arrangements are taken for granted. Historical and comparative analyses then become particularly important in reminding us that educational institutions like other social institutions come into being at specific historical junctures and reflect the purposes of those who created them. When dramatic changes occur in a society, it is sometimes the case that the creation of an education system is accompanied by a rhetoric containing a very clear articulation of social, moral and political values. In countries like Russia and China, where the socialization of the young is seen as a vital part of the process of building a new order in society, the relationship between the children's social experience at school and the values of the wider society is clearly spelt out in educational writings and perceptible in educational practices.[1]

Traditionally (typically) the British prefer not to think about this relationship too closely. In a society committed in its political rhetoric to pluralism and toleration it is more comfortable to consider the social organization of education as governed by administrative convenience and efficiency than to examine the hidden messages the system conveys to children about the hierarchical nature of society, the lack of participation by the majority in decision-making processes and the dragging weight of traditional authority. (We do not even attempt to ensure, as for example, the Germans do, that our children routinely learn about the nature of democracy; significantly, the only subject statutorily required in schools is religious education, not political education). Nevertheless, it is a deeply rooted belief within British culture that the experience of school should play a central part in the character formation of the young person. In both historical and fictional accounts of schooling, it often appears that the enrichment of the mind is only a secondary function of the British school[2]; its primary value lies quite explicitly in the social experiences the child must learn to negotiate. Through this process he (generally) will internalize a range of social values which cannot successfully be imparted by the family or even the local community. The genealogy of this belief undoubtedly goes back to the origins of organized educational establishments, but its peculiarly British delineation comes of age in the development of boys' public schools in the nineteenth century.

The Nineteenth Century Public School

There is no lack of evidence to suggest that the ideas and beliefs which created the 'monolith' (Gathorne-Hardy, 1977) of the boys' public school system between approximately 1824 and 1900 have permeated popular educational discourse throughout the twentieth century. In 1982, a report by the West Midlands Conservative Women's Advisory Committee could criticize teachers in these terms:

> they have learned to deride the simple values of disciplines exemplified in the school stories of our earlier generation from Tom Brown to Greyfriars, but these values and disciplines were the cement of our civilization.[3]

To understand the problems faced by those educationalists who feel the cement may have set the wrong way, we need to take a brief look back at these ideas and beliefs, and the institutions which embodied them. And, lest we are seduced ourselves by the power of images absorbed since childhood, we need to remember for whom these institutions were intended; the sons of a small ruling elite who were to be trained to inherit the roles of leaders of men irrespective of the talents and capacities they might individually possess. Just as the existence of social hierarchies was accepted without question, the notion of a universal right to education was completely alien to these men who founded the 'great' public schools. Even those who attempted in the course of the nineteenth century to extend the availability of this form of schooling thought only of broadening and supporting the existing elite with the well-socialized offspring of the prosperous middle classes.[4]

Honey's (1977) meticulous survey of the development of public schools in the nineteenth century corrects the tendency to see a unified conception of the nature and purpose of such schooling from Arnold of Rugby onwards. Nevertheless, through the diversity of concerns and strategies some common themes emerge. Many of those who founded or developed educational establishments in the nineteenth century shared a deep sense of dismay about the state of society, its depravity, anarchy and profanity, and felt an urgent need both to strengthen the young to resist its influence and to prepare them as the agents of reform. Their confidence in the ability of schooling to change society varied (then as now); Arnold himself, a deeply religious man with a strong conviction of the reality and power of original sin, appears to have been highly sceptical of the possibility of achieving such a goal. (*ibid*, p. 24)

In terms of the organizational strategies intended to achieve these goals, some generalizations can be made. Throughout the nineteenth century, belief in the value of organized games gained currency, as a means of developing a habitual tendency in the pupil to see himself as part of a team, relying on the contribution of other members but not failing to play his own part. Off the field the boys typically experienced a strongly hierarchical structure intended to foster a ready acceptance of authority and later, as prefects, the responsible exercise of it. The strength of this structure was increased through the frequent use of house-systems, the breaking up of institutions into smaller units to encourage in-group identification and loyalty. Partly as a consequence of this, pupils experienced almost no privacy. Honey suggests that this organizational characteristic of school life contributed to rigid denial of the expression of feeling, especially feelings of weakness and vulnerability, which has become part of the British upper-class stereotype.

Since the ideals of these Victorian educationalists still cast their influence over our modern conceptions of the functions of schools, it is valuable to remind ourselves of the problems they encountered. The available evidence suggests that most schools failed with many pupils for much of the time in establishing obedience, chastity and a concern for the pain and suffering of their fellow men. On the other hand, outright revolts by pupils became less common, relations between masters and pupils became closer and more human, and the capacity of the institution to induce identification and loyalty to itself increased. While the Victorian public school may have been rather unsuccessful at fostering the individual moral values it prized, it clearly had powerful effects on the social values of its pupils. Intense commitment to the institution, usually implying a particular relationship of obligation to fellow alumni, could last throughout an ex-pupil's adult life. It is worth considering again the factors which helped to create this commitment, a phenomenon which still exerts a powerful hold on our imagination. The humanizing of staff-pupil relations has been mentioned, as has the effect (through membership of the school, the House or both) of belonging to a small selective group which encourages solidarity within itself and competition with outsiders. Honey also notes that both the age range and social class range of pupils narrowed over the period, fortifying the sense of community. And it is worth considering that the sufferings and humiliations so frequently inflicted as a matter of tradition on the younger pupils by the older had the psychological effects of initiation into tribal societies, in invoking total identification with a social world they could not escape.

However, this success in itself revealed a weakness in the school-as-a-microcosm-of-society model. The very clarity of the rules and boundaries, achievements and rewards of this tightly-knit society was not necessarily the best preparation for the uncertainties of adult life. Coupled with the intensity of adolescence, it seemed to many ex-pupils like a high point of experience to which the rest of life never really compared. Cyril Connolly's brilliant description of this feeling in his Theory of Permanent Adolescence is well known[5]. Perhaps this became a special problem for the public schoolboys of Connolly's era, with the Empire breaking up, the masses (including women) all the time demanding a greater say in the running of their affairs and the availability of a role for the ruling elite dwindling.

To what extent did the public school founders and heads consciously use the social organization of their school to instil certain values and beliefs about society? Arnold used to refer to Rugby as a 'little commonwealth' and other writers used the image of the school as a microcosm of society. If the social and political ideology fostered by the system is not as clearly articulated as the moral and religious values, this is perhaps because from time to time individuals became uncomfortably aware of conflicts between the Christian virtues they preached and those values which the system encouraged. One potential area of contradiction was the almost universal encouragement of competitiveness, the spirit of 'lawful rivalry' or 'emulation' as Arnold called it, one of the 'organizing principles of Victorian society (*ibid*, p. 15).

Another conflict of values thrown up by the system was that between solidarity with one's fellow pupils, obedience to authority and respect for truth. Readers of *Tom Brown's Schooldays* will note that it was considered far more unethical to lie to a fellow pupil than to a master. There remains an ambivalence within the British system about the relative importance of solidarity with one's peers and conflicting moral principles, such that 'tale-telling' is a worse crime than refusing information to a teacher in the full knowledge of a sin committed by one's classmate. It is interesting to speculate on the extent to which this attitude stems from class loyalty (the perception by the boys of a difference in social status between themselves and those paid to teach them), or how far it is an inevitable consequence of living as the less powerful group within a hierarchical institution. From time to time, schools have deliberately attempted to overcome this ethic of peer solidarity by advancing the interests of the community as a whole. However, this concept appears to be unattractive to the British psyche, at least in regard to schooling. There is generally a slight revulsion against the stereotype of Communist education, where a 'defaulter is likely to find himself at a meeting of his classmates ... where they solemnly discuss his shortcomings, point out the error of his ways, appeal to him to remember his duty to the class, the school, the Motherland, the building of Communism' (Grant, 1964, p. 58). Commenting on the 'honour' system introduced at Gresham's in the early twentieth century and its later manifestations, Gathorne-Hardy (1977) evinces his own distaste for 'the excessive use of ... community shame' as a disciplinary device even where this replaces the use of corporal punishment (p. 322).

Counter-Tendencies: The 'Progressive' Movement

Undeniably the values and practices of the public schools system have exerted a strong influence on the subsequent development of education for the masses. Against the weight of this tradition we have barely four decades of attempting to work out an appropriate model of universal secondary education. There were, of course, countervailing influences in the development of working-class educational movements throughout the nineteenth century, which sought different educational goals and developed correspondingly different forms of organization.[6] Yet the effects of those alternative traditions of popular education have been muted in comparison. Ironically, more attention has been given to counter-tendencies within the elite system itself, where conflicting ideas and beliefs gave rise to a number of institutions with organizational characteristics markedly different from the mainstream. These exceptional institutions could arise from a fundamentally different view of human nature, believing the child to be essentially good rather than steeped in original sin; or from a desire to achieve a more equitable, just and democratic society; or from the more pragmatic influence of an open-minded individual genuinely seeking more effective methods of teaching and learning.

Two examples from the late eighteenth and early nineteenth century, which Gathorne-Hardy (1977) claims to have been extremely successful for a limited period, were Cheam, founded by William Gilpin in 1752, and Hazelwood under the Hill brothers:

> [Gilpin's] overriding principle was that a school should be a microcosm of, and training-ground for, society as he saw it. Thus there should be no tyranny, no arbitrary master rule, but the boys should be involved with the law and understand it. There could be no hierarchy, no fagging system, since all should be equal under the law. A code was drawn up and regularly read out. If it was transgressed, Gilpin would mete out punishment. But a boy could appeal if he felt he had been treated unjustly and disputed cases were heard by a jury of twelve boys. If the appeal were successful Gilpin paid compensation (p. 275).

Similar ideas inspired the organization of Hazelwood in the 1820s:

> The school was self-governing, with the laws made by a committee of boys, and enforced by an elected court presided over by a judge. Corporal punishment, public disgrace and lines were abolished. Instead marks were awarded for everything — work, behaviour, voluntary labour — and a boy's standing in the school judged by his marks. The punishment of the court was to fine marks; extreme cases were kept in on holidays (p. 276).

Both Gilpin and the Hill brothers believed in the capacity of their pupils to respond to fair treatment and participatory government by developing a commitment to justice and the common good. It is valuable to be reminded that such beliefs have been embodied in educational practice at various points in history, even though the influence of Cheam and Hazelwood was to be submerged for a time by the rise of very different ideas about schooling.

In the present century it is still the case that the most widely-known attempts to create an organizational climate in schools compatible with liberal-democratic values have taken place outside the state educational system, as the inspiration of an individual educationalist. Freed from many of the constraints of LEA and DES control, such institutions have been better able to select and train their own staff in accordance with their philosophy, placing their own requirements on both teachers and pupils. Certain independent schools, of which Dartington in Devon is perhaps the most extreme example, have become renowned for their attempts to change the nature of the school experience, the relations between staff and pupils and the definition of the purpose of education. Depending on one's point of view, such schools have been seen as the vanguard of a move towards genuine liberatory education suited for a democratic society, as hotbeds of permissive morality and anarchy, or as yet another more hypocritical manifestation of the elitism of the ruling classes.

Probably the most internationally famous is the school founded by A.S. Neill, Summerhill, which still continues after his death to attract educationalists from all over the world. Neill himself was influenced by the ideas of Homer Lane, an American educationalist who tried unsuccessfully to establish a school in Dorset modelled on an institution called the Junior Republic, a self-governing community for young delinquents which existed in the United States at the beginning of the century. Lane's school was called the Little Commonwealth and was based on the belief that children learn the need for law and order through the anarchy resulting from allowing them complete freedom. His experiment ended disastrously before it had a chance to prove itself. Neill's attempt in 1924 to implement a similar philosophy survived, and gave rise to a number of highly influential books on his experience.

This is not the place to attempt an evaluation of the success of Neill's school. However, it is important to note that the pupils at Summerhill were a highly unrepresentative group, not only because their parents could afford to pay for their education, but because many of them were extremely difficult and unhappy children. Although Neill may have wanted to make his own contribution towards changing the world, the dominant theme of his work is the development and happiness of the individual child. The most direct inheritors of his ideas have been some of the independent special schools catering for the 'maladjusted' pupil, run as 'therapeutic communities'[7]. Independent special schools yield some interesting examples of the deliberate manipulation of organizational climate to achieve their aims. Again, we have institutions created by individuals inspired by particular beliefs about human nature and society. Staff can be specially selected and trained to contribute towards the creation of a specific part of the treatment process.

Some important lessons could be learned from comparative studies of the effects of these institutions. However, there are serious drawbacks to generalizing from their experience. They cater for an unusual client group, consisting of children who for a variety of reasons could not be tolerated within the state system. But the general criteria by which children are put into what Tomlinson (1982) calls 'non-normative' categories of special need (maladjusted, educationally subnormal etc. as opposed to blind, physically handicapped etc.) have been shown to be highly suspect[8]. In addition, very little research has been done on the process by which children are selected for *specific institutions* within special school provision, whether independent or state and with whichever treatment orientation. Consequently it is very difficult to evaluate the effects of different regimes and make comparisons.

Innovation Within the State System

However exciting we may find the institutions discussed so far, their influence is restricted by the fact that their clientele is drawn from a small and mainly privileged section of society. Their ability to experiment with different forms of organization depends on their success in an education marketplace to which the majority of the population have no access. If they succeed, the unrepresentative nature of the pupils they process can be used as an argument against the wider application of their ideas to affect all sections of society. This is why it is so important to have before us examples of 'ordinary' schools which have, nevertheless, attempted to offer a different kind of educational experience to a wide range of children, against the mainstream of the educational system. Let us look first at what they are attempting to change.

> Until very recently it was true to say that the overwhelming formative influence upon the English concept of the 'school' was the model furnished by the boys' 'public' boarding-school which grew up in Victorian times (Honey, 1977, p. xiii).

What kind of influence was this? To the extent that grammar schools tried to ape the mores of the public school, they adopted rituals intended to increase the pupils' identification with the institution, and solidarity with each other as alumni. The importance of competition was stressed, both on the games field and for academic honours. Strict rules on uniform were the norm, with attendant regulations about acceptable behaviour for wearing the uniform outside school. House systems and prefects, often with differentiating marks of dress, fostered both group identity and the acceptance of hierarchy.

This clearly worked to a limited extent when pupils were aware that they had been selected for a given institution, thus helping to create the spirit of an 'in-group'. Inevitably, it has been much less successful under a comprehensive system where, in principle at least, no school's population is any more an 'elite' than any other. Attempts to create the feeling of group membership through such rituals as uniform are quite likely to be resented by that section of the school population who know that they will never attain positions of authority within this particular hierarchy — the big payoff under the most repressive and tyrannical prefectorial system. Many influential studies of state schools in recent times document the importance of different pupil cultures within a school, some of which are increasingly alienated from and in opposition to the values of the school as they move up the age range.

It is only in part a response to the problems created by this alienated and apparently growing minority that some educationalists have reconsidered the role of schooling in a modern democracy, and in particular, the appropriateness of traditional models of social organization. If all children are to be prepared emotionally as well as intellectually to play a full role as responsible citizens (including the capacity to voice criticism and attempt to bring about change), they need the experience during their schooldays of participation in the decisions affecting their communal life. They need to experience what it means to be part of a group in terms of mutual trust, cooperation and consideration. A particularly important lesson to learn is the operation of justice within a group of equals, where all agree to be bound by a rule that has been jointly formulated and is intended to further the common good.

An early attempt (in terms of the relatively new 'comprehensive tradition') was made in London in 1960, when four schools were amalgamated in Islington to form a new, multiracial, coeducational comprehensive school, Risinghill. Its head, Michael Duane, attempted to establish a caring community of teachers and pupils who would treat each other with friendliness, respect, tolerance and fairness. Risinghill lasted as a school for five years before being closed down. Its fate, emotionally documented by Berg (1968) has passed into educational legend. It seems from her account that one important factor which finally helped to shake the school apart was the conflict between the head's philosophy and those staff who wished to preserve the traditional degree of distance between teacher and pupil. The specific issue which focussed the conflict was the use of corporal punishment, which Duane refused to countenance.

Risinghill was, of course, the result of a forced marriage between institutions with rather different educational traditions. This is rarely a happy state within which to hammer out a new philosophy (see, for example, Ball, 1985). Almost without exception, those schools which have become renowned for their attempts to redefine educational goals within the constraints of the state system have begun as new schools, with a corresponding degree of freedom to choose appropriate staff to work out new structures and procedures (Moon, 1983).

Undoubtedly the best-known of these is Countesthorpe Community College in Leicestershire.

> When Countesthorpe first opened in 1970 it was acclaimed in the *Times Educational Supplement* as 'the most advanced working model in Europe of the theories of secondary education that have developed in the last few years, as a result of the practical experience of universal secondary education.' It was the jewel in the crown of its instigator, Stewart Mason, the Director of Education for Leicestershire ... (Moon, 1983, p. 9).

Clearly, Countesthorpe began its life carrying a tremendous burden of responsibility for progressive educational ideas. And it had no easy ride; it had to withstand considerable public opposition including a hostile press at the same time that it was trying to find its way, upholding its beliefs about new forms of schooling while being able to recognize and learn from them.

The watchfulness of the media for any signs of failure was reminiscent of the problems faced by Dartington but with this difference; unlike Dartington pupils, the children attending Countesthorpe had little choice but to go to their local community comprehensive, thus failure met with more bitter attack. Nevertheless, the school has established itself and developed as a significant example of practical innovation.

At first sight the features which differentiate Countesthorpe from more conventional comprehensive schools seem to involve staff more than pupils:

> One of the more unusual features of the school is the commitment of the staff to democratic government. The principal does not take the policy decisions (though he is ultimately responsible for them), neither do an oligarchy of senior members of staff. Such decisions are made at meetings of the staff, ancillaries and students which we (rather quaintly) call 'Moots'. Moot policy provides the framework within which a rotating standing committee deals with the weekly business thrown up by the normal functioning of the school. When it comes across an item which cannot be dealt with within existing policy, a moot may be called and the framework changed or amended ... the democratice ethos pervades teams and departments as well as the relationship with students ... (*ibid.*, p. 6)

While pupils share to a considerable extent in the overall decision-making, and enjoy considerable autonomy over their own pursuits, this is not taken to the lengths that Summerhill attempted. It is arguable that in a state comprehensive school the abandoning of a hierarchical structure of authority among the staff alone is a sufficiently radical difference to change significantly the experience of the pupils. The precise extent of pupils' participation is not easy to determine from the outside and has no doubt varied over the fourteen years of the school's existence. Still, it is accepted as a valued principle, against which the school's practice can be continually assessed.

It is not easy to assess the influence on mainstream education of the experience of these schools. While there is a limited amount of filmed and written material available, a more important process is probably the slow infiltration of ideas through teachers moving around, who find themselves frustrated and constrained within a traditionally organized school and know that a workable alternative exists.

Democratic Schooling in the U.S.: The 'Just Community'

We have so far concentrated exclusively on British examples of the deliberate utilization of organizational structure to reflect and develop certain values. However, the British experience reflects a problem faced by all Western democracies over the socialization of the young. The same contradictions emerge between the desire to ensure the continuation of existing forms of society and the rhetoric of a freely choosing citizenry, prepared by their education to exercise their right to a voice. It seems inevitable within such societies that individuals and groups should from time to time attempt to establish new forms of schooling which they perceive as more in line with the values of a liberal democracy. Of particular interest and importance are examples from the USA, since these have developed within a rather different social and political climate, and their influence has spread to many other Western countries.

Scharf (1977) claims that attempts to establish democratic forms of schooling are a relatively recent phenomenon in the United States:

> Early American educators clearly did not intend nor believe that students should have a voice in their own education. The colonial school was authoritarian, teacher-directed and often punitive. The meaning of 'democratic education' implied the problem of entrance (i.e. that all children should be able to enter

the 'common school') and not the problem of substance (i.e. that education should be structured democratically). (p. 89)

The great educationalist Dewey argued repeatedly the importance of 'this fundamental principle of the school as a form of community life'. Current interpretations of the Deweyite philosophy take a number of different forms, from the 'free school' movement through community-based education to school self-government involving teachers, students and administrators. Scharf notes that 'such efforts to genuinely involve adolescents in the political processes of the school have been rare' and 'the failures associated with the school democracy movement clearly outweigh its successes' (p. 91). He attributes this failure to the lack of a properly articulated theoretical basis to the development of democratic values. Such a theoretical basis can be found, he believes, in the 'Just Community' approach. The approach has explicitly 'articulated the role of community within a theory of moral education' (Power, 1983). The body of theory guiding this approach has been provided by the work of Lawrence Kohlberg and his associates, on the process of the development of moral judgment.[9]

A typical example of the Just Community approach in action is the Cluster School in Cambridge, Massachusetts (Wasserman, 1976). As a natural extension of his work on moral judgment, Kohlberg became interested in the possibility of setting up a school, designed to develop the moral maturity of its pupils through the experience of shared responsibility for all aspects of the school's communal life. The opportunity arose to put his ideas into practice in part of a large, urban comprehensive school in 1974. The renamed 'Cluster School', around seventy volunteer students and seven staff, has a curriculum which integrates moral discussions into English and social studies, and a governance structure based on participatory democracy. Decisions are made at community meetings preceded by small group discussions. The school has proved itself capable of handling such potentially destructive issues as marijuana use and stealing within the school, both initially commonplace. The reasons for and against such behaviour and the possible responses of the community are discussed in group and community meetings, and the idea of community responsibility has slowly evolved. Staff and students are equally bound by the decisions of these meetings and have an equal say in the discussions.

The Effects of Schooling in the Development of Values

For all the institutions which have been discussed, those involved in their establishment and operation have regarded the social experience of the members as crucially significant in the development of values. As we have already remarked, there may be a number of different motivations underlying the establishment of such schools. Some of the founders and teachers are primarily concerned with the development of the individual child, others have a broader perspective of schooling for the needs of society. Sometimes the justification is couched in moral terms, sometimes it is more clearly socio-political. The common theme running through the ventures described in the preceding pages which differentiates them from the school experience of the average child seems to lie in the breakdown of hierarchical authority, giving each person within the social group a share in the decisions affecting his or her life.

It remains to be asked if these institutions have been effective in achieving their aims. What evidence do we have that the social experience of schooling has any significant effect on the social development of children? This is even more difficult to answer than the more frequently raised question of the academic effects of different forms of schooling[10]. We have some evidence that under certain types of school regime children are less likely to be disruptive in class or avoid school altogether by truanting, but this only suggests a degree of tolerance on the part of the child rather than the active acquisition of certain values. The evidence is minimal of any long-term effects of school on the understanding of society or the development of ethics. It remains largely an act of faith by those who believe in the importance of educational experience that new projects and experiments continue to be established.

Clearly any such evaluation of the effects of different forms of school organization is far from easy to carry out. There are considerable difficulties involved both in assessing school ethos or 'climate' and in measuring the development of values and attitudes. Not least of these is the necessity to carry out careful comparative studies of the processes of schooling within different institutions. Recently some encouragement has been given to this type of research through the publication of *Fifteen Thousand Hours* (Rutter, *et al.*, 1979), a comparative study of twelve London comprehensive schools. This has been the most systematic attempt in British research to explore the relationship between school factors and educatonal outcomes, and clear differences emerged between the institutions studied which could not be accounted for in terms of the 'quality' of their pupil intake. Although the study has been criticized in many respects, not least for the lack of an attempt to theorize the relationship between organizational factors and pupils' experience, it has reawakened interest in this important area of research[11]. However, attempts to conceptualize organizational 'climate' will inevitably run into the kinds of value-laden issues raised in this chapter, and the possibility of making clear statements from research findings still seems at some distance. Fortunately this is unlikely to deter those who have taught within the type of institution we have been discussing and experienced a different relationship between teacher and pupil from continuing to experiment and work towards radical changes in the traditional forms of schooling. Whether their ideas are influential or ignored is an important question for all concerned with values education.

Notes

1 The educationalist Krupskaya, wife of Lenin, wrote 'Since socialism is a particular organization, it is of special value to children to become exposed in school to some organizational experience'. Ungoed-Thomas (1970) cites this in a discussion of the Soviet 'concern to teach socialist morality by controlling the school structure'.
2 At least when the fiction belongs to the genre of the public school tale. The influence of this stereotype depends not only on novels but even more significantly on children's magazines from the late nineteenth century onwards, whose readership extended far beyond the echelons of society from whom the clients of private education were drawn. That such an attitude existed in reality is nicely illustrated by Honey's (1977) quote from General Plumer addressing an Old Etonian dinner in 1916: 'We are often told that they taught us nothing at Eton. It may be so, but I think they taught it very well.' (p. 228)
3 Quoted in the Staffordshire *Evening Sentinel*, 19 May 1982.
4 See Honey, *op. cit.*, chapter 2 on the efforts of J.L. Brereton and Nathaniel Woodard 'to extend the provision of public-school education to a very much wider section of the middle classes'.
5 '... It is the theory that the experience undergone by boys at the great public schools, their triumphs and disappointments, are so intense as to dominate their lives and arrest their development ... Early laurels weigh like lead and of many of the boys whom I knew at Eton, I can say that their lives are over. Those who knew them then knew them at their best and fullest; now in their early thirties they are haunted ruins ...' (Connolly, 1961, p. 271).

6 See, for example, *Unpopular Education*, pp. 34–40, by the Education Group of the Centre for Contemporary Cultural Studies.
7 Therapeutic communities such as New Barns or Peper Harrow draw many of their ideas on treatment from neo-psychoanalytic or other psychodynamic theories of personality development. See HANVEY (1980) for a discussion of their growth and characteristics.
8 'The major sociological interest in the categories of special education lies in the conflation of *normative* with *non-normative* conditions ... there can be some normative agreement about the existence of certain categories of handicap, or special need, particularly those which fall into what is currently defined as a medical sphere of competence ... on the other hand, the categories of feeble-minded, educationally subnormal, maladjusted and disruptive are not, and never will be, normative categories ... the answer to the question 'what is' an ESN.M child or a maladjusted child will depend more on the values, beliefs and interests of those making the judgment than on any qualities intrinsic to the child ... from a sociological point of view it becomes very important to ask what sort of children, in terms of social class and background, are being selected for the non-normative categories' ... (Tomlinson, 1982, pp. 65–7)
9 Kohlberg's theoretical work has developed over a considerable period of time and has been published in many different places. Changes in the formulation of his theory and the difficulties which may be encountered in tracing the different versions can create problems for a British audience. Useful sources are KOHLBERG (1984); WEINREICH-HASTE (1983); WEINREICH-HASTE and LOCKE (1983); MODGIL and MODGIL (1985); MOSHER (1980).
10 See, for example, REYNOLDS' (1982) review of school effectiveness, and OUSTON (1985).
11 See STRIVENS (1985) for a discussion of the conceptualization of school climate, and ANDERSON (1982) for a review of research.

References

ANDERSON, C.S. (1982) 'The search for school climate: a review of research', *Review of Educational Research*, 52, pp. 368–420.
BALL, S. (1985) 'School politics, teachers' careers and educational change: a case-study of becoming a comprehensive school' in WALKER S. and BARTON L. (Eds.) *Education and Social Change*, London, Croom Helm.
BERG, L. (1968) *Risinghill: Death of a Comprehensive School*, Harmondsworth, Penguin Books.
Centre for Contemporary Cultural Studies (1981) *Unpopular Education*, London, Hutchinson.
CONNOLLY, C. (1961) *Enemies of Promise*, Harmondsworth, Penguin Books.

GATHORNE-HARDY, J. (1977) *The Public School Phenomenon*, London, Hodder and Stoughton.
GRANT, N. (1964) *Soviet Education*, Harmondsworth, Penguin Books.
HANVEY, C. (1980) 'What is a therapeutic community?' *Mind Out*, No 43.
HONEY, J.R. DE S. (1977) *Tom Brown's Universe*, London, Millington.
KOHLBERG, L. (1984) *Essays on Moral Development: Vol. 2 The Psychology of Moral Development*, New York, Harper and Row.
MODGIL, S. and MODGIL, C. (Eds.) (1985) *Kohlberg: Consensus and Controversy*, Lewes, Falmer Press.
MOON, B. (Ed.) (1983) *Comprehensive Schools: Challenge and Change*, Windsor, NFER-Nelson.
MOSHER, R. (1980) *Moral Education: A First Generation of Research*, New York, Praeger.
OUSTON, J. (1985) 'Issues in the assessment of school outcomes' in REYNOLDS, D. (Ed.) *School Effectiveness*, Lewes, Falmer Press.
POWER, C. (1983) 'Evaluating just communities: towards a method for assessing the moral atmosphere of the school' in KUHMERKER, L. MENTKOWSKI, M. and ERICKSON, L. (Eds.) *Evaluating Moral Development*, Schenectady, NY, Character Research Press.
REYNOLDS, D. (1982) 'School effectiveness research — a review of the literature', *School Organization and Management Abstracts*, 1, pp. 5–14.
REYNOLDS, D. (Ed.) (1985) *School Effectiveness*, Lewes, Falmer Press.
RUTTER, M., MAUGHAN, B., MORTIMORE, P. and OUSTON, J. (1979) *Fifteen Thousand Hours*, London, Open Books.
SCHARF, P. (1977) 'Moral development and democratic schooling', *Theory into Practice*, 16, 2, pp. 89–96.
STRIVENS, J. (1985) 'School climate: A review of a problematic concept' in REYNOLDS, D. (Ed.) *School Effectiveness*, Lewes, Falmer Press.
TOMLINSON, S. (1982) *A Sociology of Special Education*, London, Routledge and Kegan Paul.
UNGOED-THOMAS, J. (1970) 'Moral education in the Soviet Union', *Moral Education*, 2, 1, pp. 3–10.
WASSERMAN, E.R. (1976) 'Implementing Kohlberg's "Just Community Concept" in an alternative school', *Social Education*, 16, pp. 203–7.
WEINREICH-HASTE, H. (1983) 'Developmental moral theory, with special reference to Kohlberg', *Educational Analysis*, 5, 1, pp. 5–15.
WEINREICH-HASTE, H. and LOCKE, D. (1983) *Morality in the Making: Judgment, Action and Social Context*, Chichester; John Wiley and Sons.

Values Teaching: Some Classroom Principles

Peter Tomlinson

Having looked at the central aims and issues of values education (Richard Pring's chapter) and then at the important question of school ethos/atmosphere (Janet Strivens' chapter), the present chapter will complete this tightening of focus in considering the interaction of teacher and taught in the classroom. It will deal, as we might say, with 'getting through' to the pupil or, in more formal terminology, with psychological and social-psychological aspects of value influences.

Starting with aims and going on to means and process, as these chapters have tended, seems only logical. But it should also be noticed that effective psychological understanding not only illuminates the processes by which we might seek to influence our pupils, but also provides the terms in which we might formulate our aims and gives us an idea of which aims are realistic in a particular setting, for a given age-group, and so forth. For example, a starkly rational view of human action as generated systematically and deliberately by conscious thought (very much a strand of traditional common sense) will yield a rather different conception of moral and social maturity than a somewhat more messy view which accepts also that people can be skilful, habitual and relatively automatic in their sensitivities, dispositions and reactions. So the emphasis here will be on process, though the chapter has relevance for product: after all, the process-product distinction *is* only a distinction, not a separation.

The issues seem to reduce at base to the twofold question of action and insight: *what* can/should I as a teacher *do* to further my chosen educational aims and *why* should I do it that way rather than some other way? These are general issues for all teachers, but in this book and this chapter we will consider their application to value-related aspects of subject teaching. And of course, however relevant its insights and prescriptions might hopefully be, a written offering like the present one is more orientated to the consideration of generally applicable insights than to the direct influencing of action through concrete recipes. For the insights being sought by the teacher who would develop the value-related aspects of his or her subject teaching concern such questions as: how do people, especially young ones in schools, respond to particular teaching processes and settings; how may they learn or change or perhaps rebel in the face of particular approaches or as a result of given experiences, tasks, ways of being treated; how can one gauge the difficulty or accessibility of particular perspectives, decision-making approaches, ideas, forms of awareness which it might be thought desirable to promote; what are the roles of formal and informal aspects of the teacher and teaching situation? And virtually any human being, hopefully every teacher, must know that such questions have no simple, universal concrete answers on which one could build a foolproof (or at least teacher-proof) recipe for successful action. Pupils vary, teachers vary, different pupils are different with different teachers, and so forth. On the other hand, despite the complexity and variation, there are perhaps general insights and principles that may be applied flexibly and adaptively to varying contexts. What can teachers turn to in the hope of gaining such insights?

In the first place they can and will consult their own experience and that of others known to them and facing similar tasks. This goes almost without saying, but its importance perhaps needs emphasizing in the face of some teachers' apparent tendencies to downgrade their own experience in the face of formal theory and research (of which they seem to have equally unrealistic requirements, paradoxically, that it deliver the goods of specific-yet-universally-applicable-prescription and insight). Having said this, there is always the need to critically appraise the scope and validity of personal experience, so as to apply its lessons intelligently to further tasks.

Second, they may learn from new techniques and approaches which they see as relevant and adaptable to their own situations. Such possibilities would include new teaching ideas in their subject, the application of pastoral and counselling-type activities in teaching, the transfer of new approaches from other subject area developments, to mention but three. The perceived relevance of such practical initiatives surely stems in large part from the fact that they are pitched in terms close to teachers' own ways of thinking about their teaching and that their aims are such that teachers can identify with them. Once again, however, there is the need not only to be open to such possibilities, but also to be critically aware of their potential limitations.

This brings us to our third area of potential resources for the teacher, namely formal theory and research. The connection is that formal theory represents no more than the systematic elaboration of ideas, testing of possibilities, and qualifying of their application potential. So, whilst personal experience and practical innovation can to some extent be evaluated informally and in their own terms, pursuit of criticality and sound insights will tend to lead towards systematic research and formal theory. But because systematic pursuit tends towards precision, depth of treatment and the development of abstractions specific to particular issues which may become far removed from the original impetus of practical educational problems, it is not surprising that formal theory is so often seen as irrelevant by practising teachers — although there are also other reasons, as hinted above. The underlying problem is that issues in teaching are not simple: on examination they are seen to be typically complex and subtle, needing particular attention to context and care not to overgeneralize. For education involves people and people are, putting it mildly, relatively complex realities. More complex still: education always involves people interacting with each other in purposive ways, with there being no guarantee that pupils' purposes are the same as their teachers', let alone their preferred means for furthering them! All of which implies that developing and appraising realistic educational insights is no easy matter — though it an unavoidable task if intelligent teaching is to take place. A further problem is that the systematic precision of educational and social science research has tended to spawn ideas and schools of thought which, though they each have a certain coherence and self-sufficiency (think of any of the great psychological paradigms, for instance, such as Skinnerianism or Piagetian cognitivism), really deal only with certain aspects of the person. In the real classroom, however, one meets whole persons, not parts ready-labelled for theoretical pigeon-holing and treatment!

This means that in facing available educational theory the teacher needs to be intelligently and critically eclectic, open to insights from the various sources, but vigilant as to their potential scope, internal consistency, and actual supporting evidence. For intelligent deployment, he will need to see how these various ideas relate to each other, especially when they have been emphasized by different approaches. This last task is actually not quite so difficult as it sounds, since it can and does occur that essentially similar ideas are sometimes dressed up in very different terminology and supported by apparently different kinds of evidence when presented by different psychological schools (see Tomlinson and Smith, 1985). All of which will help combat any tendency towards simple-recipe-seeking, as well as directing towards a coherent set of manageable insights, around which more specific issues can be considered.

The remainder of this chapter will attempt to draw out just such a small number of central principles; that is, to draw out some relevant insights confirmed across a number of psychological approaches, to show their links with what is implicit in practical innovations and approaches, and to very briefly suggest some implications for value aspects of subject teaching.

Issues, Topics, Perspectives, Learning Tasks Vary in their Difficulty as a Function of their Complexity and Subtlety

This point might seem an obvious one that is picked up by all teachers, who, especially if they trained in the last couple of decades, will have had heavy doses of Piagetian theory stressing the progressive acquisition of more complex forms of thinking by children. Even if this were so, it would still be worth pointing out its centrality and the fact that there is considerable formal evidence to support the view. But in looking at classroom practice (one's own included, I must admit), one is constantly finding instances where the complexity of a task or communication is being overlooked, especially when it is more or less incidental or implicit with respect to the formal content of one's planned lesson (an opportunistic illustration, for example). And in any case, some teachers seem very slow to pick up the idea. The fact that Piagetian work has featured so strongly in teacher training courses does not at all guarantee that any, even the most relevant of its teaching implications will have been grasped and applied, especially when one remembers that Piaget seems so often to be misrepresented as a maturationist describing the inevitable sequence of intellectual acquisitions all children attain with increasing age. Even taking account of recent critiques of what Piaget did actually have to say (for example, Brown and Desforges, 1979), the other side of the Piagetian coin seems more useful educationally, namely that the order of acquisition of the different types of thought operation described by Piaget be seen as an ordering of their difficulty (i.e. tasks characteristic of later stages are more difficult than those defining earlier stages).

Unfortunately, there are at least two difficulties in the way of practically applying Piagetian characterizations of task difficulty to personal, social and broader value-related aspects of curriculum subjects. The first is the formal-symbolic logical terms in which Inhelder and Piaget (1958 and 1964) characterized developmental stages of reasoning and the second is that their original and major applications have been to the content matter of physical sciences. However, there have been developments in both of these aspects which should assist their educational application to the domains of interest in this book.

Regarding the developmental difficulty of different kinds of thought tasks, neo-Piagetian researchers such as Pascual-Leone (1970) and Case (1981) have proposed a general model in which difficulty is related to (a) the number of items of information that must be taken into account at any one time in order to solve a problem, as well as to (b) the ease with which such aspects can be discerned. Of even more direct relevance to assessing the difficulty of educational tasks is the recent SOLO taxonomy put forward by Biggs and Collis (1982), which these authors illustratively apply to the teaching of history, elementary mathematics, English, geography and modern languages.

Likewise, over the last decade or so cognitive developmental research has expanded from its original physical science and mathematical focus to take in the domain of social cognition (cf. Flavell and Ross, 1981). Of central relevance to the concerns of this book is the monumental work of Lawrence Kohlberg on the development of moral reasoning (see Scharf, 1978 for a very readable introduction and set of discussions). Kohlberg's work indicates that there is a developmental sequence of perspectives on the terms and nature of social justice, in which individual, pre-moral outlooks are prior to a second level in which conventionality underlies the perspective, which is in turn followed by a post-conventional, moral outlook in which consideration is extended to all persons. Conversely, this work can be taken to indicate that these three levels and the two stages at each of them constitute a rank ordering of difficulty of the sorts of social and value-related considerations one might want to bring into treatments of value aspects of curriculum subjects.

Whilst Kohlberg's ideas have spawned a vast amount of research, including their application to classroom social and moral education, they have not been without their critics, and the reader who wishes to consider their possible application to her subject and its value aspects is recommended to consult not just an introductory treatment but also Modgil and Modgil's recent collection *Lawrence Kohlberg: Consensus and Controversy* (1985).

The point, then, is that value-related aspects of particular subjects are themselves likely to involve varying difficulty for pupils, just as much as are the traditionally central concepts and principles of those knowledge domains. The teacher who would develop such aspects of his subject must therefore look quite closely at what he is going to ask of his pupils in dealing with them, with the above-mentioned sources offering one possible line of assistance in doing so.

Importance of Specifics for Comprehension and Interest

The point was made above that the difficulty of a thought task depends heavily on its complexity and that there are various formal characteristics of such complexity whereby its extent may be assessed. But it is not necessarily true that all tasks of a given level of complexity pose the same ease or difficulty to pupils. There is now much evidence (see Tomlinson, 1981, chapter 3) for the view that although human beings internally represent their world in organized, economical ways — since their cognitive limitations and its richness demand this — nevertheless, they do so in terms that are relatively specific. For instance, logical reasoning about concrete subject matter with which we are familiar is easier than dealing with abstract general terms. It is not as if we carried a manual of logic around inside our heads and applied it with equal ease to any problem of a given complexity, or that we consulted internal dictionaries to tell what counts under a given concept (for example 'Is it a person, is it a bird?' etc.), rather, we understand and think very much in terms of our existing experience in relatively specific terms, in whose recording familiarity and significance will have played a large part (see Claxton, 1984, for some good illustrations). Recent work in science teaching, for instance Driver (1982) has confirmed this in showing how pupils typically bring their own *very varied* implicit ideas and theories regarding what the teacher may be wishing to treat formally and generally. This emphasis on the individual nature of people's perspectives and ways of making sense has been central to the cognitive theory of personality put forward by George Kelly (see Pope and Keen, 1982, for an introduction to Kelly's personal construct theory in the educational context).

This suggests, as proponents of meaningful learning and teaching have long advocated, that to maximize the chances of really getting through to our pupils, we must sooner or later make connections with things, events and issues with which they are familiar and which interest them. Other aspects of learning theory (Tomlinson, 1981, chapter 4) would support the notion that interest and relevance are not just optional extras to be used by 'romantic softies', but enhance actual comprehension and effective learning as such. This in turn requires a potentially high degree of learner-centredness in the sense that what one pupil is familiar with, another isn't necessarily: it is individuals who have and store experiences, so that what makes sense and what appears relevant varies from pupil to pupil. 'Naturally', many would say, but one suspects that it is not just class size that makes too many teachers teach as if to a collective mind whose background experience approximates to their own. If we want our pupils to take seriously value-related aspects of our subject, therefore, we shall not have much impact unless we can find ways into *their* experiences, which can turn out surprisingly different from our own.

Finding such ways in will not suffice on its own, however. In fact, especially in the area of values, it can be downright dangerous to leave things at that — for instance, their existing experience may be severely restricted and narrow and their mode of thinking socially stereotyped. Having gained access to what makes sense to the pupil, one then has to get them thinking about it, developing and reflecting upon it, seeing its advantages and shortcomings. Otherwise one runs the risk of merely practising current knowledge and reinforcing existing prejudices. This needs to be done whilst keeping in mind a related point also emphasized by modern psychology, namely:

The Active Nature of Pupil Learning Processes

By this I mean that whether in their sensory awareness of physical surroundings or in their perception of meaningful communication, let alone their treatment of significant problems, human beings (including school pupils!) stamp their imprints at various stages and in various ways. Modern psychology has established very clearly that even in simply attending to physical events around us, we are selective, perceiving what we can, what we expect, what we wish — all of which is typically far less than what is available to us in reality. We make sense by relating to what *we* already know and understand. We go about resolving *our* uncertainties according to *our* resources, which may be relatively specific. This notion of an active subject has been particularly emphasized by Piaget, with his notion of assimilation (balanced by the receptive notion of accommodation), although the hard supporting evidence from modern experimental psychology is seldom presented in educational treatments of Piaget.

The basic implication of this insight is that teaching cannot simply consist of telling. It must enlist the pupil's own active participation since, as the psychology of skill acquisition shows us, what gets processed gets learned. The trick is then to ensure that the pupil indeed processes what one wishes to have him acquire: meaningfully rather than in a rote or superficial way, on task rather than off task. This means considering the teaching process very much as a conversational process, as Gordon Pask puts it, in which the pupil's participation is encouraged and monitored by non-threatening opportunities to show what he or she has made of the process so far. One form such a conversational approach may obviously take is the small group discussion. The need to keep pupils 'on task' and deploying useful thinking skills (which I suspect to be the concern that makes quite a few teachers wary of discussion methods) is underlined by at least two studies in the moral education research area. Maitland and Goldman (1974) found that small groups discussing moral and social dilemmas only made progress as indicated by Kohlberg moral judgment maturity levels when they were required to come to a consensus. Similarly, through carefully monitoring small group discussions of similar dilemmas, Berkowitz and Gibbs (1981) found that progress in moral perspective level tended to require active probing of each other's reasoning, as opposed to mere repetition, agreement or disagreement with what had been simply heard. Small group (and for that matter, moreso large and class group) discussion does require considerable subskills and attitudes of its participants, such as waiting one's turn, attentive listening, control of emotional reaction, and so on — and this is even more of a requirement for the sort of thorough processing indicated by Berkowitz's studies. The fact that many children do not seem to bring such skills and attitudes with them imposes a preliminary educative task on the teacher who would reap the considerable benefits of guided group discussion. Ways of implementing such a task include playing communication games, having clear initial rules of turn-taking with firm chairmanship, and a range of other tactics now gaining popularity under the label of lifeskills teaching.

If the traditional teacher-dominated 'dustbin-filling' approach is insufficient from an intellectual point of view, then it is likely to be even more disadvantageous from a motivational perspective, which is of paramount importance where value influences are at stake, though this too needs balancing comment. One of the basic personal motives recognized by modern social psychology is *reactance*, that is, our tendency to restore and maintain a sense of freedom. Without pretending that there aren't other somewhat offsetting motives within young humans, it is clear that any constraint associated with teachers' attempts to promote such aims as open-minded reflection, respect for other points of view, and so forth, is likely to have negative effects, especially with secondary school adolescent pupils. This leaves the teacher, particularly the secondary teacher, in a difficult position. Not only is schooling compulsory, but adolescents have well-developed and shrewd defences with which they are capable of combatting not just the perceived invasions by others but also their own short and longer term interests (compare, for instance, the good old standby reaction 'Boring!'). Many of the ways of countering such problems involve the notion of social definition, which will be introduced under the next heading.

Varying Levels of Awareness and Their Consequences

The common-sense psychology shared implicitly by many of us still seems to portray people and their actions in a *dualistic* way which leads to a *rationalistic* view. That is, it sees the person as consisting of mind and body: the mind as a totally aware chamber of mainly verbal thoughts, which direct our actions in a rational manner — we 'know what we're doing' (unlike animals) and so we are responsible for those actions. It is difficult to know just how clearly and widely this view is held, in spite of its contradictions in much of our everyday experience and behaviour, but there is informal and formal evidence (cf. Henry, in progress) for its prevalence. My impression is that teacher trainees are confirmed in their dualistic views and rationalism by their encounters with Piaget's cognitive psychological ideas, which do after all start from the notion that children do think. And in any event, when one turns to such an important influence in moral and social development research as Kohlberg, one finds him stressing the central role of conscious thinking in both moral evaluation and action (see Tomlinson, 1985).

It is important to realize that whilst this mind-body view may be nice and clean, even obvious, it is in fact far too simple and clearcut to account for many aspects of our everyday experience and behaviour, aspects which have been studied systematically by experimental psychology. From experimental research (see Tomlinson, 1981, chapters 2 and 3) it is very well established that human beings can pick up and process information, including guiding their actions systematically, at a number of different levels of awareness. The fully self-aware *focal attention* that seems most familiar to us as we 'look out from just behind our eyes' or 'talk to ourselves inside our heads' is only one mode of processing information, and it is very limited: in this mode we can only attend to one thing at a time and the rate at which we can consciously deal with new items is quite limited (about three per second on some estimates). We could not achieve most of our everyday actions unless much of what we do was *unconsciously automatic*. Put differently, most of our everyday activity is *skilled*, it has become relatively effortless, systematically automatized — and this applies not just to our movements and actions, but also to the picking up and linking of information to direct and coordinate such moves. A link between these two very different levels of processing is provided by yet another form of awareness, the *pre-attentive* or out-of-the-corner-of-the-eye way we have of keeping tabs on the horizons of our conscious field. And there are various forms of evidence that these unconscious and pre-conscious forms of awareness are particularly important in the values domain, that is, where it is a question of pleasure or pain, preference or aversion. For instance, it has been shown that when people are already consciously processing an incoming spoken message, they will not be able to identify words from a separate source which are accompanied by mild electric shock, yet these words will later elicit an emotional arousal response, which the person cannot account for.

This is not the place to go further into these sorts of finding, but the above points strongly underline the importance of pupils' *total* (not just their conscious) reactions to and incidental learning from contexts. They give us a more specific grasp on the effects of school atmosphere and ethos mentioned by Richard Pring and discussed by Janet Strivens; both pupils and teachers are all the time soaking up far more than they are consciously aware. However, in the present chapter my focus is limited to face-to-face interaction within the classroom, laboratory, gym and other teaching settings, and the above points have various implications for such face-to-face situations (though these too have their forms of atmosphere).

A first implication concerns our stances towards pupils. They do not simply respond to the content of our words, but, potentially anyway, to anything we present them with. Most of us 'know' this in a conscious, 'informally theoretical' way, but the skilled, automatic quality of our social interactions means that our nonverbal channels such as facial expression, voice tone, etc. (see Tomlinson, 1981, chapter 8 for a systematic coverage) may be communicating messages that are not what we would want ('nonverbal leakage' as it has been termed), or at least that are being misconstrued — perhaps also unconsciously — by pupils, who are thereby 'put off' or otherwise missed. Perhaps as a legacy of the dualism mentioned earlier, with its myth that normal humans know all of what they're doing, there does not seem to be much of a tradition of systematic, constructive self-examination in the teaching profession, at any level, though the notion of a 'hidden curriculum' of implicit messages (Hargreaves, 1978) is by now well-established in educational thinking. It is important to point out, however, that whilst analyzing the possible significance of particular formal arrangements may pose its difficulties (for instance, the nature and role of school assembly — see

Bailey, 1978), the sorts of informal, incidental classroom-based features mentioned above are not going to be picked up and corrected without systematic efforts by teachers to gain feedback on their teaching, whether they use audio- or video-recording, or the informal appraisals of trusted colleagues on the team.

A more positive application of these insights concerns the way that *social definition* may be used as a management technique to further the teacher's aims. By social definition is broadly meant the way that people's actions stem 'naturally' from the way they perceive and define a situation. Such perceptions and definitions are complex and often subtle, and they are not typically done in a purely conscious, deliberate way; rather, features of the situation are picked up and reacted to in the usual skilful, relatively automatic way mentioned earlier. If one can get another person to (implicitly, remember) define a situation in a given way, so that certain expectations and actions naturally follow, then one may have exerted a powerful and implicit form of influence. For instance, Danziger (1976) gives as examples the role of social definitional influences in the selling of encyclopaedias and the obtaining of police confessions. The point of application in the present context is that management and guidance of pupil activities, especially secondary pupil activities, would be a precarious and disjointed affair indeed if it were all regulated by conscious confrontation and influence: even in those cases where the normal expectations of school-type behaviour seem to have broken down, it may still be possible to influence pupils into the types of discussion or other exercise one wishes to promote, by various means of implicitly signalling the naturalness of so doing and by making the experience a meaningful and happy one as far as possible. This may sound as if it is verging on the romantic, but consider the likely ineffectiveness of a 'parade ground' approach with respect to all but the crudest of social dispositions. When it comes to value-related areas the positive involvement of pupils is so essential that the sorts of suggestions for constructive approaches offered by Roberson (1981) cannot seriously be ignored. I am aware that to say this is to court accusations of indoctrination from some quarters. What one says about that depends on one's concept of indoctrination (see Snook, 1972), but the central point here is that implicit social definitional means may be required in order to get pupils taking the trouble to use their personal powers in the pursuit of critical appraisal which will form a basis for their rational autonomy. The familiar point could also be made that, as the evidence quoted earlier indicates, implicit processes are inevitable by virtue of the skilled nature of human action, so that one had better make sure they serve defensible aims rather than random or negative outcomes.

A further implication of varying levels of awareness and processing relates to assessment. Some aspects and aims of value-related teaching are so subtle or so long-term, or both, that it appears impossible to imagine how they could ever be systematically assessed. But insofar as one can hope to see results in, say, the direction of the sorts of aim suggested by Richard Pring elsewhere in this volume, one is sooner or later faced with the question of pinning down some sorts of indicators of such outcome possibilities. It seems worth pointing out here that the points made in the present section make the conscious-verbal types of assessment items so typical of schooling inadequate, at least on their own — though the development of other forms of assessment, whether formal or informal, systematic or intuitive, will require all the more analysis and cross-validation, for as well as its aims being amongst the most subtle, the area of values is also just about the most prone to personal reaction and subjective bias.

Insight and Skill

Many of the points made in the preceding pages might be combined under a heading such as 'implications of applying the concept of skill to values education' — though that would announce a more systematic treatment than space has allowed, for the modern psychology of skill does begin to do justice to the complexity of human beings, and what it gains in validity, it loses in simplicity. Pupils and teachers, we are all multifaceted and our learning progress is not typically smooth and direct; four steps forward and three back is nearer the usual mark. The point, on which I will close, is that even a small set of principles such as those suggested here will take time to become implemented in our actions: we do not become skilled overnight. We only do so by attempting to apply our knowledge, insights and best hunches, by monitoring the process and its outcomes, and by attempting to modify our next efforts on that basis. And we need to do this repeatedly, using whatever means of feedback and guidance our situation offers. Whatever resources, principles and experience may be available from elsewhere, the situation we face in a given classroom on any particular occasion is always unique in important respects. As teachers we therefore need considerable open, flexible skills. Insights and possibilities such as those offered by this book will hopefully be of assistance, but it is up to the individual teacher to apply them intelligently in skilled practice.

References

Bailey, J.R. (1978) 'Implicit moral education in secondary schools', *Journal of Moral Education*, 8, pp. 32–40.

Berkowitz, M.W. and Gibbs, J. (1981) 'Transactive communication as a condition for moral development', paper read at the SRCD Conference, Boston.

Biggs, J.B. and Collis, K. (1982) *Evaluating the Quality of Learning: The SOLO taxonomy*, London, Academic Press.

Brown, G. and Desforges, C. (1979) *Piaget's Theory: A Psychological Critique*, London, Routledge and Kegan Paul.

Case, R. (1981) 'Intellectual development: A systematic re-interpretation', in Farley, F.H. and Gordon, N.J. (Eds.) *Psychology and Education: The State of the Union*, Berkeley, McCutchan.

Claxton, G. (1984) *Live and Learn*, London, Harper and Row.

Danziger, K. (1976) *Interpersonal Communication*, New York, Pergamon.

Driver, R. (1982) *The pupil as Scientist?* Milton Keynes, Open University Press.

Flavell, J.H. and Ross, L. (Eds.) (1981) *Social Cognitive Development: Frontiers and Possible Futures*, Cambridge, Cambridge University Press.

Hargreaves, D.H. (1978) 'Power and paracurriculum', in Richards, C. (Ed.) *Power and the Curriculum*, Nafferton, Nafferton Books.

Henry, I.C. 'The concept of 'person' in children and adolescents', PhD study in progress, School of Education, University of Leeds.

Inhelder, B. and Piaget, J. (1958) *The Growth of Logical Thinking from Childhood to Adolescence*, London, Routledge and Kegan Paul.

Inhelder, B. and Piaget, J. (1964) *The Early Growth of Logic in the Child*, London, Routledge and Kegan Paul.

Maitland, K.R. and Goldman, J.R. (1974) 'Moral judgment as a function of peer group interaction', *Journal of Personality and Social Psychology*, 30, pp. 699–704.

Modgil., S. and Modgil., C. (Eds.) (1986) *Lawrence Kohlbery: Consensus and Controversy*, Lewes, Falmer Press.

Pascual-Leone, J. (1970) 'A mathematical model for the transition rule in Piaget's developmental stages', *Acta Psychologica*, 32, pp. 301–45.

Pope, M. and Keen, T. (1982) *Personal Construct Theory and Education*, London, Academic Press.

Robertson, J. (1981) *Effective Classroom Control*, London, Hodder and Stoughton.

Scharf, P. (Ed.) (1978) *Readings in Moral Education*, Minneapolis, Holt.

Snook, I.A. (1972) *Concepts of Indoctrination: philosophical essays*, London, Routledge and Kegan Paul.

Tomlinson, P.D. (1981) *Understanding Teaching: Interactive Educational Psychology*, London, McGraw-Hill.

TOMLINSON, P.D. (1986) 'Kohlberg's moral psychology: Any advance on the present stage?' in MODGIL, S. and MODGIL, C. (Eds.) *Lawrence Kohlberg: Consensus and Controversy*, Lewes, Falmer Press.

TOMLINSON, P.D. and SMITH, R.N. (1985) 'Training intelligent teachers: some implications of the psychology of skill', in FRANCIS, H. (Ed.) *Learning to Teach: Psychology in Teacher Education*, Lewes, Falmer Press.

Notes on Contributors

BRIAN ALLISON is Professor of Education and Head of the Centre for Postgraduate Studies in Education, Leicester Polytechnic. He has taught art and design to all age levels and abilities in schools and colleges, and gained his doctorate from the University of Reading in 1974. As well as supervising research and writing extensively on art and design education, he has been a Visiting Professor in a number of countries, receiving the USA National Arts in Education award in 1982 and the Australian Commonwealth Fellowship in 1984. He is currently World President of the International Society for Education through Art and President-elect of the National Society for Education in Art and Design.

NICHOLAS BEATTIE moved to the University of Liverpool after teaching French and German in London and Zambia. He is now Senior Lecturer in the Department of Community, Education and Policy Studies, and Senior Tutor on the PGCE course. His main research interests are in comparative education.

HILARY DAVIES graduated from Queen Elizabeth College, University of London in 1962 and subsequently took a Diploma in Adult Education and an MPhil in Education at the University of Leeds. After some years teaching in further and adult education she became involved in teacher training in home economics, becoming Principal Lecturer at Ilkley College in 1978. She is a former member of the CNAA Committee for Education and a coordinator of the EOC statement *Equal Opportunities in Home Economics*. Since 1981 she has been Adviser for 16–19 Education, Bradford Metropolitan District Council.

PETER HOLLINDALE taught at schools in Gloucester and Bristol, and is now Senior Lecturer in English and Education at the University

Notes on Contributions

of York. He specializes in children's literature, Elizabethan and Jacobean drama, and the teaching of Shakespeare at all levels in school and higher education. His current interests include the hidden assumptions and implications underlying practical work in drama teaching. He is general editor of the Macmillan Shakespeare.

ROBERT IRVINE SMITH taught history in three schools before being appointed to the staff of the University of York Department of Education. His main work has been in initial and in-service teacher education. He directed the Schools Council General Studies Project (1968–73) and since then has edited annual publications of teaching materials based on that project. Other publications include *Men and Societies: Recent Courses in the Humanities and Social Sciences* (Heinemann, 1968) and *Information Technology Revolution* (Longman, 1982).

DAVID LAYTON was Director of the Centre for Studies in Science Education, University of Leeds from 1970 until 1982. Since 1973 he has held the Chair of Science Education. His primary research interest is in the social history and politics of the science curriculum and his books include *Science for the People, Interpreters of Science, Technological Revolution?* (Falmer Press, 1984) and *The Alternative Road.*

JIM PARRY is a former teacher in schools, colleges and a polytechnic department of education. He is now Lecturer in Philosophy in the Physical Education Department of the University of Leeds, and is Course Tutor for the MA in PE. He is currently working on Gramsci's political philosophy and the ideological build-up to the 1988 Olympics.

RICHARD PRING is Professor of Education at the University of Exeter School of Education. He previously taught in two London comprehensive schools and at the University of London Institute of Education. His most recent publication is *Personal and Social Education in the Curriculum* (Hodder and Stoughton, 1984).

MARGRET QUINTON graduated from City of Leeds and Carnegie College in 1972, later taking a Diploma in Art History and an MA in Education at the University of Leeds. She has taught a wide age range and is currently teaching in a large middle school. Her main areas of concern are art, critical studies and curriculum cordination. She is currently involved in local curriculum development projects and in-service training.

JANET STRIVENS graduated from the University of Cambridge and later took an MSc at the University of Exeter. She is currently Lecturer in Education at the University of Liverpool, working with both student and experienced teachers. Her research interests include language, the social studies curriculum, moral and political development and school climate.

PETER TOMLINSON is Lecturer in the School of Education, University of Leeds, having previously attended the universities of Leuven, Oxford and Toronto, worked in a London primary school and at the Farmington Trust Research Unit, Oxford, then lecturing in education at the University of York. He is the author of *Understanding Teaching: Interactive Educational Psychology*. He has recently completed a six-year longitudinal study of moral judgment and is currently turning to the training of intelligent classroom teaching skills.

PATRICK WIEGAND is a Lecturer in the School of Education at the University of Leeds. He has taught in primary and secondary schools and has written several school textbooks. He has research interests in the field of geographical education.

BRYAN WILSON joined the Centre for Educational Development Overseas, subsequently incorporated into the British Council, after twenty years teaching mathematics in schools in Britain and Uganda. During the period 1970–1984 he had the professional oversight of Britain's international relations in the field of mathematics education: this involved short-term assignments in over fifty countries. Since late 1984 he has been working with the Church Missionary Society.

Index

acclimatization
  and geographical education, 70
adult education
  and science education, 172–3
Arnold, Matthew, 1, 34
Arnold, T., 197, 198
Art and the Built Environment Project, 21, 69–70
art and design education
  aims of, 17–18
  Anglo-European bias in, 22–3
  cultural context of, 18–27
  and environment, 16
  and external examinations, 15, 17, 18, 22–3
  functions of, 20
  as humanistic endeavour, 24, 25–7
  and multiculturalism, 22–3
  objectives in 'cultural' domain of, 23–4
  and racial prejudice, 22
  social context of, 18–27
  and values, 11–28
Assessment of Performance Unit (APU), 183
Association for Curriculum Development in Geography, 53
Association for Science Education (ASE), 160, 165, 168, 170
audio-visual methods
  in modern languages teaching, 114–16
awareness
  forms of, 219–20

ballet, 146–7
  see also dance
Basis for Choice, A, 184
Beckett, S., 30
Becoming Human Through Art, 19
Better Road to Peace, A, 163
Bloom, B., 3
Boyson, Dr Rhodes, 70–1
Brazil
  art and design education in, 25
British Association for the Advancement of Science, 158
Bulgaria
  aesthetic education programmes in, 20
  'Banner of Peace' movement in, 26
Bullock Report, 31

Cambridge School of English, 34, 38–9, 40
Cambridge Modern and Medieval Languages Tripos, 110–11
Certificate of Pre-Vocational Education, 184
Certificate of Secondary Education (CSE), 15, 23
  see also examinations
Chapman, L., 20
Cheam [school], 200
child-centred curriculum, 12–15
child development, 13–15, 122, 214–16
children
  and literature, 35–7

Index

Children and Their Books, 47
China
  social organization of schooling in, 195
Chorley, R. and Haggett, P., 51
Christian Aid, 70
City and Guilds of London Institute, 184–5, 189
classroom principles
  and values teaching, 211–24
classroom tasks
  complexity of, 214–16
Cluster School (Cambridge, Mass.), 206
Cockcroft Report, 97–8, 104–5, 107
Commission for Racial Equality, 63
Committee of Inquiry into the Teaching of Mathematics in Schools (Cockcroft Committee), 97–8
Commonwealth Association of Science, Technology and Mathematics Educators (CASTME), 95
community
  and values in schools, 190–1
comprehensive schooling, 116–17, 202–5
  and modern languages teaching, 116–17
Connolly, C., 198
Contemporary Issues in Geography and Education, 53
Council on National Righteousness, 169
Countesthorpe Community College, 204–5
Creative and Mental Growth, 13–14
'Critical Studies in Art Education' project, 21
cultural context
  of art and design education, 18–27
culture
  and modern languages teaching, 112–14, 115, 116, 123
Culture and Environment, 39
curriculum, *passim*
  see also entries for particular subjects
  content of, 192–4
  context of, 181–94
  potential, 6–8
  values across the, *passim*
Curriculum 11 to 16, 183
Cyprus
  art and design education in, 25

Dainton Report, 96–7
dance, 146–7, 150, 154
  see also ballet; physical education
Dartington [school], 201, 204
Dartmouth
  seminar on English at, 30–1
democratic schooling
  in United States of America, 205–6
Department of Education and Science (DES), 72, 126, 184
development stages
  and task complexity, 214–16
Devon
  local education authority in, 184
Dewey, J., 1, 206
Discovery, or the Spirit and Service of Science, 164
Dixon, J., 30–3, 36
drama teaching
  aims of, 30–3
  compared with English teaching, 29–31
  and values education, 29–50
Duane, M., 203

Ebony Tower, The, 42
economics
  values and, 81–2
education
  see also values education
  aims of, 3–4, 13, 183–5
  effects of, 3, 4
  means of, 3, 4
  political context of, 182–3, 185
  process of, 3–4
  and values of society, 181–3, 185
Education through Art, 13
Education in Schools (Green Paper), 183–4
End to Autumn, The, 43
English teaching

229

Index

aims of, 30–3, 44, 45–6
compared with drama teaching, 29–31
and literature, 34–49
models of, 30–3, 35–6
and New Left, 38–41
and structuralism, 40–1
and values education, 29–50
environment
  and art and design education, 16
  and geographical education, 72

environment issues
  and values education, 65
Equal Opportunities Act, 22
essay writing, 45–6, 47
European Economic Communities (EEC), 22, 118
evolution
  theory of, 169–70
examinations
  and art and design education, 15, 17, 18, 22–3
  and geographical education, 57–65
  and mathematics education, 107
  and modern languages teaching, 111, 114, 116–17, 127–8
  and physical education, 140, 141, 154
  and science education, 165–7
  and 16+, 57, 58–9

Factor, L. and Kooser, R., 163–5
Feldman, E.B., 19
Fenton, Edwin, 77, 78, 80, 82
Fifteen Thousand Hours, 207–8
fitness training, 149
  see also physical education
Flanders and Swann, 51, 53
Foods, Farming and Famine, 65
Fowles, J., 42
Framework for the School Curriculum, A, 184
French
  in the curriculum, 110–11
Frontiers in Geographical Teaching, 51

games

in public schools, 197
and values, 142–5
Garner, E., 126–7
gender
  see also sex bias; sexism; women
  and modern languages teaching, 131n21
  and physical education, 141
  and science education, 166
General Certificate of Education (GCE), 15, 23
  see also examinations
General Studies Project, 82–3
geographical education
  and acclimatization, 70
  assessment in, 62
  and bias, 62–3
  and environment, 72
  and ethnocentricism, 62–5
  examination syllabuses and, 57–65
  hidden values in, 57–65
  overt values in, 57–65
  and political education, 68–9
  and procedural values, 57–65
  and race bias, 62–3
  and sex bias, 64–5
  and substantive values, 57–65, 72
  teaching strategies for, 65–73
  and value analysis, 66–7
  and value-biased material, 72
  values in, 51–76
  and values clarification, 65–6
  and values enquiry, 67
  and values probing, 67–8
  and visual images, 71–2
geography
  humanistic, 51–2, 54
  and landscapes, 53–7
  quantitative, 51, 52
  radical, 52
  and relationship between people and places, 53–7
  and social problems, 52
Geography 14–18 Project, 59–61
Geography Report on Assessment in a Multicultural Society, 63–4
Geography 16–19 Project, 60–1, 67
Geography for the Young School Leaver Project, 58, 61, 63–4, 82

Development Education Project of, 64
German
　in the curriculum, 124
Getty Foundation, 19
Gill, D., 63-4
Gilpin, W., 200
grammar schools
　ethos of, 202-3
Greek
　in the curriculum, 110-11
Gregory, Sir Richard, 164
Gresham's, 199
gymnastics, 147-8, 150
　see also physical education

Haggett, P.
　see Chorley and Haggett
Handbook for Economics Teachers, 81-2
Hawkins, E., 128
Hazelwood [school], 200
Henry, J., 105-6
Her Majesty's Inspectorate (HMI), 58, 72, 183
　Geography Committee of, 58
herbicide 2, 4, 5-T, 172
hidden curriculum, 6, 174, 189
Hidden Persuaders, The, 11
Hill brothers, 200
history
　political bias in, 81
　racism and, 81
　sexism in, 81
history teaching
　and behavioural values, 77, 78-80
　content of, 84
　learners' perceptions and, 85
　objectives of, 84
　and procedural values, 80-2
　resources for, 84
　skills and, 84-5
　and substantive values, 82-6
　values in, 77-86
History 13-16 Project, 82
Home Affairs Committee, 167
home economics teaching
　aims of, 88-9, 90-2
　content of, 89-90, 91
　criticisms of, 89-90
　history of, 87-90
　and sexism, 89-92
　values in, 87-93
housing
　availability of, 54-6
human movement studies, 139-40
　see also physical education

Humanities Curriculum Project, 1, 82-3, 186
Hüllen, W., 128-9

Indo-European languages, 119
Inner London Education Authority (ILEA), 189-90
Intelligence of Feeling, The, 14
International Society for Education through Art (INSEA), 24-5
　themes of World and Regional Congresses of, 25
Islamic values
　and mathematics, 101-2
Israel
　art and design education in, 25

Japan
　science teaching in, 168
Joint Council for 16+ National Criteria, 58-9
Jonson, Ben, 39
Jude the Obscure, 42
'Just Community'
　and schooling, 205-6

Kelly, G., 216

Kellner-Solvay cell, 161
Kepler, J., 101
Kill a Mockingbird, To, 47
King Lear, 43-4
Kirkhamgate/Dishforth motorway scheme, 68-9
Kohlberg, L., 171, 190, 206, 209n9, 215, 218, 219
Kooser, R.
　see Factor and Kooser
Kuhn, T., 95, 158, 164

231

Index

landscapes
    as value laden, 53-7

Lane, Homer, 201
language
    compared with literature, 34-40
language skills, 37-8
languages
    see also modern languages teaching
    values of particular, 124
Latin
    in the curriculum, 110-11, 117
Lawrence, D.H., 41-2
Learning Through Drama, 31-2, 33
Leathes Committee, 111-13
Leathes Report, 124
    see also Leathes Committee
Leavis, F.R., 34
Leavis, Q.D., 39-40
Lewis, J.L., 170
lifeskills, 2, 8, 85
literature
    compared with language, 34-40
    and moral values, 34-5, 39-44
    as radical, 41-4
    response to, 48
    and social values, 38-40
    teaching of, 34-40
    value of, 34-8
    and values, 34-40
Little Commonwealth, 201
local education authorities
    and mathematics education, 98-9

Lowenfeld, V., 13, 14

McLuhan, M., 12
Manpower Services Commission (MSC), 184, 189
Mansell Report, 184
maps and values, 56-7
Mathematical Association, 97
mathematical learning
    authority in, 100-1
mathematical truths
    as objective, 94-5
mathematics
    and competitive social values, 105-6
    in the curriculum, 95, 96
    intrinsic authority of, 100-1
    and Islamic values, 101-2
    respect for ability in, 106
    in society, 104
    as unique among school subjects, 94-5
mathematics education
    aims of, 96-9, 101-2
    and Christian values, 107
    content of, 102
    and cooperative social values, 105-6
    and examinations, 107
    local education authorities and, 98-9
    methodology of, 102-5
    planning of, 106-7
    and respect for truth, 99
    and social convention, 106
    textbook examples used in, 102-4
    values in, 94-108

Mathematics 5-11, 97-8

Mathematics in Society Project (MISP), 104

Mill, J.S., 83
Ministry of Defence, 163
Modern Language Association, 110
modern language learning
    average pace of, 123
    and child development, 122
    nature of early stages of, 122
Modern Langauge Teaching, 111
modern languages
    definition of, 110
Modern Languages, 111
Modern Languages in the Curriculum, 128
modern languages teaching
    aims of, 111-14, 125-30
    and audio-visual methods, 114-16
    and comprehensive schooling, 116-17
    cultural value of, 121-2
    and culture, 112-14, 115, 116, 123
    and curriculum change, 127-8

Index

as 'Eurocentric', 125
and European studies, 127–8
and examinations, 111, 114, 116–17, 127–8
history of, 110–13
perceptual value of, 119–20, 123
and social values, 124–5
sociopolitical value of, 120–1, 123
as utilitarian, 118–19, 123
and values, 109–33
moral education, 186–9
  see also values education

multicultural education
  and science education, 167–70
Multi-ethnic Education, 167

National Science Teachers'
  Association (NSTA) [USA], 169
Neill, A.S., 201
New Barns, 209n7
New Left
  and English teaching, 38–41
nuclear power issues
  in geographical education, 68
Nuffield Programme in Linguistics and English Teaching, 37

Oppenheimer, R., 159
Ordnance Survey maps, 57, 58
Orwell, G., 83
outdoor education, 148–9, 154–5
  see also physical education
Overseas Development
  Administration, 64

Paffard, M., 31, 32, 46–7
pastoral care
  in schools, 2
Pauling, Linus, 162–3
Peace Game, The, 163
peace studies, 187
people
  and relationships with places, 53–7
Peper Harrow, 209n7
personal development, 183–5
personal education, 187–9
physical education
  see also dance; fitness training;
    gymnastics; outdoor pursuits;
    swimming and life-saving
  and aesthetic dimension, 137
  aims of, 151–3
  and competition, 143–4
  compulsion and, 142
  content of, 134, 142–9
  and different conceptions of
    education, 134–6
  as 'different' subject, 141–2, 150–1
  educational ideologies and, 134–5
  and examinations, 140, 141, 154
  and gender, 141
  general features of, 141–2
  and health, 155
  and human movement studies, 139–40
  and leisure, 138
  method in, 149–51
  and moral values, 142–4
  and 'movement' movement, 137
  opportunities in the future for, 153–5
  and popular culture, 141, 154
  and recreation, 138
  and skills, 138, 151
  and understanding, 138–9
  values in, 134–57
  views of, 135–6
Piaget, J., 190, 214–16, 217, 219
places
  people's relationship with, 53–7
Plato, 101
political context
  of education, 182–3, 185
Popper, K., 95

Power, C. and Reimer, J., 190–1
pre-vocational courses, 184–5, 189
'progressive' movement, 199–202
public schools
  aims of in nineteenth century, 197
  boys' experiences of, 208n5
  in nineteenth century, 196–9
  organization of in nineteenth
    century, 197
  and social values, 197–8
  stereotypes of, 208n2

233

Index

and values, 198–9
pupils
  active learning processes of, 217–19
  and awareness levels in values learning, 219–22
  comprehension and values education of, 216–17
  and perceptions of drama in the curriculum, 44–5
  and perceptions of English in the curriculum, 44–7

Race Relations Act, 22
Racial Disadvantage, 167
racism
  in art and design education, 22
  and geographical education, 62–3
  in history, 81
Rampton Committee, 167
Read, H., 13, 14
Reimer, J.
  see Power and Reimer
religious education, 7–8

Risinghill [comprehensive school], 203–4
Royal Society of Arts, 184
Russell, Bertrand, 100
Russia
  social organization of schooling in, 195
Russian
  in the curriculum, 124, 132n32
Rutter, M. *et al.*, 189–90

Sapir-Whorf hypothesis, 116, 119
School Curriculum, The, 167, 184
school ethos
  see schools, ethos of
School Geography, 63
schooling
  aims of, 183–5
  and character formation, 196–9
  and 'Just Community', 205–6
  'progressive' movement and, 199–202
  and social development, 207–8
  social organization of, 195–210

and values, *passim*
schools
  as 'childminders', 2
  and community, 190–2
  and educational outcomes, 189–90, 207–8
  ethos of, 189–92, 207, 210
  influence on outcomes of, 189–90, 207–8
  values affected by, 188–9
Schools Council, 1, 17–18, 21, 22, 31–2, 37, 47, 59–61, 63, 67, 82, 141, 167
  Art and the Built Environment Project of the, 21
  Art Committee of the, 17–18
  Drama Teaching Project of the, 31–2
  Humanities Curriculum Project of the, 1, 82–3, 186
  Lifeline Project of the, 1
  Startline Project of the, 1
  Writing and Learning Across the Curriculum Project of the, 37
science
  constitutive values of, 173–4
  and the curriculum, 161–5
  as value-free, 158–9
  and value systems, 95
science education
  aims of, 159–60
  and cognitive outcomes, 176–7n7
  and evaluation, 165–7
  and examinations, 165–7
  'facts' and 'values' in, 161–5
  and gender, 166
  and hidden curriculum, 174
  individual practical work in, 166–7
  methodology of, 168
  and multicultural education, 167–70
  and pedagogy, 165–7
  practical work in, 166–7
  values in, 158–76
Science in a Social Context project, 104

Science in Society project, 104, 165, 170–1

Index

science, technology and society
 courses, 170–3, 174–6
science textbooks
 values in, 163–5
Scientists Against Nuclear Arms
 (SANA), 163
Scottish Central Committee, 126
Second World Conference on Muslim
 Education (Islamabad, March
 1980), 101
sex bias
 see also gender; sexism
 in geographical education, 64–5
sex education, 169

*Sex Education in the Science
 Classroom*, 16
sexism
 see also gender; sex bias
 in history, 81
 and home economics teaching,
  88–92
Shakespeare, William, 43–4
simulations
 and geographical education, 68–9,
  70
16+ National Criteria for Art and
 Design, 16
Sloane Ranger Handbook, 57
social context
 of education, 181–3, 185
social development, 183–5, 207–8
social education, 187–9
 see also values education
social organization
 of schooling, 195–210
social studies teaching
 and behavioural values, 77, 78–80
 content of, 84
 learners' perceptions and, 85
 objectives of, 84
 and procedural values, 80–2
 resources for, 84
 skills and, 84–5
 and substantive values, 82–6
 values in, 77–86
social values, 1, 8, 11–28
 see also values education
socialism

and mathematics education, 102–3
and schooling, 208n1
Socialist Mathematics Education,
 102–3
SOLO taxonomy, 215

special education, 201–2, 209n8
sport, 142–5
 see also physical education
 and popular culture, 145
Standard Average European (SAE)
 languages, 119
state schools
 see also comprehensive schooling
 innovation and, 202–5
State of the World Atlas, 56
structuralism
 and English teaching, 40–1
subject teaching
 see also entries for particular
  subjects
 and values, 4, 5–8, 11–178, 192–4
Summerhill [school], 201, 205
Swann
 see Flanders and Swann
swimming and life-saving instruction,
 145–6
 see also physical education
Tavor course, 114
teacher education
 and values education, 2
teachers
 and art and design education, 18
 and classroom behaviour, 78–80
 and English teaching, 31–4, 36–7,
  41, 42–9
 experience of and values education,
  212
 and formal theory regarding values
  education, 212–13
 and geographical education, 59–61
 and history teaching, 82–6
 and mathematics education, 96,
  104–5
 and modern languages teaching,
  109, 116–17, 129, 131n28
 and physical education, 149–51
 and science education, 175–6
 and science, technology and society

235

Index

courses, 172
and skill in values education, 222
and social definition, 221-2
and social studies teaching, 82-6
stances towards pupils of, 220-1
and subject specialism, 2-3
and techniques and values education, 212
and values education, 2, 192, 211-24
Teachers for Peace, 163
Teaching Geography, 53
Teaching the New Social Studies, 72
Technical and Vocational Education Initiative, 185, 189
Teller, Edward, 162-3
Third World
and geographical education, 62-5

Tom Brown's Schooldays, 198-9
trails
and geographical education, 69-70

UNESCO, 24, 25, 26
World Congress on Culture (1983) of, 24
Union of Soviet Socialist Republics *see* Russia
United States of America
art education in, 19-20
deaths from heart attacks in, 149
democratic schooling in, 205-6
'Using Pictures with Children', 21

value analysis
and geographical education, 66-7
Valued Environments, 54
values
see also values education
and art and design education, 11-28
and child-centred curriculum, 12-15
and developmental stages, 214-16
and English and drama teaching, 29-50
and environment issues, 68
in geographical education, 51-76
in history, 77-86

in home economics teaching, 87-93
and housing, 54-6
in mathematics education, 94-108
in modern languages teaching, 109-33
in physical education, 134-57
in science education, 158-76
and social organization of schooling, 195-210
values clarification
as curriculum policy, 186
and geographical education, 65-6
values education
see also values
approaches to, 171
and assessment, 222
and classroom principles, 211-24
conceptual problems of, 187-9
ethical problems of, 186-7
and particular subjects, 192-4, *see also* entries for particular subjects
political problems of, 187
problems of, 185-9
and pupil comprehension, 216-17
and pupil learning processes, 217-19
and pupils' awareness levels, 219-22
and skill, 222
and social definition, 221-2
values enquiry
and geographical education, 67
values probing
and geographical education, 67-8
visual images, 11, 19, 22, 23-4
see also art and design education
vocational education, 182, 183-5

Walkabout, 47
War Game, The, 163
West Midlands Conservative Women's Advisory Committee, 196
Witkin, R., 14
women
see also gender; sex bias; sexism
and geographical education, 64-5
and home economics, 87-93

Index

Wordsworth, W., 35
World Studies Project, 70
Writing and Learning Across the Curriculum, 37

youth training programmes, 184